People who make decisions are usually leaders, and those whom we call leaders are always engaged in the decision-making process. Nevertheless, for historic reasons, these two subjects are usually treated separately in the academic literature. The contributions in this book, by eminent practitioners in their fields from the USA, Great Britain, the Netherlands, and Australia, begin to point the way towards a theoretically more policy-oriented approach in which our knowledge of the decision and leadership process can be shown to overlap. Once this overlap is appreciated and taken into account, both subject areas become enriched.

The contributions address themselves to the leadership–decision-making process at various levels of social reality, from global problems of foreign policy, via analyses of what happens in business organizations, to research findings and theories that operate at the level of individuals and small social groups. This book will be of interest to students and scholars of business management, decision theory, organizational and social psychology, and sociology.

DECISION-MAKING AND LEADERSHIP

DECISION-MAKING AND LEADERSHIP

Edited by

FRANK HELLER

Tavistock Institute, London

CAMBRIDGE
UNIVERSITY PRESS

Published by the Press Syndicate of the University of Cambridge
The Pitt Building, Trumpington Street, Cambridge CB2 1RP
40 West 20th Street, New York, NY 10011–4211, USA
10 Stamford Road, Oakleigh, Victoria, 3166, Australia

First published 1992

Printed in Great Britain by The Bath Press, Avon

British Library cataloguing in publication data
Decision-making and leadership.
1. Decision-making
I. Heller, Frank A. (Frank Alexander) 1920–
153.83

Library of Congress cataloguing in publication data applied for

ISBN 0 521 40370 7 hardback

CE

This book is dedicated to the memory of Irving Janis, who died in November 1990, having spent some time meticulously revising his chapter, which proved to be his last scientific work.

Irving Janis' distinguished contribution to applied social science covers half a century of pioneering work in several distinct areas. In relation to this volume, which contains three contributions linking leadership and decision-making to stress, it is worth pointing to Janis' important 1951 work 'Air War and Emotional Stress' and his widely quoted 1958 'Psychological Stress', which has been hailed as the beginning of an important new approach to health psychology.

His earliest work concerned the empirical investigation of attitude change, the dynamics of persuasion and political propaganda. His polymath interests and capacity led to the use of varied methodologies covering the range from rigorous experimental work to insightful case analysis. Broadly based training enabled him to choose different methods to suit the subject matter he was studying. I believe it was this eclecticism, combined with creativity and intellect, that allowed him to make his seminal contribution to the complex field of decision-making. It enabled him to move from controlled experiment to an in-depth case analysis of catastrophic decision errors due to Groupthink.

In his most recent work, including the chapter in this book, Janis integrated his life-long varied experience to give us a prescriptive model of effective problem solving which combines cognitive decision rules with requisite leadership characteristics. We are deeply indebted to him.

F.A.H.

CONTENTS

BIOGRAPHICAL DETAILS OF AUTHORS

BERNARD M. A. BASS is Distinguished Professor of Management and Director of the Center for Leadership Studies at the State University of New York at Binghamton. He is the author of close to 300 research publications as well as thirteen books and is editor of six others. His most recent books were Bass and Stogdill's *Handbook of Leadership* (1990), *Advances in Industrial Organizational Psychology: An International Review* (1987) and *Leadership and Performance Beyond Expectations* (1985). In the past decade, he has concentrated on the application of transformational leadership to management development.

LEE ROY BEACH holds the McClelland Chair of Management and Policy in the College of Business and Public Administration, University of Arizona, Tucson, Arizona. He received his Ph.D. from the University of Colorado-Boulder, did post-doctoral work at the University of Michigan, was a Professor and Chair of Psychology at the University of Washington, and has been a visiting scholar at Cambridge University, the University of Leiden, and the University of Chicago. He is currently a principal in the Interdisciplinary Program in Behavioral Studies in Judgement and Decision Making at the University of Arizona.

FERGUS BOLGER is a research fellow in the Department of Psychology at University College, London. His interests are in expert judgement and judgemental forecasting. With George Wright, he recently published *Expertise and Decision Support* (New York: Plenum Press).

CARY L. COOPER is currently Professor of Organizational Psychology and Deputy Chairman of the Manchester School of Management, University of Manchester Institute of Science and Technology. He is the author of over fifty books and has written over 200 articles for academic journals, and is a frequent contributor to newspapers, including The Guardian, The Daily Telegraphy, The Times, and International Herald Tribune on topics of managerial and organizational behaviour. He is

Editor of the international *Journal of Organizational Behaviour* and has been an adviser to two United Nations agencies: the World Health Organization and the International Labour Office, in the area of occupational stress.

MICHAEL CRAWFORD is an adjunct Senior Research Fellow at the Australian Graduate School of Management, with commitments in the School's Centre for Corporate Change and Executive Programs. He also heads CorEx Ptd Ltd, a management consulting firm. In 1985 he received the Academy of Management's award for best paper based on a dissertation in Organization and Management Theory. In the last ten years, he has concentrated on developing concepts and techniques for measuring organizational characteristics and the use of that information in organizational change to improve commercial effectiveness in large organizations. This work has focused on change appropriate to the organization given its strategic position.

PIETER J. D. DRENTH is professor and head of the department of Work and Organizational Psychology at the Vrije Universiteit, Amsterdam. He has published extensively on various subjects within his field. Among other publications, he is co-author of the *Handbook of Work and Organizational Psychology* (Wiley, 1989) and *Decisions in Organizations: A Three-Country Comparative Study* (Sage, 1988). He participated in the cross-national studies *Industrial Democracy in Europe* (Oxford, 1981), and *The Meaning of Working* (Academic Press, 1987). Among his extra curricular activities were terms as Rector Magnificus (Vice Chancellor) of the Vrije Universiteit (1983–7) and he is currently President of the Royal Netherlands Academy of Arts and Sciences.

FRED E. FIEDLER is Professor of Psychology and of Management and Organization at the University of Washington in Seattle. He received his AM (1947) and Ph.D. (1949) at the University of Chicago, taught at the University of Illinois, Urbana, from 1951–69 and since that time, at the University of Washington in Seattle. His main research interests have been in the field of leadership. He has authored over 200 scientific papers and has received a number of awards for his research. He has held visiting appointments at the Universities of Amsterdam, Louvain, Oxford and the Technion, as well as holding the S. L. A. Marshall Chair in the US Army Research Institute for the Behavioral and Social Sciences. He is currently President of the Organizational Psychology Division of the International Association of Applied Psychology.

FRANK A. HELLER is Director of the Centre for Decision Making Studies at the Tavistock Institute of Human Relations. He received his Ph.D. in Psychology from the University of London; previously took a degree in Economics and Sociology from the London School of Economics. Has been Visting Professor at the University of California at Berkeley; Stanford University; INSEAD; the University of Surrey and Hangzhou University, China. He is Executive Editor of a series of Yearbooks published by John Wiley & Sons and a current series of Handbooks published by Oxford University Press. He has initiated and been a member of a number of cross-national research projects on Managerial Decision-making and Leadership.

DAVID HICKSON is Research Professor of International Management and Organization at the University of Bradford Management Centre (UK), and Eldon Foote Visiting Professor of International Business at the University of Alberta, Canada. He holds visiting appointments jointly with the departments of Sociology and of Business at the State University of New York-Albany. Before becoming an academic he worked in administration. His principal research is and has been on the structures of managerial decision-making processes; power within organizations; and on international differences in a variety of organizational features in a number of countries. He is Editor-in-Chief of the supranational research journal *Organizational Studies*, was a founder of the European Group for Organizational Studies (EGOS) and also a founder member of the British Academy of Management. He has published in numerous research journals and is joint author or editor of five books, notably *Top Decisions*.

ROBIN M. HOGARTH is the Wallace W. Booth Professor of Behavioral Science, and Director of the Center for Decision Research at the University of Chicago's Graduate School of Business. He previously held appointments at INSEAD (Fontainebleau, France) and the London Business School (UK). His research centres on the psychology of judgement and decision-making processes and, in particular, issues related to causal reasoning and the assessment of uncertainty. He has published five books (including *Judgement and Choice*, 2nd edition (Wiley, 1987) as well as many articles in leading professional journals.

IRVING JANIS died in November 1990 when he was Adjunct Professor of Psychology at the University of California-Berkeley. He was Professor Emeritus of Psychology at Yale University where he had taught for nearly fifty years. He had long been a contributor to research on stress, attitude change, and decision-making. His earlier research on stressful personal decisions was published in collaboration with Leon Mann in *Decision Making* (1977). During the past decade he had concentrated his research and theoretical analyses on sources of error in crisis management and foreign policy decisions reported in his books on *Groupthink* (1982) and *Crucial Decisions* (1989). He received the Distinguished Scientific Contributions Award from the American Psychological Association in 1981, the Kurt Lewin Memorial Award from the Society for the Psychological Study of Social Issues in 1985, and the Stanford Award for Distinguished Professional Contributions to Political Psychology in 1990. His chapter in this book is based on research supported by the National Science Foundation in Washington and the Carnegie Foundation of New York.

PAUL KOOPMAN is Professor of the Psychology of Management and Organization in the department of Work and Organizational Psychology at the Vrije Universiteit, Amsterdam. In 1980 he finished his Ph.D. study at the same university on the subject 'Decision making in organizations'. He is co-author of *Decisions in Organizations: A Three-Country Comparative Study* (Sage, 1988) and has written many articles and handbook chapters on this subject, for instance in the *Handbook of Work and Organizational Psychology* (Wiley, 1984) and in the *International Review of Industrial and Organizational Psychology* (1990).

HOWARD KUNREUTHER is the Meshulam Riklis Professor in Practice of Creative Management, Professor of Decision Sciences and Public Policy and management, as well as Director of the Wharton Risk and Decision Processes Center at the University of Pennsylvania. His current research is concerned with the role of insurance compensation, incentive mechanisms, and regulation as policy tools for dealing with technological and natural hazards. He is author and co-author of numerous scientific papers concerned with risk and policy analysis, decision processes, and protection against low-probability/high-consequence events, as well as numerous books and monographs, including *Integrating Insurance and Risk Management for Hazardous Wastes* (1990).

Dr Kunreuther has an AB degree from Bates College and a Ph.D. in Economics from the Massachusetts Institute of Technology.

Major MARK A. McGUIRE, United States Army was an assistant professor on the faculty of the Department of Behavioral Sciences and Leadership at the United States Military Academy, West Point, New York. He received his BS from the United States Military Academy in 1977 and an MS in social psychology (organizational research) from the University of Washington in 1987. He is currently attending the Command and General Staff College at Fort Leavenworth, Kansas.

SUSAN MILLER came into academic life after spending almost ten years gaining commercial experience with a number of companies in the public and private sectors. Her first degree was in Organizational Behaviour, which added a theoretical base to her practical knowledge of organizations, and she followed this by taking an MBA. Research for her Ph.D., carried out at the University of Bradford, investigated the ways in which top-level decisions in organizations are put into effect. She is now Research Fellow at Bradford, working with David Hickson on further research on the making and implementing of strategic decisions.

TERENCE R. MITCHELL is Carlson Professor of Management and Organization at the University of Washington, Seattle and has published extensively in decision-making and organizational behaviour. THADDEUS F. PALUCHOWSKI is completing his Ph.D. research in policy and strategic planning at the Graduate School of Business at the University of Washington. EMILY VON ZEE is an Assistant Professor of Psychology at the University of Washington. Her research interests include both decision-making and communications.

EARL H. POTTER III received his Ph.D. in Organizational Psychology from the University of Washington and is currently Professor of Management at the United States Coast Guard Academy in New London, Connecticut. For over twenty years he has been a commissioned officer in the US Coast Guard, serving in staff and line positions from Alaska to the Antarctic. Dr Potter's research on leadership and stress has been published in the *Journal of Applied Psychology*, *Academy of Management Journal*, and *Journal of Personality and Social Psychology*. As a teacher and consultant to public and non-profit organizations he has focused on leadership development, team performance, and creating effective organizations.

GENE ROWE is a research fellow at Bristol Business School. His interests are in behavioural and mathematical ways of aggregating individual judgements. He recently published a review of Delphi in the journal *Technological Forecasting and Social Change*.

MIKE SMITH graduate from Liverpool University (B.Sc. (1966), Ph.D. (1970)) and was in a research unit attached to the Department of Psychology before going to work in industry as head of a small research unit on training. He then continued his specialisation in the areas of selection and management at the Department of Applied Psychology at University of Wales Institute of Science and Technology before joining UMIST in 1976, becoming Senior Lecturer in 1979. He has served on a number of professional bodies and has authored and co-authored several books and articles.)

GEORGE WRIGHT is Professor of Business Administration at the Graduate School of Business, University of Strathclyde. He has published in such journals as *Management Science, Current Anthropology, Journal of Forecasting, Memory of Cognition, Organizational Behaviour and Human Decision Processes, Journal of Cross-cultural Psychology*, and *Technological Forecasting and Social Change*. He is editor of the *Journal of Behavioral Decision Making* and has co-authored six books on the human aspects of decision-making and forecasting.

PHILIP YETTON is Professor of Management and Director of the Fijitsu Centre for the Management of Information Technology in Organizations at the Australian Graduate School of Management. He has extensive consulting experience in Australia, Europe, UK, and the USA in areas as diverse as the computer, chemical, textile, and banking industries as well as in health, the prison services, and the military. Phil Yetton has been a consultant on strategic leadership to a number of major organizations, including the State Bank of New South Wales. He has co-authored the market leaders in text books – *Managers in Australia*, written numerous research papers and co-authored, with Professor Victor Vroom, the internationally acclaimed text *Leadership and Decision Making*. He is a graduate of Cambridge, Liverpool, and Carnegie-Mellon Universities and was appointed Professor at the Australian Graduate School of Management, New South Wales, in 1983. In 1989 he won the Vice-Chancellor's Teaching Award at the University of New South Wales.

I

INTRODUCTION AND OVERVIEW

FRANK HELLER

INTRODUCTION

The two topics joined in the title of this book: decision-making and leadership, are usually treated separately and it is therefore necessary to put forward a reasonable case for bringing them together. Minimally the case is this: while the pursuit of academic progress – for the subject matter of a discipline as well as the person working in it – often requires a relatively narrow specialization, the requirements of students and practitioners are different. Students of social science or of management need a broad understanding of the landscape before they can plan their itinerary towards a desirable goal.

Similarly, those who apply social science findings to leadership and decision-making in organizations – and this includes scholars, consultants, and practitioners – should benefit from explorations of similarities, overlaps, and boundary disputes, some of which may lead to new flashes of insight. Finally, as my introduction will demonstrate, the majority of authors in this book already take account of both topics.

Social science debates in the last thirty years or so seem to have moved away from the previous emphasis of differences between pure and applied work. At the same time, there has been substantial growth in theoretically informed and methodologically sound empirical work that sets out to satisfy intellectual curiosity without spurning practical applications. I believe this trend will continue and strengthen over the next half century.

Scholars working with decision-making and leadership clearly have a great opportunity to develop new ways of examining the theoretical and practical developments of organizational processes that contain or relate to their topic. In fact, in retrospect, the separation between these subject areas may seem strange. Leaders are nearly always involved in making decisions and the organizational process of making decisions usually involves those who are formally designated as leaders or who emerge informally in such a role. This is illustrated by many of our chapter writers.

Nevertheless, there is obviously much scope for investigating different facets of a tremendously complex area of human behaviour. It is also clear that no single book can get anywhere near to covering the enormously extensive and fertile fields of work in leadership and decision-making; this would require a mini encyclopaedia.

Instead, the assemblage of contributors to this volume is intended to whet the appetite and provide the reader with an opportunity to survey a limited number of important recent approaches to theory and practice. The choice of authors did not follow a scientific schema, but once the authors were chosen, they were free to develop the topic with their own interpretation of what was currently important. This explains why several leadership chapters use stress as a central theme. Some may see this as an example of fashion invading a scientific discipline, while others will observe that, throughout the ages, stress has been a shamefully neglected central fact of life that has only now begun to attract the attention it deserves.

In any case, bodies charged with funding research in this field will observe that, while theory remains important in most cases, the emphasis is on the practicality of the findings and a recognition that there are critical problem areas to which the social scientist can make a contribution.

OVERVIEW

The urgency of a social science contribution to the solution of very serious current problems is well illustrated by Irving Janis. He talks about the potentially lethal consequences of major policy decisions flawed by failure to use available information and by a cavalier, over-confident, and unsystematic approach. He proposes a descriptive model of *vigilant problem solving* that pinpoints the essential steps for avoiding defective decisions causing major accidents, pollution, or the threat of nuclear conflict.

Incidentally, his chapter shows the significant overlap between the two concepts joined in the title of this book. The first half of Janis's chapter describes vigilant problem solving and its major constraints operating in policy-making groups within a decision-making framework. Then, in the second half, he puts forward eight hypotheses for improving problem solving, but he sees them as prescriptive leadership practices. While the model describes mainly structural aspects of decision behaviour which are identified as the major contributors to vigilant problem solving, in the end he finds it useful to draw attention to the existence of personality deficiencies in leaders and therefore the need to incorporate personal leadership characteristics in the final model.

Several other authors find it convenient or even necessary to use both decision-making and leadership to describe their research, although of course it is not always necessary to use these terms. Hickson and Miller, for instance, differentiate between pre- and post-decision processes. However, when they use the empirical evidence to extract ten specific pre-decision processes, five are clearly aspects of leadership: expertise, effort, formal–informal interaction, and authority level.

Fiedler is best known for work on leadership and uses this term in the heading of his chapter. However, the study he reports (in table 3.1) on the relationship between intelligence and stress uses the leader's decision-making performance as the description of behaviour and differentiates decision-making from other tasks, like training subordinates or communicating with the public. The results show that stress deriving from a person's superior correlates negatively with the leader's intelligence when he engages in decision-making behaviour, but not when he carries out non-decision-making tasks.

Similar conceptual overlap or interchangeability between leadership and decision-making can be found in the chapters by Cooper and Smith, Bass, Drenth and Koopman, Heller, and Yetton and Crawford.

There is no need to summarize every contribution in this introductory overview, since each chapter starts with a summary. Instead, I will draw out certain themes and arguments which are central to this area of study.

The interesting diversity of approaches by our authors suggests that we are nowhere near a paradigm or even a noticeable convergence of the literature. Is this something to worry about? It certainly increases the intellectual challenge, but I believe that it does not prevent the current state of the art from being of practical significance in certain specified areas of work. Janis, for instance, starts by noting the considerable 'variety of uncoordinated theories' and quotes James March with approval for saying that there are 'no clear universals' in decision-making. Nevertheless, Janis then goes on to notice some 'promising hypotheses' from a variety of sister social science disciplines which he has attempted to utilize and he finishes by claiming that these bits and pieces can be 'put together to form a fairly coherent view of strategic decision-making processes'.

While other authors do not express their optimism in such global terms, many seem to be quietly confident that their work deserves to be taken seriously, has practical implications, and is supported by a useful degree of cross-validation. Heller, Drenth, and Koopman for instance, have found empirical evidence for the utility of dividing the longitudinal decision cycle into a number of distinct phases because they discovered that the behaviour of managers as well as lower-level employees varies significantly in different phases. This increases our understanding of the role of leaders and followers in a variety of decision-making tasks; it also gives social scientists and managers who design systems of communication and decision-making a much wider choice. Furthermore, while previously most decision analysis was content to finish up with the decision itself, they found that the post-decision implementation phase is of considerable theoretical and practical significance.

Hickson and Miller's work seems to lead to similar conclusions, and they divide the total process into pre- and post-decisions. Their analysis of decision implementation introduces several refinements. In the first place, there are three different constituents: those who have authorized the decision, those who implement it, and those who are affected by the implementation. There are at least four criteria for success: speed, ease, completion, and the extent to which the leadership's intentions are fulfilled. The implementation process is illustrated with two case examples.

If some form of phase model were recognized as an important structure in the analysis of leadership and decision-making behaviour, it would affect a considerable part of the existing literature. For instance, most writers on strategic decision-making, including our chapter writers, are agreed about the importance of *ambiguity* and *uncertainty*, although the operationalization of these terms differs substantially. Cooper and Smith use these concepts as one of the sources of managerial stress, but they are also central to the classical area of formal decision theory and refinements such as those described by Hogarth and Kunreuther. It may be reasonable to speculate whether ambiguity and uncertainty are more important at the beginning of a strategic decision process, or later on. How much uncertainty remains at the point of decision and does it diminish during implementation? If there were substantial differences over the longitudinal cycle, as Drenth and Koopman claim, then it might be useful to introduce several probability estimates in formal decision models.

In field studies, like those described by Bass, Hickson and Miller, Cooper and Smith, and Drenth and Koopman, the assumption is frequently made that uncertainty is a characteristic of strategic decisions and inevitably affects leaders involved in such a process. Bass talks about the problem of groups faced with 'threats to their steady states of well-being' and claims that appropriate leadership will reduce stress and burnout. The critical word is, of course, 'appropriate'. If uncertainty is low at the beginning of a decision cycle, which may last twelve months, but is high at the end, should the method of leadership adjust to this factor? Drenth and Koopman think so. Bass argues that, under certain circumstances strong, even autocratic leadership, helps to reduce stress, while a different situation might require a more participative approach. From extensive evidence, he concludes that, while the contingent nature of the relationship between leadership style and stress is established, we do not yet know enough about the specific contingency conditions. It therefore seems plausible that the use of phases in leadership behaviour research is a neglected contingency. The evidence from Drenth and Koopman (tables 4.1 and 4.2) suggests this may be a fruitful area to investigate. They show that for long- as well as medium-term decisions, top managers use a significantly more centralized method of leadership in the finalization phase than in either the events leading up to it or during implementation. This fits in well with Bass's analysis.

It seems that a phase hypothesis on stress reduction should be investigated. In any case, this example shows once again that the artificial separation between the literature on leadership and decision-making is potentially counterproductive for both.

Further convergence between leadership and decision-making comes from the chapters by Fiedler *et al.* and Heller. They are interested in the utilization of competence. Fiedler *et al.* were intrigued by the extensive evidence of a low relationship between the intelligence and experience of leaders and their performance. Commonsense would lead one to expect a strong relationship between competence (intelligence and experience) and effective performance. Although the puzzle has not yet been completely solved, the evidence shows that leaders do not or cannot use their intelligence when interpersonal relations with their superior put them under stress. This factor, called 'boss stress', affects leaders' intelligent contribution to decision-making. However, it does not affect tasks like communicating, executing orders, and routine activities. When 'boss stress' is low, leaders use their intelligence.

Heller, too, stresses the role of experience, intelligence, and work-relevant skills. He uses the term 'competence' to describe these multiple requirements and cites research evidence to show that the most important outcome of genuine rather than pseudo participative decision-making is an improved utilization of competence. At the same time there is evidence that leaders who do not recognize that their colleagues or subordinates have the relevant experience and skill will not use participative practices.

Since it can be shown that leaders often under-estimate the skill and experience of their subordinates and consequently fail to involve them, they reduce the achievement and efficiency of the decision outcome.

Competence therefore plays a critical part as an antecedent as well as a consequence of effective decision processes and Heller suggests the need for a new theoretical model to describe these relationships.

Yetton and Crawford also come to the conclusion that attempts to change leadership practices will be unsuccessful unless certain contingencies, including competence, are taken into account. They had the unusual opportunity of measuring the before and after effect of a leadership change programme introduced by consultants who used the Blake and

Mouton grid method. The training was successful in making leaders espouse a more democratic style but failed to affect their behaviour to the same extent. This gap between belief and practice created problems and the research demonstrates the need to devise change programmes based on a careful pre-change research using contingency rather than universalistic models.

The theoretical work of Beach and his colleagues is distinct from the previously described contributions but seems to relate more closely to the two chapters on decision theory and decision modelling by Hogarth and Kunreuther and Wright *et al*. Beach and colleagues concentrate their attention on the socio-psychological framework within which the individual decision-maker operates. They are aware that individuals often find themselves in groups and are also influenced by other environmental factors, but their theoretical model assumes that these influences are distilled in the minds of the decision-makers and can be identified by examining values and moral and ethical considerations. These values, which they call 'principles', influence, motivate, and help to design the outcome of the decision process, which they call 'goals'.

To move from 'principles' to 'goals' requires a plan, and to accomplish this it is necessary to imagine what has happened in the past, what is happening now, and what will happen in the future. This process of 'imaging', gives the name to their theory, which can become quite complex and abstract. Image theory is descriptive rather than normative and it pays special attention to the precise identification of the problem for the solution of which a decision is needed. They claim that the more usual approach is to assume that naming a problem is equivalent to identification.

Although classical and formal decision theory uses quite a different vocabulary, it also relies heavily on the capacity of individuals to filter and condense in their minds the multitude of external influences which impinge on individual actors. Actors have to weigh up and, if possible, integrate their images of past events, present experience, and future expectation. Since uncertainty is a prevalent condition in a complex world, actors weigh up the pros and cons of existing alternatives, which include values and moral considerations (principles), by comparing them with the attractiveness of goals in view of the likelihood of attaining these outcomes.

In the absence of uncertainty, there would be little need for imaging or internally weighing up principles in making plans towards the achievement of goals. Decision theorists use the term 'mental simulation' to describe the process of imaging and they argue that, as perceived ambiguity and uncertainty increases, so one would expect mental simulation to increase.

Hogarth and Kunreuther's chapter aims at exposing the inadequacy of classical decision theory, which holds that the decisions people make should not be influenced by the accuracy or ambiguity of a probability. They use three experimental case studies to test their prediction that, contrary to the classical model, ambiguities affect decision behaviour. Instead of using the traditional concept of probabilities, they use the notion of 'subjective weights' which are more flexible because they allow the imaging (mental simulation process) to adjust estimates of the probability up or down as a function of perceived ambiguity.

Like most current theories on leadership or decision-making, Hogarth and Kunreuther use a contingency model. In their case, the contingencies are the structurally different situations people find themselves in and the roles they assume, rather than idiosyncratic personality factors. They argue that ambiguity can be defined as a 'lack of knowledge of prob-abilities and outcomes' and this makes it possible to predict a number of real life situations, for instance whether and in what circumstances plaintiffs and defendants engaged in legal proceedings will prefer to settle out of court.

In spite of many specific successes, decision theory has not yet learnt to cope adequately with the limitations of human competence and with the inadequacies of the models of man from which formal theory derives its inspirations. Several authors remind us of the important distinction made by Herbert Simon's early analysis of the managerial decision process, namely the difference between the classical postulations about 'economic man', who operates through a rational, and therefore predictable, calcu-lus and 'administrative man', who has to work with very imperfect knowledge and can cope with time and other pressures only by limiting his assessment of all the existing possibilities (Simon, 1945, 1982). While the stated assumptions by those who work with the theory of 'economic man' are severely constrained, the administrative decision-maker is often overwhelmed with complexity as well as with political pressures and the subtle operation of human motives. He has neither the time nor the ability to go beyond a 'best under the circumstances' solution, which Simon calls 'satisficing'.

The two case studies given by Hickson and Miller bear this out very neatly. Nevertheless, it is worth dwelling on the fact that though Simon's theory of 'bounded rationality' was put forward in 1945, and almost certainly contributed to his Nobel Prize, both theorists and practitioners still find it difficult to accept the full consequences of the bounded rationality model.

Drenth and Koopman make the interesting point that the modern decision-maker cuts through complexity, uncertainty, and lack of full information, by choosing the alternative 'that gives him just enough satisfaction for his level of aspiration'. The term 'level of aspiration' is rarely used in this context, but could constitute an important operational refinement for an understanding of optimization. There is a wide range of scientific work, including controlled experiments, relating to level of aspiration behaviour. It goes back to work by Hoppe (1930) and was elaborated by Kurt Lewin and colleagues (Lewin *et al.*, 1944).

There are substantial individual differences in levels of aspiration behaviour and they can be measured fairly precisely, for instance in relation to job competence (Heller, 1952). It may be that future work which distinguishes between decision-making optimality based on 'satisficing' behaviour and more rational maximality assumptions, will be able to include the level of aspiration concept in an attempt to predict leadership behaviour.

Certain kinds of judgements, including those used in levels of aspiration procedures, can be evaluated objectively. You can ask people how well they expect to perform in a test of accuracy or speed and the judgement can then be compared with the actual performance, but there are many judgements which cannot be compared with an objective reality; for instance judgements or interpretations of dreams, or judgements about the artistic value of a painting or novel.

Decision theory makes very extensive use of judgements, most usually in estimating the probability of events that have not yet occurred and the probable usefulness of expected outcomes. Decision modelling can lead to important theoretical conclusions in many fields of human activity, as long as one can be assured that judgements are reasonably accurate. This subject is given extensive analysis in the chapter by Wright *et al.* The outcome of the review is not entirely reassuring.

The basic assumption of decision theory is that improved understanding of a problem can be achieved by making the best possible use of the subjective information available to the decision-maker, rather than by giving him more and more information. It is therefore essential to investigate how good people's judgements are. Wright *et al.* review the extensive literature on laboratory and field studies on the quality of human judgements in a variety of situations. They give telling examples of the way the media can seriously distort our ability to make realistic assessments on important subjects, like cancer. Media coverage induces a belief that lung cancer is a more likely cause of death than stomach cancer, although 'in reality the latter is twice as likely as the former'. From this it would seem probable that experts would be able to make better judgements. It is therefore sad to record that investigations on expert judgements lead to the conclusion that, in general, they 'exhibit the same biases as naive subjects'.

The struggle to overcome these difficulties has only just begun. The approach reported by Hogarth and Kunreuther is based on a model which assumes that people are capable of adjusting to ambiguities by assessing certain situational variables, like size of outcome. In the face of high risk situations, the average person shows caution, but, faced with the possibility of losses, for instance as a result of installing a new technology, they become less cautious.

This approach to decision-making, like that of several other contributors to this volume, leaves little room for the traditional psychological literature, which sees personality as the major determinant of leadership behaviour.

I believe that, as research on leadership and decision-making begins to converge, it will be seen that an assessment of personal as well as structural and situational factors becomes necessary to yield the most predictive model of behaviour.

REFERENCES

Heller, F. A. (1952), 'Measuring motivation in industry', *Occupational Psychology*, 26, 1–10.

Hoppe, F. (1930), 'Erfolg und Misserfolg', *Psychologische Forschung*, 14 (1–62).

Lewin, K., Dembo, T., Festinger, L., and Sears, P. (1944), 'Levels of aspiration', in J. McV. Hunt (ed.), *Personality and the Behavior Disorders* (New York: Ronald), pp. 333–78.

March, James (1988), 'Bounded rationality, ambiguity and the engineering of choice', in David Bell, Howard Raiffa, and Amos Tversky (eds.), *Decision Making* (Cambridge University Press).

Simon, Herbert A. (1945), *Administrative Behavior* (New York: Macmillan).

Simon, Herbert A. (1982), 'Rational decision making in business organization', in Herbert Simon, *Models of Bounded Rationality*, vol. 2 (Cambridge, MA: MIT Press), pp. 474–94.

2

CAUSES AND CONSEQUENCES OF
DEFECTIVE POLICY-MAKING: A NEW
THEORETICAL ANALYSIS

IRVING JANIS

ABSTRACT

Despite our current state of ignorance about how and why strategic decision-making is likely to be 'rational' or 'irrational', the time seems ripe for attempting to bring a bit of order out of the theoretical chaos. This chapter presents a synopsis of a recently developed 'constraints' model for analysing the causes and consequences of low- versus high-quality policy-making. A key assumption is that, when confronted with vital issues, policy-makers will fail to use high-quality decision-making procedures if they are aware of salient constraints that they regard as unmanageable. Constraints include three well-known types of obstacles to using the high-quality procedures of vigilant problem-solving: cognitive constraints (e.g., limited resources for collecting or analysing information), affiliative constraints (e.g., conformity pressures from powerful constituencies), and egocentric constraints (e.g., personal need to alleviate psychological stress).

Another important assumption is that failure to use the procedures of vigilant problem-solving increases the likelihood of making avoidable errors that result in undesirable outcomes. Because this assumption has been challenged by a number of social scientists, a brief review is presented of new evidence on the relationship between the quality of decision-making process and the attainment of objectives, from a recent correlational study of international crisis management.

Implications of the 'constraints' model are discussed for management studies that seek to find the probable causes of policy fiascos with an eye to making recommendations about preventing recurrences in the future. The potential value of the model for generating original, plausible hypotheses is illustrated for three areas of basic inquiry: *effective leadership practices* that promote vigilant problem solving, *organizational norms and structures* that reduce the adverse effects of the three types of constraints, and *personality characteristics of top-level executives*, pertinent for selecting leaders who are likely to be effective as policy-makers.

Recent surveys of pertinent social science research repeatedly call attention to our current state of ignorance about how crucial decisions are made by governments, business corporations, and public welfare organizations, as well as by individuals. For example, in a comprehensive review of social psychological research published in 1985, Abelson and Levi state that many conflicting views have emerged from the existing research as to how 'rational' or 'irrational' decision-making is likely to be. They assert that 'The human decision-maker has been variously seen as a corrigible rationalist, a bounded rationalist, an error-prone intuitive scientist, a slave to motivational forces, or as the butt of faulty normative models' (p. 233). Their main conclusion is that no definite conclusion can be drawn as to which of these views is correct. No one of these views, they point out, is able to account for all the relevant findings, but, on the other hand, none of them seems to be completely wrong.

James March (1981) came to a similar conclusion a few years earlier when he commented on the extensive research literature on policy-making in large organizations. Speaking about the way crucial decisions are arrived at, March asserts that 'there are no clear universals'. Individuals and groups in organizations, according to March, often choose the first barely acceptable alternative that comes along rather than maximize, but not always. When major policy changes are needed, they frequently stick to obsolete policies by making only small incremental modifications, yet on occasion they make 'heroic leaps'. Sometimes they take account of a broad spectrum of objectives and long-term considerations when it seems required, sometimes they fail to do so. Certain of their new decisions reflect learning from past mistakes, others do not.

If March's comments about the absence of universals are correct – and from my own observations as well as from my reviews of the literature on organizational decision-making, I believe that they certainly are – we must acknowledge that at present we have no simple generalizations describing how major policy decisions are made. Nor do we have any valid theory that describes and accounts for linkages between procedures for arriving at policy decisions, and good versus poor outcomes, from which we could extract dependable prescriptions for improving the quality of policy-making in government, business, and public welfare organizations. What we do have, as Abelson and Levi, March, and many other experts point out, are numerous unintegrated hypotheses that are subject to debate and disagreements among social scientists. So far as the development of theory is concerned, this area is still in a very early stage. There are all too many contending theorists, some of whom clash head on while others simply ignore or bypass their rivals without bothering to analyse points of divergence or convergence, all of which creates an atmosphere of theoretical chaos.

To counteract all this bad news, there is hardly any good news. The main piece of good news is that our ignorance is absolutely complete. If you look around very hard, you can gather together scattered research findings that can be used to evaluate and consolidate some of the most promising hypotheses from the work of psychologists, political scientists, sociologists, economists, historians, management scientists, and scholars in other social science disciplines. For the past several years I have been trying to exploit this little bit of good news to the maximum extent. I have found that, despite all the fragmentation and lack of agreement in the research literature, there are many bits of theorizing and pieces of sound empirical evidence that can be fitted together to form a fairly coherent view of strategic decision-making processes. So it looks to me that the time to start integrating the seemingly divergent theoretical perspectives and empirical findings is now at hand.

Perhaps the pessimists are right when they tell us that we shall never have a comprehensive theory that encompasses fully all the complicated psychological, sociological, political, and economic factors that influence the making of consequential policy decisions. But I see no reason for being inhibited about taking steps in the direction of bringing more order out of the chaos of clashing concepts by sketching a rough outline of an integrative theoretical framework that describes the social and psychological determinants of policy-making procedures and their consequences. In any case, that is what I have attempted to do in a book titled *Crucial Decisions: Leadership in Policymaking and Crisis Management* (1989), which I shall summarize briefly in this chapter.

REMINDERS ABOUT WHAT IS AT STAKE

While working on my most recent research project, which concentrates on crisis management by US leaders in eight presidential administrations since the end of the Second World War, I have been struck by a number of common features. Those features began to loom very large in my mind when I realized that I had already encountered them here and there in the research literature and also in my prior psychological studies of crucial decisions made by executives in business corporations and in public welfare organizations. Like other investigators of decision-making in large organizations, I have been especially impressed by the high frequency of policy decisions that are flawed by failure to take account of available information about the probable consequences of the chosen course of action. And, like many citizens all over the world, I worry about defective policy decisions that could have lethal consequences.

Over and beyond deleterious effects on an organization's success and survival, defective policy-making can be lethal in the literal sense of the term for an industrial plant's employees and for people in a local community when the plant's executives decide to ignore the serious problems of preventing industrial accidents and pollution. Avoidable fatalities are likely to result from their decisions to continue using relatively cheap but dangerous ways to dispose of toxic chemicals or other wastes that pollute the air, the water supply, or the food chain for local produce, despite experts' impressive warnings about cumulative effects expected to become disastrous in subsequent years. More widespread loss of lives results when local and state governments, federal regulative agencies, and public health organizations fail to arrive at sound governmental policies to prevent wholesale pollution that causes cancer or other fatal diseases. And it has long been apparent to large numbers of scientists and policy planners that the continuation of increases in industrialization, exploitation of limited natural resources, and applications of new technologies throughout the world, if unregulated by new and more sensible national and international policies, will sooner or later exact intolerable costs in the form of eco-catastrophes. Two of the most publicized threats are depletion of the ozone layer of the atmosphere from chlorofluorocarbons and drastic changes in climate resulting from the 'greenhouse effect'; there are many other dangers as well.

The only realistic source of hope for avoiding the lethal consequences is *sound leadership by policy-makers* – those who have sufficient power and influence to counteract the powerful political and economic forces that maintain the status quo. The same must be said about the set of policy issues generally regarded as urgent for the survival of civilization and perhaps of all human beings: how to avoid a lethal nuclear war?

Unfortunately, the bad news I have just been talking about is not offset by the little bit of good news I mentioned: the social sciences have relatively little to offer as yet for solving the gravest of public and international policy problems. Nevertheless, I expect that many social scientists who recognize this state of affairs share my belief that it is worthwhile for investigators and theorists in all the social science disciplines to give priority to working on research topics that have at least a chance of contributing a little something to our very limited knowledge that could be pertinent to preventing gross errors when the most crucial types of policy decisions are made.

One pertinent area of scholarly inquiry has to do with the processes of arriving at major policy decisions, including analysis of the conditions under which miscalculations, faulty implementation, inadequate contingency planning, and other such errors are most probable. That is the area dealt with by my theoretical analysis. If it succeeds in stimulating research that leads to increased understanding of when, how, and why avoidable errors in policy-making and crisis management occur, it could prove to have useful prescriptive implications.

KEY QUESTIONS

My theoretical analysis draws upon the research literature on policy-making and my own prior research investigations and intensive interviews of policy-makers in a variety of different kinds of organizational settings. My prior investigations have included comparative case studies of foreign policy decisions by heads of state and their advisors, domestic policy decisions by executives in government agencies, major business decisions by executives in large corporations, and strategic decisions by managers of hospitals, social service agencies, and other public welfare organizations. All of these studies of policy-making and crisis management have focussed mainly on social and psychological factors that give rise to miscalculations. One of the main goals of my research and theory construction is to try to answer the following fundamental questions: *When and why do leaders of nations and other large organizations make policy decisions of poor quality that result in avoidable errors? How can the quality of policy decision-making be improved so as to prevent such errors or at least keep them to a minimum?*

Since my main approach involves analysing the causes and consequences of *poor-* versus *good-quality* policy-making, the first key question that needs to be answered is: What are the characteristics of good-quality policy-making? To put it another way: What are the high-quality procedures that policy-makers *fail* to use when they make defective decisions that contain avoidable errors?

To start with, a fairly definite answer is given by Herbert Simon in his highly influential book on *Administrative Behavior* (1976). His descriptive account of how good executives make policy decisions calls attention to the major steps in effective problem solving. One involves listing alternative courses of action or choices; another is to examine the major consequences that can be expected to follow from each of the choices; yet another is to carry out a comparative evaluation of the various consequences. Simon points out, however, that an objectively rational approach cannot be carried out fully because of the limited knowledge and capabilities of all human beings because

'knowledge of consequences is always fragmentary', 'values can be only imperfectly anticipated', and 'only a very few of . . . [the] possible alternatives ever come to mind.' (Simon, 1976, p. 81)

There are other well-known cognitive limitations as well. For example, the nature of the threat or opportunity that poses the policy problem may

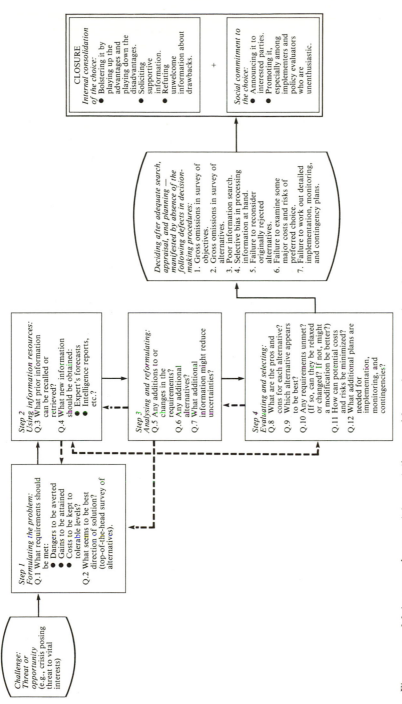

Figure 2.1 Main steps characterizing a vigilant problem-solving approach to decision-making. *Source:* Janis, 1989, p. 91.

not be well understood because the available information is too ambiguous or incomplete. And, even if the essential information about every viable option and its expected consequences were available, there is no valid way to combine all the various organizational, political, economic, ideological, and personal values that might be at stake into a single utility criterion of scale.

In agreement with many other observers of organizational behaviour, Simon concludes that, in practice, good policy-makers who are striving for high-quality decisions engage in analytic problem solving, but they do so in a way that only crudely approximates the requirements of a normative rational model. Their procedures, which I refer to as *vigilant problem solving*, involve working to the best of their limited abilities, within the confines of available organizational resources, to exercise all the caution they can to avoid mistakes in the essential tasks of information search, deliberation, and planning.

The essential steps of vigilant problem solving are summarized in figure 2.1. This figure is not intended as an ideal model for the making of policy decisions but as a realistic *descriptive* model of what most executives demonstrate by their actions that they are *capable* of doing when they try to do the best job of decision-making under the circumstances. The model describes what executives can do within the confines of incomplete knowledge, unresolvable uncertainties, limited capacity to process information, bureaucratic power struggles, and all the other usual constraints that can hamper sound thinking about the generally ill-defined policy problems that require crucial decisions. The hallmark of high-quality decision-making is that, by the time the policy-makers arrive at their final choice and move towards closure, they have carried out the essential steps of vigilant problem solving (by answering all the key questions listed in figure 2.1) sufficiently well that they do not display any of the symptoms of defective decision-making (listed in the fourth column of the figure). By doing so, their policy decision is likely to be far better than if they were to use one or another of the alternative approaches (which I shall describe shortly) – better in that they are more likely to obtain a comprehensive view of the options, to recognize trade-offs among competing values, to choose a course of action that meets the essential requirements for a satisfactory course of action, and to develop alternative fallback options in case the chosen option unexpectedly proves to be unworkable or ineffective.

All too often policy decisions made by top-level national leaders display many of the gross symptoms of defective decision-making listed in the fourth column of figure 2.1 (see, for example, George, 1980; Janis, 1986, 1989; Lebow, 1987; Neustadt and May, 1986). An intensive study of the way international crises have been managed by United States presidents and their main advisors who have served since the end of the Second World War indicates that there was an absence of gross symptoms in only a small percentage of the crises throughout the nuclear age (Herek, Janis, and Huth, 1987). And, as will be described later in this chapter, the research findings show that symptoms of defective decision-making are related to two types of unsuccessful outcomes – failure to protect national interest and failure to promote international stability by lowering the level of super-power conflict. Obviously, during super-power crises there are grave risks of gross miscalculations that can have catastrophic consequences. In a future confrontation, miscalculations could lead inadvertently to all-out nuclear war, even though the leaders on both sides want to avoid it.

This brings us to a key question: why is it that top-level policy-makers often fail to carry out the steps of vigilant problem solving to the best of their abilities when making crucial decisions, even though the vital interests of their nation or organization are at stake? The answer to this question forms the nucleus of my theoretical analysis of the causes of defective policy-making.

CONSTRAINTS THAT INTERFERE WITH VIGILANT PROBLEM SOLVING

In his insightful analysis of *Presidential Decisionmaking* (1980), Alexander George calls attention to the 'ever-present constraints' that often require the chief executive to consider 'trade-offs' in 'the search for high-quality decisions in foreign policy, as in domestic policy' (p. 1). He discusses many different kinds of constraints, almost all of which can be classified into one or another of the three main types in figure 2.2.

In order to take into consideration the requirements posed by any of the constraints represented in the figure, policy-makers generally have to make a trade-off in the form of sacrificing something that reduces at least slightly the quality of the decision-making process. For example, in order to take account of a deadline that imposes a time limit, the search for relevant information is likely to be much less extensive than desired; in order to take account of the need for acceptability among powerful factions within the organization, a very good alternative might have to be eliminated even though it looks like the best solution to the policy problem.

Constraints in each of the three categories shown in figure 2.2 have been described by social scientists in many different disciplines. The major constraints are listed in the upper half of table 2.1. The lower half of table 2.1 lists typical decision rules that policy-makers use to cope with each type of constraint. (All three types of constraints and all the cognitive,

Irving Janis

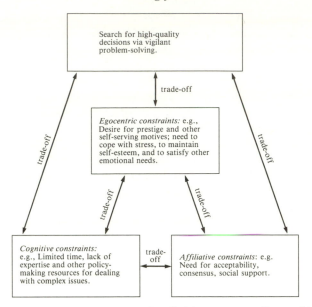

Figure 2.2 Constraints creating trade-off dilemmas in policy-making. *Source*: Janis, 1989, p. 16, adapted from A. L. George, 1980, *Presidential Decisionmaking in Foreign Policy: The Effective Use of Information and Advice*, Boulder, CO: Westview Press.

affiliative, and egocentric decision rules named in this table are described in detail in Janis, 1989, chapters 2, 3, and 4.)

Policy-makers fairly often rely upon one or another of the simple decision rules when a constraint looms so large that it dominates their thinking. This is one of the main observations that has emerged from my own research on high level policy-making, including comparative case studies of presidential policy-making during international crises. My observations on this point bear out suggestive surmises by other social scientists. In a substantial number of instances, what the policy-makers do is tantamount to giving one of the constraints top priority; they select a course of action by using a simple decision rule that enables them to deal satisfactorily with the dominating constraint at the cost of neglecting other objectives. They do not engage in adequate information search or appraisal of alternatives and fail to carry out other essential steps of vigilant problem solving.

From these observations, I have formulated a major postulate concerning the effects of constraints: *The vigilant problem-solving strategy will be used only if the policy-maker expects (consciously or preconsciously) all the salient constraints to be manageable. If he or she perceives*

Table 2.1. *Major constraints that can obstruct vigilant problem solving and some typical decision rules used to cope with them*

Cognitive constraints	Affiliative constraints	Egocentric (self-serving and emotive) constraints
Limited time	Need to maintain:	Strong personal motive:
Perceived limitations of available resources for information search and appraisal	power status compensation social support	e.g., greed, desire for fame
		Arousal of an emotional need: e.g., anger, elation
Multiple tasks	Need for acceptability of new policy within the organization	Emotional stress of decisional conflict
Perplexing complexity of issue		
Perceived lack of dependable knowledge		
Ideological commitments		

Cognitive decision rules	Affiliative decision rules	Egocentric (self-serving and emotive) decision rules
Availability	Avoid punishment	Personal aggrandizement: 'What's in it for me?'
Satisficing	'Rig' acceptance	
Analogizing	Exercise one-upmanship in the power struggle	Angry retaliation
Nutshell briefing		Audacity: 'Can do!'
Operational code	Group think: preserve group harmony	Elated choice: 'Wow! Grab it'
		Defensive avoidance: procrastinate, pass-the-buck, or bolster
		Hypervigilant escape: 'Get the hell out fast'

Source: Janis, 1989, p. 149.

any one of the constraints as being so crucial that it must be allowed to play a dominant role in making a choice, the policy-maker does not carry out the successive steps of vigilant problem solving.

Whenever a decision involving vital interests of the organization is under consideration, a policy-maker is likely to be keenly aware of at least a few of the powerful constraints that could be obstacles to a vigilant problem-solving approach, such as the need to avoid over-using the valuable time of top-level personnel within the organization. Any of the constraints listed in table 2.1 can become so salient when a policy decision is being made that the policy-makers cannot ignore it. But being keenly aware of one or another of the three types of constraints does not always prevent an executive from carrying out the steps of vigilant problem solving. From the standpoint of effective problem solving, there certainly is nothing wrong with paying close attention to the various constraints. On the contrary, as indicated in figure 2.1, the essential first step of vigilant problem solving involves specifying all the various requirements to be met in order to arrive at a good solution to the problem. These requirements include taking account of deadlines, conformity pressures from dominant powerholders within the organization, one's own emotional feelings, and all sorts of other cognitive, affiliative, and egocentric constraints that could affect the way the decision is arrived at, the substance of the policy decision, or both. Thus, when a constraint is salient but does not interfere, it nevertheless influences the policy-making process right from the outset, because the requirements essential for dealing with each of the salient constraints are added to the other requirements posed by the threat or opportunity that constitutes the challenge requiring a policy decision. The added requirements may be dealt with, in part, by means of trade-offs.

A policy-maker who adopts a vigilant problem-solving strategy concentrates on a complex set of objectives:

1. The primary objective is to work out a good solution to satisfy – as well as can be done under the circumstances – the major requirements posed by the threat or opportunity that constitutes the challenge, with due regard for potential risks that could result in disastrously high losses to the organization or nation. The constraints represented in table 2.1 can be viewed as incorporating three additional objectives that a vigilant powerholder is likely to strive for whenever he or she participates in the making of a major policy decision.

2. To arrive at a policy solution with minimum expenditure of time, cognitive effort, funds for intelligence operations, and other organizational resources available for policy-making.

3. To find a solution that will be accepted by various other powerholders and implementors within the organization, with no substantial recriminations, so as to retain (and possibly expand) power, status, compensation, and social support for the powerholder personally and for his or her primary group of close associates (if any) within the organization.

4. To satisfy his or her own egocentric motives and emotional needs, such as those evoked by the psychological stress of decisional conflict.

The four types of objectives are interrelated in that gross failure to meet any one of them is likely to lead to failure to meet one or more of the others.

The objectives in three of the above four categories tend to be almost completely neglected when one of the constraints is seen as being so crucial that it is allowed to play a dominant role in making a choice. For example, if the managers on an executive committee believe that the complexities of the policy issue confronting them exceed their capabilities or that the organization lacks adequate resources for working out a high-quality solution to an important problem, they will make a crucial policy decision by 'the seat-of-their-pants', without bothering to examine carefully the pertinent information that is readily available and without even making any phone calls to consult with appropriate outside experts. They would use a *simplistic approach* rather than vigilant problem solving. For example, they might rely almost entirely upon the answer that immediately comes to the focus of their attention when they apply one or two simple cognitive decision rules – such as 'analogize' or 'satisfice' – instead of using these decision rules as supplementary aids to vigilant problem solving in a way that does not interfere with careful search, critical thinking, and planning.

Managers react in a similar way when extremely concerned about the threat of social punishment – for example, from rival powerholders or from the leader of a powerful affiliated constituency (such as a bloc of voters or stockholders) who wants to tell them which policy option to choose. If the managers judge the danger to their power position to be great because they can see no way to protect themselves, they will immediately rely upon the affiliative decision rule to conform in order to avoid punishment. Each member of the group who expects that this affiliative constraint cannot be managed in such a way as to keep the potential damage to a tolerable level feels that he or she has no choice but to give in to the social or political pressure.

A dominating constraint need not necessarily be one that the policy-maker is consciously aware of. Emotional stress, for example, typically operates as an internal constraint at the preconscious level. A chief executive might fail to adopt a vigilant problem-solving strategy because of this constraint, despite being very confident that he or she can effectively manage all the main external and internal constraints – such as the complexities of the issue, limited organizational resources, conformity demands from other officials and from representatives of powerful constituencies, and the chief executive's own inner desire for personal fame (see Janis and Mann, 1977).

Top national leaders may sincerely believe that none of the constraints needs to be given priority over the search for a high-quality solution to the problem posed by an international crisis that could result in outbreak of war. And yet, their own intense emotional reactions to the distressing dilemma could play such a dominant role that they resort to a simplistic strategy (see Janis, 1989, chapter 4). In such instances, they use either the 'hypervigilance' decision rule (get the hell out of the dilemma fast) or the 'defensive avoidance' rule (don't think about it: procrastinate, pass-the-buck, or bolster whichever alternative seems least objectionable at the moment). During a major crisis the more constraints a leader is aware of, the more agonizing the decision dilemma will be and the greater the likelihood that the level of emotional stress will rise above the threshold for becoming a dominating emotive constraint.

VARIABILITY IN THE WAY A POLICY-MAKER ARRIVES AT A DECISION

In my research on policy-making, I have encountered numerous instances of the *same* chief executive or the *same* executive committee using a very crude, simplistic approach for some policy decisions and using the highly sophisticated vigilant problem-solving approach for others. My observations, which are strongly supported by reports from other investigators, have led me to formulate a second major postulate: *The vigilant problem-solving strategy as well as simplistic strategies, along with various intermediate or mixed strategies, are in the repertoire of almost every policy-maker.*

Although executives may make many decisions by simplistic, quick-and-easy procedures, it should not be at all surprising that from time to time they use a vigilant problem-solving approach. Almost all executives who arrive at top-level positions in national governments, in major corporations, or in large public welfare organizations are likely to know how to carry out the essential steps of problem solving as a result of having had ample opportunities to learn from all sorts of socialization training in our culture, including on-the-job apprenticeship training as junior executives, even if they have not taken any formal courses in management.

My variability postulate contradicts a point of view that seems to be fairly widely held among social scientists who write about organizational management. Many of them make an assumption that I regard as an over-generalization stemming from valid critiques that have challenged the old 'rational actor' model, which used to be accepted by large numbers of economists, political scientists, and management scientists, but has repeatedly been called into question. The current over-generalization represents an extreme pendulum swing in the opposite direction from the old model. The most extreme anti-rationalists evidently believe that Aristotle was completely wrong, man is *not* a rational animal, certainly not when making policy decisions. Among some social scientists, the old comfortable notion that the policy-makers who decide our fate generally behave like rational actors, making full use of their resources to obtain information and to appraise the pros and cons of available alternatives, seems to have been replaced by the extremely uncomfortable assumption that policy-makers practically *never* do so. This assumption, in effect, replaces the obsolete 'rational actor' model with a 'non-rational actor' model that supposedly holds true for almost all policy decisions.

Those who take the 'non-rational actor' model seriously as universally valid are likely to be surprised when they discover that a chief executive, not at all noted for pursuing an analytic intellectual approach, demonstrates his capability of obtaining very high ratings on the criteria for sound decision-making that go along with a vigilant problem-solving strategy. President Dwight D. Eisenhower, for example, showed considerable variability in the way he arrived at major policy decisions. Often he relied upon a quick-and-easy approach, but not always. In *The Hidden Hand Presidency*, Fred Greenstein's (1982) revisionist analysis of Eisenhower as a national leader, we get a picture that is completely at odds with the popular image of Ike as a pleasant but fuzzy-minded chief executive, unwilling to read any memorandum longer than one page, and unable to explain his policies, except in terms of vague platitudes worded ungrammatically. Greenstein presents evidence that clearly shows Eisenhower's high level reasoning ability and his use of a vigilant problem-solving approach in his confidential analyses of complex, controversial issues posed by a major international crisis.

Other examples can be cited of high-quality decision-making by well-known statesmen and executives who engaged in vigilant problem solving. A prime example is the development of the Marshall Plan in 1947 by US government leaders in the State Department, which was largely the work of an analytic problem-solving group headed by George Kennan, whose deliberations I have analysed in a detailed case study (Janis, 1982, pp. 159–72). Such examples, however, would be surprising only to those who believe that satisficing, creeping incrementalism, and other 'non-rational' processes are so pervasive in organizational decision-making that an analytic problem-solving approach is hardly ever used.

Earlier I cited James March's conclusion that there is no universal way that executives arrive at decisions. That is exactly what would be expected if the assumption is correct that practically every policy-maker shows considerable *variability* in the way he or she arrives at policy decisions – often relying almost entirely upon 'satisficing' and other cognitive heuristics, sometimes giving priority to affiliative rules, sometimes to egocentric (self-serving or emotive) rules; at still other times using a mixed approach with partial reliance on simple decision rules; once in a while carrying out all the essential steps of vigilant problem solving.

QUALITY OF POLICY-MAKING AS A DETERMINANT OF SUCCESSFUL OUTCOMES

There is one more key question pertaining to the consequences of defective policy-making to which I have alluded but not yet discussed sufficiently: does it really make any difference whether policy-makers show few or many symptoms of defective decision-making? Some social scientists claim that it does not. It seems quite fashionable these days, especially among leading theorists in management studies and political science, to take a very jaundiced view of the prospects for improving policy-making in government, corporations, and other large organizations. For example, William Starbuck (1983, 1985) argues in favour of a very pessimistic view, drawing especially upon the critique of analytic problem solving by Charles E. Lindblom (1980). Top-level policy-makers, Starbuck asserts, very seldom engage in 'reflective' (vigilant) problem solving, even though the executives may pay lip service to the value of this approach and even though they may retrospectively try to make it look as if they had been conforming to it. Starbuck goes on to say that the 'reflective' (vigilant) problem-solving approach would not be effective even if it were often used by policy-makers because organizational problems are usually too complicated to solve and, besides, it leads to strong rationalizations that make for more inflexibility in response to policy failures than when executives take action without thinking carefully about the consequences of alternatives. Starbuck cites numerous studies to support his generalizations, but the evidence is weak and inconsistent. In fact, many of the studies he mentions actually point to the opposite conclusion (see Janis, 1989, chapter 6).

The specific hypothesis that I propose as an alternative to the views of pessimists like Starbuck is this: *For consequential decisions that implicate vital interests of the organization or nation, deliberate use of a problem-solving approach, with judicious information search and analysis (within the constraints usually imposed by limited organizational resources), will generally result in fewer miscalculations and therefore better outcomes than any other approach.* To put it another way, in terms of the components shown in figure 2.1 (p. 15): *The fewer the steps of vigilant problem solving that are carried out adequately – as manifested by symptoms of defective policy-making – the higher the probability of undesirable outcomes from the standpoint of the organization's or nation's goals and values.*

Until recently there has been practically no dependable evidence bearing directly on this hypothesis. Direct evidence of a positive relationship between quality of policy-making and outcome is provided by a systematic study by Herek, Janis, and Huth (1987). The main purpose of

Table 2.2. *Process and outcome scores for 19 major international crises*

Crisis	Quality of process — Total symptoms of defective policy-making	Outcome — Internat'l conflict	US interests
Indochina (1954)	0 ⎫	+1	+1
Quemoy-Matsu II (1958)	0 ⎬ 16%	+1	+1
Laos (1961)	0 ⎭	+1	0
Greek Civil War (1947)	1	−1	+1
Quemoy-Matsu I (1954–5)	1	+1	+1
Berlin Wall (1961)	1 ⎬ 26%	0	0
Cuban Missile Crisis (1962)	1	+1	+1
Yom Kippur War (1973)	1	+1	+1
Invasion of South Korea (1950)	2	0	+1
Suez War (1956)	2 ⎬ 16%	+1	−1
Jordan Civil War (1970)	2	+1	+1
Berlin Blockade (1948–9)	3 —— 5%	−1	+1
Tonkin Gulf Incidents (1964)	4 ⎬ 10%	−1	0
Vietnam Ground War (1965)	4	−1	−1
Vietnam Air War (1964–5)	5	0	−1
Arab-Israeli War (1967)	5 ⎬ 16%	0	0
Cambodian Incursions (1970)	5	0	−1
Korean War Escalation (1950)	6 —— 5%	−1	−1
Indo-Pakistani War (1971)	7 —— 5%	0	0

Note: The cases are ordered according to total number of symptoms of defective decision-making displayed by the President and other top-level leaders of the United States government. Outcome scores of −1 indicate both outside experts agreed that the crisis outcome was unfavourable, +1 indicates agreement that the outcome was not unfavourable, and 0 indicates disagreement. Table 3 in Herek, Janis, and Huth (1987) is the source for the outcome ratings shown in this table, but a number of typographical errors in the former table have been corrected in accordance with the corrected table, which was published in the December 1987 issue of the *Journal of Conflict Resolution*, 31, 672) under the heading of *Erratum.*
Source: 'Decisionmaking during international crises: is quality of process related to outcome?' by G. Herek, I. L. Janis, and P. Huth, 1987, *Journal of Conflict Resolution*, 30, 517.

our study was to determine the extent to which favourable outcomes in international crises affecting the United States are related to the quality of policy-making by the nation's leaders. In order to investigate the relationship between quality of decision-making processes and outcome of policy decisions, we assessed the US government's management of each of nineteen international crises by making detailed ratings of the presence or absence of each of the seven symptoms of defective policy-making listed in the fourth column of figure 2.1 (see p. 15). We imported into this research on international relations some of the methodological refinements that have been developed in systematic research in the field of social psychology

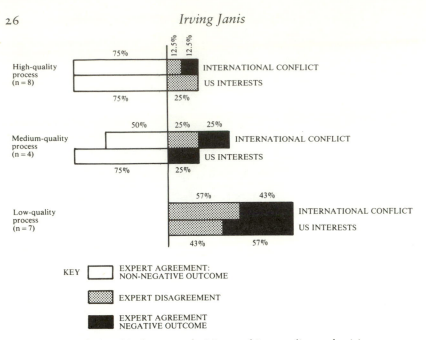

Figure 2.3   Relationship between decision-making quality and crisis outcomes. *Source*: Adapted from G. Herek, I. L. Janis, and P. Huth, 1987, 'Decisionmaking during international crises: is quality of process related to outcome?', *Journal of Conflict Resolution*, 30, 517.

– including special procedures designed to prevent contaminated judgements and to control for other artefacts that can give rise to spurious results.

The results in table 2.2 show a strong relationship between quality of decision-making as manifested by the number of symptoms of defective decision-making (rated by the investigators) and unfavourable outcomes (based on the average ratings of the two outside experts). The relationships between the process and outcome scores, which are displayed graphically in figure 2.3, were sizeable and in the predicted direction. Quantitative correlational data show that higher symptom scores are significantly related to more unfavourable outcomes for US vital interests ($r = 0.64$, $p = 0.002$), and to more unfavourable outcomes for international conflict ($r = 0.62$, $p = 0.002$). These results clearly indicate that crisis outcomes tended to have more adverse effects on US interests and were more likely to increase international conflict when the policy-making process was characterized by a large number of symptoms. The findings are consistent with the expectation that when policy-makers use vigilant problem-solving procedures they tend to make decisions that are likely to meet their goals. Contrary to the generalization asserted by Starbuck

(1983, 1985) and contrary to the expectations of other pessimists, the quality of the decision-making process *is* related to the policy decision's outcome.

While the correlations between process and outcome support the hypothesis that low-quality decision-making leads to unfavourable outcomes, they do not prove this causal relationship. One type of alternative explanation is that the significant correlations result from the influence of a third (unobserved) variable. It is possible, for example, that more serious crises are usually associated with more defective decision-making and with less favourable outcomes because more serious crises are more stressful and involve more difficult decisions with higher stakes than do less serious crises. In order to check on this possible type of third-factor explanation, we obtained ratings from two additional experts on seriousness of the crises and difficulty of the decision-making. To test the extent to which the correlations between process and outcome were affected by these variables, we constructed step-wise regression equations for each of the two outcome variables (US vital interests and international conflict). This method can be used to control statistically for the effects of any third factor for which ratings are available. The results of this statistical analysis indicated that the substantial correlations we obtained between process and outcome could not be accounted for by a third factor of the type we examined – seriousness or difficulty of the crisis.

Although we were able to rule out seriousness of the crisis and difficulty of decision-making as hidden third variables responsible for the results, there is always the possibility that other hidden factors we did not look into could be responsible for the observed correlations. Because our data are correlational, we cannot conclude that the quality of decision-making processes, as indicated by the number of symptoms of defective decision-making, plays a causal role in producing the policy decision outcomes. It is a plausible interpretation, however, not contradicted or disconfirmed by any of the results.

The findings of the Herek, Janis, and Huth (1987) study thus bear out the surmises of those social scientists who have concluded that poor-quality procedures used in arriving at a policy decision give rise to avoidable errors that increase the likelihood of obtaining an unsatisfactory outcome (see, for example, George, 1980; Lawrence, 1985; Neustadt and May, 1986; Stein and Tanter, 1980).

There are, of course, many different causes for unsuccessful outcomes of crucial policy decisions, including unforeseeable obstacles to effective implementation and uncontrollable events, such as counter-moves by adversaries or competitors, which can drastically interfere to such an extent that a policy decision does not work out the way it was intended. Nevertheless, it appears warranted to assume that among the major causes of unsuccessful outcomes is one that is very much under the leaders' control: *the quality of the decision-making procedures used either to arrive at a new policy or to reaffirm the existing policy.* Taking account of the research evidence just cited together with many other bits of evidence from research by other investigators, I have adopted the following assumption as a third main postulate: *the quality of the procedures used to arrive at a fundamental policy decision, as indicated by the number of symptoms of defective decision-making, is one of the major determinants of a successful outcome.*

The constraints model of effective and ineffective policy-making

Figure 2.4 presents a preliminary descriptive model that embodies the three key postulates discussed in the preceding sections. It also includes a minor fourth postulate which is quite familiar to social scientists and widely accepted: *when policy-makers are confronted with any threat or opportunity that poses a challenge to continuing business as usual, they will not devote their time or other resources to seeking a high-quality solution (which requires carrying out the essential steps of vigilant problem solving) if they personally judge the problem to be unimportant.* This figure shows the main social and psychological components that are determinants of vigilant problem solving. The model also highlights the determinants of three other procedural strategies, involving reliance on three different types of simple decision rules, each of which is likely to lead to errors as a result of failing to carry out the essential steps of vigilant problem solving in dealing with serious challenges that affect vital interests.

As in most flow charts, this one starts at the upper left and terminates (in one or another of the four 'END' boxes) in the lower right, with mediating processes represented in between. If you look at the box in the upper left, you can see that the psychological processes that enter into the making of a policy decision begin when powerholders become aware of a challenge in the form of a threat or opportunity that poses a problem because the powerholders' organization or nation will suffer losses (or opportunity costs) if it continues business as usual without making any changes. The challenge may occur precipitously as a result of a single dramatic event or communication (such as an ultimatum threatening war from a rival nation) or it may build up gradually from a series of relatively unobtrusive events or communications (such as gradual blocking by a rival nation of access to foreign markets).

Illustrative types of informational inputs that are among the main antecedent conditions are shown in the first column. (Additional types of antecedent conditions not shown in the first column – organizational norms and traditions, personality predispositions of policy-makers, and leadership practices – will be discussed later in this chapter.)

The core of the model consists of the mediating psychological processes represented in the second and third columns of the figure: the second column shows the key questions evoked by the challenge; the third column shows the type of procedural strategies that policy-makers will adopt as a result of the answers they give to the key questions. The fourth column shows the expected consequences of each of the four procedural strategies designated in the boxes in the third column. The overall evaluation of the adequacy of the management of the problem, as indicated in the final column, depends on whether or not the problem actually turns out really to be serious (according to the consensus of honest judgements of knowledgeable observers – which are not necessarily the same as their public pronouncements). If the problem actually is serious, the use of any of the three procedural strategies involving a quick-and-easy approach that relies on simple decision rules (represented by the upper three boxes in the third column of figure 2.4) would be judged as extremely deficient. The low cost of arriving at the policy decision would be far outweighed by the high danger of serious losses to the organization resulting from the poor procedural strategy used.

As policy-makers go through the process of answering the key questions shown in the second column of the model, they do not necessarily verbalize to themselves either the question or the answer. The process may occur at a preconscious level, which can be detected by observing indirect verbal and non-verbal indicators (see Janis, 1989, pp. 190–200).

Policy-makers' answers to the key questions about the importance of the challenge and to the key questions about constraints may frequently be quite unrealistic as a result of gross misunderstandings of warnings, misperceptions, and faulty inferences based on misleading ideological assumptions. Also they may be misled by incorrect information and deliberate manipulations by interested parties who have a vested interest in steering the choice towards their own preference. Many studies in the social sciences can be drawn upon to formulate plausible propositions about the conditions under which policy-makers are likely to give unrealistic answers to the key questions.

The model can be used to analyse sources of error in the decision-making process, whether an executive is making a policy decision entirely on his or her own or is participating in a group decision with fellow members. In the latter case, the investigator would examine the procedures used by the advisory group, committee, or board that collectively participates in making the policy decision.

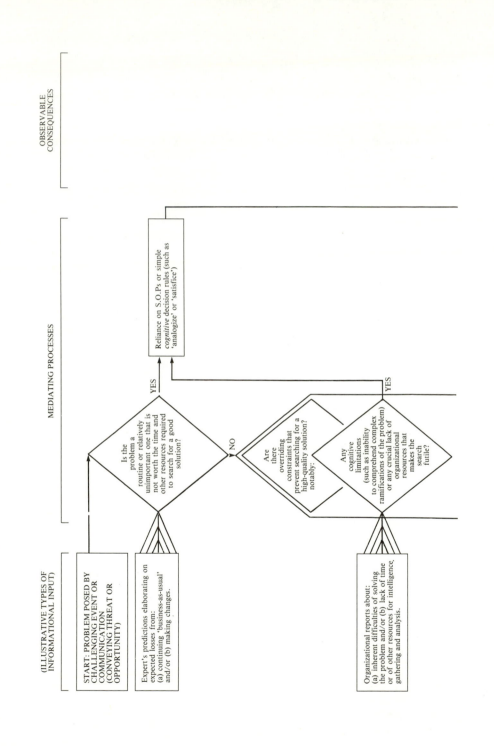

OBSERVABLE
CONSEQUENCES

MEDIATING PROCESSES

(ILLUSTRATIVE TYPES OF
INFORMATIONAL INPUT)

START: PROBLEM POSED BY
CHALLENGING EVENT OR
COMMUNICATION
(CONVEYING THREAT OR
OPPORTUNITY)

Expert's predictions elaborating on
expected losses from:
(a) continuing 'business-as-usual'
and/or (b) making changes.

Is the
problem a
routine or relatively
unimportant one that is
not worth the time and
other resources required
to search for a good
solution?

YES

NO

Reliance on S.O.P.s or simple
cognitive decision rules (such as
'analogize' or 'satisfice')

Are
there
overriding
constraints that
prevent searching for a
high-quality solution?
notably:

Any
cognitive
limitations
(such as inability
to comprehend complex
ramifications of the problem)
or any crucial lack of
organizational
resources that
makes the
search
futile?

YES

Organizational reports about:
(a) inherent difficulties of solving
the problem and/or (b) lack of time
or of other resources for intelligence,
gathering and analysis.

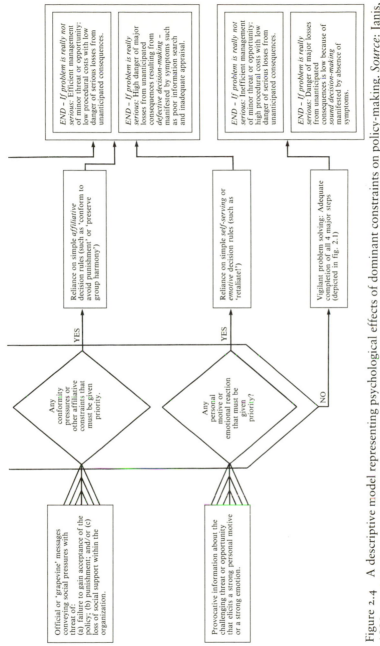

Figure 2.4   A descriptive model representing psychological effects of dominant constraints on policy-making. *Source*: Janis, 1989, pp. 154–5.

Table 2.3. *Consequences of the vigilant problem-solving approach to policy-making as compared with three other approaches*

Types of approach in policy-maker's repertoire	Amount of time and effort required	Quality of decision-making: no. of defective symptoms	Probability of avoidable errors
Vigilant problem-solving	Very large	0–1	Low
Quasi-vigilant	Moderate to large	2–3	Moderate
Quasi-simplistic	Small to moderate	4–6	Fairly high
Simplistic	Very small	7	Very high

Source: Janis, 1989, p. 163.

MIXED, INTERMEDIATE APPROACHES

For purposes of exposition, the theoretical model presented in figure 2.4 shows the pathways leading to only two end points of a continuum. At one extreme of the 'quality-of-procedures' continuum are the simplistic procedural strategies, characterized by a very large number of symptoms of defective decision-making. At the other extreme is the vigilant problem-solving approach, characterized by no symptoms at all or only one symptom (from the common-garden variety of human error to be expected whenever someone attempts to carry out conscientiously a series of complicated tasks). But there are intermediate procedural strategies to be considered that result in an intermediate number of symptoms of defective policy-making, which are not represented in the figure. A few additional assumptions pertaining to these intermediate categories need to be introduced in order to enable the basic features of the model to be applied to policy-making approaches that are neither entirely simplistic nor vigilant problem solving, but combine components of both.

The missing intermediate categories not represented in figure 2.4 are included in table 2.3, which lists the main consequences of four procedural approaches to policy-making used from time to time by policy-makers in national governments, business corporations, public welfare institutions, and other large organizations. The first and the fourth type of approach listed in the table correspond to the two extreme types of approach represented in figure 2.4. The second and third type of approach shown in the table pertain to policy-making processes of intermediate quality, characterized by some degree of reliance upon simple decision rules combined with carrying out some but not all of the essential tasks of vigilant problem solving.

IMPLICATIONS FOR RESEARCH ON MANAGEMENT

The constraints model presented in figure 2.4 and table 2.3 provides the rudiments of a theoretical framework for describing alternative procedural strategies used to arrive at policy decisions. It is intended to serve the main functions of scientific explanations. Two of the most important of those functions are to help us understand connections among diverse phenomena and to make relevant predictions about future events.

The model might prove to be especially valuable in investigations that seek to determine the probable causes of any policy fiasco for the purpose of trying to understand what has gone wrong, with an eye to making recommendations about how to prevent recurrences of such errors in the future. It offers a set of alternative explanations to be investigated, which differ markedly from popular models currently being used implicitly, if not explicitly, by many investigative committees in governments and other large organizations throughout the world. The most popular model is based on the notion that the main cause of gross policy errors usually is chronic negligence or incompetence on the part of one or more persons in positions of responsibility within the organization. Those who rely on this model expect their investigation will end up putting the finger on negligent culprits or incompetent bunglers. Their main presumption is that chronic defects in management of a major threat or opportunity can be eliminated if the leaders who botched it up are replaced by new ones with better qualifications for their leadership roles. In contrast, the constraints model does not direct investigators to confine their inquiry to looking for individuals who are chronically negligent or incompetent, when seeking to explain one or more instances of defective policy-making. The constraints model offers a number of additional causal sequences to be looked into as probable causes of error in policy-making.

Five different pathways are shown in the model, only one of which is likely to end up bringing glory and attributions of greatness to national leaders who are responsible for policy-making and crisis management. That one requires them to give negative answers to all the key questions when confronted by each major threat or opportunity. Four of the pathways depicted in the figure are mediated by a simplistic approach. Those defective pathways can be seen somewhat more easily in figure 2.5, which summarizes the essential features of the model represented in figure 2.4. It also includes another set of antecedent conditions – personality deficiencies–which are to be considered as sometimes, although not always, accounting for policy-makers' failure to make high-quality decisions.

Whether carrying out applied research for the practical purpose of preventing the recurrence of policy errors in one particular organization or basic research for the scientific purpose of understanding how and why

ANTECEDENT CONDITIONS

(1) PATHWAYS	(2) INFORMATIONAL INPUTS	(3) PERSONALITY DEFICIENCIES
Pathway 1 Under-estimating the importance of a challenging threat leads to reliance on simple *cognitive* rules	START: PROBLEM POSED BY CHALLENGING EVENT OR COMMUNICATION (CONVEYING SERIOUS THREAT) / Experts' predictions elaborating on expected losses from: (a) continuing 'business-as-usual', and/or (b) making changes.	1. Lack of conscientiousness 2. Lack of openness 3. Cool, calm, detached, coping style 4. Chronic optimism concerning stability and low vulnerability of the organization.
Pathway 2 Over-reacting to information about cognitive constraints leads to reliance on simple *cognitive* rules	START: PROBLEM POSED BY CHALLENGING EVENT OR COMMUNICATION (CONVEYING SERIOUS THREAT) / Organizational reports about: (a) inherent difficulties of solving the problem, and/or (b) lack of time or of other resources for intelligence gathering and analysis.	5. Low self-confidence with chronic sense of low self-efficacy 6. Chronic pessimism concerning the organization's ability to supply essential resources for solving complicated problems.
Pathway 3 Over-reacting to information about affiliative constraints leads to reliance on simple *affiliative* rules	START: PROBLEM POSED BY CHALLENGING EVENT OR COMMUNICATION (CONVEYING SERIOUS THREAT) / Official or 'grapevine' messages conveying social pressures with threat of: (a) failure to gain acceptance of the policy, (b) retaliation, and/or (c) loss of social support within the organization.	7. Strong need for social approval 8. Strong need for power and status 9. Chronic apprehensiveness about ruthlessness of other powerholders in the organization with supporting beliefs about their readiness to inflict retaliation 10. High dependency on a cohesive group of fellow executives.
Pathway 4 Over-reacting to information that induces egocentric constraints leads to reliance on simple *egocentric* (self-serving or emotive) rules	START: PROBLEM POSED BY CHALLENGING EVENT OR COMMUNICATION (CONVEYING SERIOUS THREAT) / Provocative information about the challenging threat or opportunity that: (a) arouses a strong personal motive or (b) elicits a strong emotion.	11. Lack of conscientiousness 12. Negativism or hostility towards the organization 13. Low stress tolerance 14. Lack of perceived control and other components of low personality hardiness 15. Ambivalence towards the organization: It deserves loyalty but is weak and vulnerable 16. Habitual externalized anger-coping style 17. Chronic hostility towards opponents.
Alternative Pathway that minimizes errors: Judging correctly the importance of the challenge and expecting to manage all constraints leads to vigilant problem solving	START: PROBLEM POSED BY CHALLENGING EVENT OR COMMUNICATION (CONVEYING SERIOUS THREAT) / Supplementary information including messages conveying or inducing cognitive affiliative, and/or ego-centric constraints	No personality deficiencies that affect responsiveness to pertinent information.

Figure 2.5   Four pathways to policy decisions of poor quality in response to major challenges, contrasted with the pathway to vigilant problem solving. *Source*: Janis, 1989, pp. 212–13.

MEDIATING PROCESSES

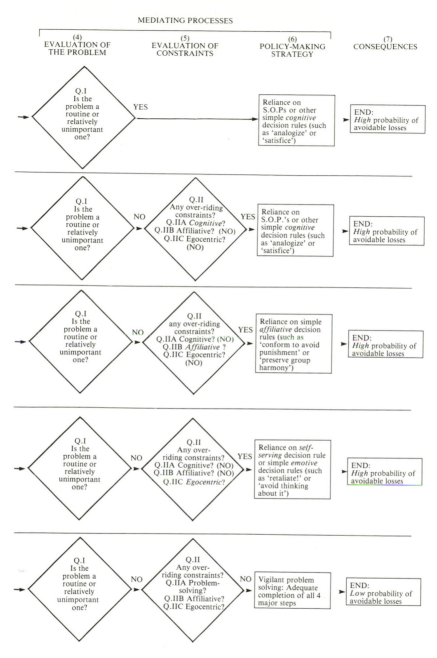

| (4)
EVALUATION OF
THE PROBLEM | (5)
EVALUATION OF
CONSTRAINTS | (6)
POLICY-MAKING
STRATEGY | (7)
CONSEQUENCES |

policy errors occur in different kinds of organizational settings, investigators using the constraints model would be prompted to start their inquiry by looking into the five alternative causal sequences summarized in figure 2.5. All five of those pathways are closely linked with existing bodies of theory in one or another of the social science disciplines.

In figure 2.5, the two columns designated as antecedent conditions – informational inputs and personality deficiencies – are useful for formulating hypotheses about the conditions under which managers will display one or another of the defective pathways (#1–#4) rather than the non-defective pathway that minimizes errors, which requires carrying out the essential steps of vigilant problem solving (shown in figure 2.1 on p. 15). A number of hypotheses can be derived from the model for three different areas of inquiry:

(1) research on *effective leadership practices* that promote vigilant problem solving among members of a policy-making group, including practices that counteract the detrimental effects of various types of information inputs (such as those listed in the second column of figure 2.5), which foster reliance on simple decision rules;
(2) research on *organizational variables* – norms, structures, and cultural characteristics that foster a vigilant problem-solving approach by top-level policy-makers whenever vital interests of the nation or organization are at stake, including organizational features that affect the flow and processing of pertinent informational inputs (like the ones listed in the second column of figure 2.5).
(3) research on *personality variables* and other dispositional characteristics of executives (such as the variables listed in the third column of figure 2.5), which might be pertinent to finding out who will be good policy-makers and who will not.

I shall present an illustrative set of hypotheses for each of the three areas, in order to point out the potential value of the constraints model for generating new hypotheses that appear to be worth pursuing. They are intended to be added to the research agendas of investigators who are interested in discovering the conditions for effective policy-making with an eye to improving the quality of policy-making in our society. Such improvements are urgently needed in the coming decades, as I pointed out at the beginning of this chapter.

HYPOTHESES ABOUT EFFECTIVE LEADERSHIP PRACTICES
DERIVED FROM THE CONSTRAINTS MODEL

Using the constraints model, I have derived a set of hypotheses about effective leadership practices (Janis, 1989, chapter 10). Some of the hypotheses are fairly well-known, having already been suggested by management experts. For these hypotheses, the constraints model provides a more comprehensive theoretical rationale than the piecemeal *ad hoc* rationales to be found in the management literature. A few hypotheses derived from the constraints model specify leadership practices that are not likely to be familiar to practitioners or to research specialists in the field of management. They provide additional examples of the potential value of the constraints model for generating original hypotheses that appear to be plausible and that warrant systematic investigation.

The hypotheses provide tentative answers to a central question for behavioural science research on leadership: what can an individual leader do to eliminate common types of error made by an executive committee or advisory group whose members participate in the formation or modification of crucial decisions, such as those made during major crises, so as to improve the quality of the policy-making process? According to the constraints model, any leadership practice that increases the likelihood that the executives who function as crisis managers or policy planners will give negative answers to the four key questions (shown in the diamonds in figure 2.4) increases the likelihood that they will use a vigilant problem-solving approach, which makes for high-quality policy decisions.

It is helpful to return to the diagram of pathways to defective policy-making shown in figure 2.5. One of the main implications is that a leader needs to *counteract* the influence of various types of informational inputs (listed in the second column of figure 2.5) that induce members of a policy-making group to give positive answers to the key questions about constraints. By inducing those participants to change so as to answer 'no' to all the key questions, according to the model, a leader will prevent them from resorting to a simplistic approach, which results in gross symptoms of defective decision-making.

Although the hypotheses about leadership practices apply most directly to the chief executive or whoever is designated as the chairperson of the policy-making group, they also apply to any influential member who takes the lead in directing the group's activity. That is to say, the leadership practices pertain not only to the actions of the *formal* leader but also to the actions of any member who functions temporarily as an *informal* leader by attempting to insert a new business item on the agenda or to change the group's procedures in conducting its deliberations. Eight hypotheses about leadership practices are put forward in the expectation that by following them leaders increase the chances of reaching successful outcomes to major crises by preventing gross miscalculations and other common types of error.

The chances of successful outcomes of major crises will be increased if a leader takes steps to prevent gross miscalculations and other common types of errors by adopting the following practices:

1   *Whenever an impending threat poses a problem that members of the group believe is a very difficult one requiring an excessive drain on themselves or their organizational resources to carry out a full-scale information search and appraisal, take steps to counteract the members' judgements that there are insurmountable obstacles to finding a high-quality solution.* If a leader does this (for example, by calling attention to available expertise and other organizational resources of which the members are unaware), the likelihood that the group will make a poor-quality decision based on using simple decision rules will be reduced.

2   *Whenever members of a policy-making group assert that it will be very difficult or impossible to gain acceptance within the organization for certain options that they regard as strong potential candidates for dealing effectively with the problem, take steps to counteract their tendency to over emphasize this organizational constraint* (for example, by asking the participants to consider the potentialities of their group for persuading others in the organization to accept the best available option on its merits and by calling attention to comparable instances in the past when opposition melted following adoption of a high-quality solution). If a leader does this, the likelihood that the group will abandon a vigilant problem-solving approach essential for working out a high-quality solution will be reduced.

3   *Whenever the members of a policy-making group show signs of relying upon a simple decision rule to conform in order to avoid recriminations or punishment from others in the organization, take steps to counteract the strong social pressures* (for example, by making an effort to persuade powerful persons to desist if they are subjecting members of the group to demands for conformity). If a leader does this, the likelihood that the group will abandon the search for a high-quality solution will be reduced.

4   *Whenever the members of a policy-making group are moving towards a consensus on a policy option that will give priority to a self-serving motive or an emotional need, defer a final decision, and introduce counteracting incentives by making salient their accountability to other powerholders who will object.* If a formal or informal leader does this, he or she will tend to prevent an ill-conceived policy choice.

5   *During a severe crisis, when the members of the policy-making or crisis management group are undergoing considerable stress, present*

*communications that are likely to alleviate acute feelings of appre-
hensiveness so as to reduce the tendency to give priority to the internal
constraint imposed by the need to cope with anxiety or other strong
emotions.* If the formal leader (or else one of the members with sufficient
stress tolerance who is capable of functioning as an informal leader) does
this, he or she will reduce the chances that the members will adopt a
defective coping pattern of defensive avoidance or hypervigilance.

6 *During any long drawn-out crisis, whenever members of a crisis
management group are undergoing prolonged emotional stress, present
communications that are likely to build up a realistic basis for hope.* If a
formal or informal leader does this, particularly at times when an
attempted course of action has failed to resolve the crisis and some
members are starting to express pessimism about finding a satisfactory
solution, he or she will tend to prevent the disruptive effects of the internal
constraint that is imposed when demoralization occurs under conditions
of high emotional stress, which makes for reactions of defensive avoidance and thereby greatly impairs the quality of decision-making.

7 *Whenever a policy-making group appears to be reaching the end of its
deliberations, after settling upon a consensus as to the best available
course of action, make a rapid, rough-and-ready diagnosis of residual
symptoms of defective decision-making, and then take steps to eliminate
them.* If a formal or informal leader does so, he or she will tend to improve
the overall quality of the policy decision. Even without knowing which
particular constraint may be responsible for a persisting symptom, such as
biased assimilation of new information, a few measures such as the
following could be sufficient to eliminate it: call each symptom of
defective decision-making to the attention of the group and ask the
members to discuss the appropriate key questions that enter into the
vigilant problem-solving strategy (shown in figure 2.1 on page 15); when
the persisting symptom is failure to work out implementation and plans,
elicit and discuss critical feedback from key implementors by inviting
representatives of the main organizational units responsible for implementing the policy decision to give the group their frank appraisals of the
options under consideration along with information concerning
implementation obstacles or setbacks to be expected.

8 *Whenever the leader surmises that the group of policy-makers is not
functioning at its highest potential level, despite his or her repeated,
corrective efforts (including measures of the type to which the preceding
hypothesis refers), make a careful diagnosis of the constraints that are
sources of resistance, call them to the group's attention, and take steps to*

counteract their adverse influence (for example, if there are indications that members of the group are being excessively constrained by time pressures, attempt to 'buy' more time by negotiating an extension of the deadline). If a leader does this, the likelihood of the process continuing to be of poor quality right up to the point of final closure will be reduced.

HYPOTHESES ABOUT ORGANIZATIONAL NORMS AND STRUCTURE DERIVED FROM THE CONSTRAINTS MODEL

It should be noted that the hypotheses about leadership practices have direct implications for *organizational norms*, including leadership role prescriptions. That is to say, any of the specified leadership practices that stand up well when investigated could be incorporated into prescriptive hypotheses about standard procedures and changes in the operational code of an organization's top-level policy-makers. If they prove to be feasible and effective in the judgement of well-qualified observers, including the top-level policy-makers themselves, those leadership practices could be consolidated by formulating new institutionalized norms and accountability requirements, rather than leaving such choices entirely up to each individual leader. The new norms and requirements would pertain directly to the organization's policy-making procedures by specifying who is expected to do what in order to arrive at sound policy decisions.

Aside from norms about leadership practices, it is possible to directly change organizational structure, procedure, and staffing patterns to facilitate problem diagnosis and management. The potential changes pertain to advocacy structures, staff specialization and development, implementation processes, and accountability procedures.

Vigilant problem solving would be facilitated if an organization were to adopt the system of 'multiple advocacy' recommended by Alexander George (1972, 1980). He proposes that organizations adopt a three-tier structure when making important decisions. First, the chief executive or top-level leader presides over the system, taking the role of a magistrate, and evaluating the relative merits of the competing positions. Second, there is a custodian of the decision-making process. This is usually a vice president or special assistant, whose job as honest broker is to maintain and supervise the adversarial and collegial nature of policy-making within the organization. Finally, there are the advocates who are chosen by the custodian to argue competing positions in policy-planning meetings with the chief executive.

George (1980) points out that multiple advocacy does not guarantee a good decision-making process in every instance. The system can malfunction if the advocates do not cover the full range of options, if no advocate can be found for an unpopular option, if advocates for a minority position do not have full access to secret intelligence reports and other essential organizational resources, or if the advocates thrash out their disagreements privately, bringing a unanimous recommendation to the chief executive. That is the reason for the 'custodian' role, the person who is responsible for protecting the organization against incomplete or sham multiple advocacy.

If there is no system of multiple advocacy, the quality of strategic decision-making would probably be enhanced by adding a decision-process expert to the staff and by adding a 'threat screening' staff. For purposes of diagnosing defects in the policy-making process and taking steps to correct the defects, the top-level managers might benefit if a skilled decision-process expert were available to serve as a consultant or as a member of their policy-making groups (see Wheeler and Janis, 1980). And, if an organization has an efficient staff for screening potential challenges, it would be possible to reduce the number of problems policy-makers have to deal with, which would give them more time to do the necessary homework on the crucial problems they work on.

The constraints model also has some important implications for improving the implementation of policy decisions. Social scientists who study organizations have become increasingly aware of the inadequacies of the so-called 'classical' hierarchical model of the exercise of power in policy-making. According to that model, policy formulators at the top choose and instruct policy implementors who, as subordinates, proceed to carry out the directives obediently in a 'non-political' way. In a detailed critique of the 'classical' model, Nakamura and Smallwood (1980) cite a large number of research investigations indicating that the process of implementation often does not unfold in a sequential 'unidirectional' fashion such that policy formulation precedes policy implementation (e.g., Bardach, 1977; Lipsky, 1978; McLaughlin, 1976; Pressman and Wildavsky, 1973; Radin, 1977; Rein and Rabinovitz, 1978; Van Meter and Van Horn, 1975).

All the studies they cite emphasize limitations of the policy-makers at the top who supposedly run things. The circular rather than linear view of the sequence, as these authors describe it, calls attention to feedback loops between policy formation and implementation. Feedback comes not only from implementors but also from other evaluators, some of whom are likely to be interested parties who are self-appointed monitors. As Lindblom (1980, p. 4) says, 'one group's solution becomes another group's problem'. He points out, as an example, that if the federal government comes out with a new economic policy that raises prices of agricultural products, it solves the farmers' problems but evokes protests from consumer groups.

The feedback model of organizational power, when combined with the constraints model, also has major implications for the leadership role of the top-level powerholders. Effective leadership requires policy-makers to be especially responsive to feedback from implementors and others affected by any of their policy decisions (see Heller, Drenth, Koopman, and Rus, 1988). Because no organization is ever a perfect representative democracy, policy-making groups are always unrepresentative in various ways. Most often there is inadequate representation of the lower-level personnel in the organization who are expected to implement the new policy. A large organization can at least partially overcome this deficiency if there is a standard organizational rule to have knowledgeable representatives of the various groups of implementors in every policy planning or crisis management group, and if careful attention is paid to the information they supply about the pitfalls to be expected from attempts to implement various policy alternatives. If representation is still not complete, vigilant information search needs to be carried out by consulting with spokesmen from the various groups that will be called upon to implement the new policy.

HYPOTHESES ABOUT PERSONALITY DEFICIENCIES DERIVED FROM THE CONSTRAINTS MODEL

With regard to personality variables, one of my main working assumptions is that leaders who differ in dispositional attributes, such as chronic level of conscientiousness, have characteristically different ways of responding to the various types of informational inputs listed in the second column of figure 2.5, which affect one or another of the answers they typically give to the key questions represented in the fourth and fifth columns of the figure. If we examine the constraints model from the standpoint of differences in *threshold* of responsiveness to warnings and to the other informational inputs in light of the research literature on personality differences, it is possible to generate a number of plausible hypotheses concerning the role of personality deficiencies. Using this approach, I have arrived at seventeen hypotheses that seem sufficiently plausible to warrant systematic investigations. These hypotheses specify *who* is most likely to display defective decision-making as a result of being generally inclined to ignore, misinterpret, or over-react to certain types of information, which increases the probability of avoidable errors. Specialists in personality research undoubtedly will think of additional personality variables pertinent to responsiveness to informational inputs, which will enable them to formulate additional hypotheses that are equally or perhaps more plausible.

The first row in figure 2.5 embodies four hypotheses about personality deficiencies. The entries in that row state, in effect, that, under conditions where a problem is posed by a challenging event or communication conveying a serious threat to vital national or organizational interests, managers who have any of four personality characteristics (listed in the third column of the first row) will tend to ignore the threat and deal with the problem as a routine or relatively unimportant one: they will rely upon standard operating procedures or other simple decision rules, which makes for a high probability of avoidable losses if the threat materializes. Each of the next three rows in figure 2.5 can be read in a comparable way as embodying additional hypotheses about personality deficiencies that make for failure to respond adequately to informational inputs pertaining to any emerging or ongoing crisis. The entire set of seventeen hypotheses represented in figure 2.5, which emphasizes the *interaction* between informational inputs and personality dispositions, may provide a fresh perspective for research on the role of personality in effective management.

The hypotheses about personality variables have their counterparts as prescriptive hypotheses that specify what can be done within an organization to improve the quality of policy-making. Each of them, if verified in subsequent research, would have something to say about the types of persons who should be recruited and promoted as promising candidates for high-level positions as policy-makers. (Further elaborations of the seventeen hypotheses and their implications for selection of managers are presented in Janis, 1989, chapter 9.)

One final comment about the constraints model of policy-making: it is very difficult to meet the requirements for a 'good' theory of complex human behaviour, notably that it should provide valid explanatory insights, account for prior empirical findings more adequately than any rival theory, make novel, non-trivial predictions that are testable, and suggest new prescriptions that are worth investigating. I hope that I am not pushing my optimism beyond reasonable limits when I allow myself to expect that within a few years we shall have a dependable answer as to whether the theoretical analysis summarized in this chapter can be developed to meet all these essential requirements.

NOTE

This chapter is based on a recent book (Janis, 1989), which presents the new theoretical analysis – referred to as the 'constraints model of policymaking' – together with extensive discussion of the research evidence bearing on all the main assumptions that enter into the analysis.

REFERENCES

Abelson, R. P. and Levi, A. (1985), 'Decision-making and decision theory', in
    G. Lindzey and E. Aronson (eds.), *The Handbook of Social Psychology*, vol. 1
    (New York: Random House), pp. 231–310.
Bardach, E. (1977), *The Implementation Game: What Happens After a Bill
    Becomes a Law* (Cambridge, MA: MIT Press).
George, A. L. (1972), 'The case for multiple advocacy in making foreign policy',
    American Political Science Review, 66 (3), 751–85.
George, A. L. (1980), *Presidential Decisionmaking in Foreign Policy: The
    Effective Use of Information and Advice* (Boulder, CO: Westview).
Greenstein, F. I. (1982), *The Hidden Hand Presidency: Eisenhower as Leader*
    (New York: Basic Books).
Heller, F., Drenth, P., Koopman, P., and Rus, V. (1988), *Decisions in Organi-
    zations* (London: Sage).
Herek, G., Janis, I. L., and Huth, P. (1987), 'Decisionmaking during international
    crises: is quality of process related to outcome?', *Journal of Conflict Resolu-
    tion*, 31, 203–26.
Janis, I. L. (1982), *Groupthink: Psychological Studies of Policy Decisions and
    Fiascoes* (revised and enlarged edition of *Victims of Groupthink*, 1972)
    (Boston: Houghton Mifflin).
    (1986), 'Problems of international crisis management in the nuclear age',
    Journal of Social Issues, 42, 201–20.
    (1989), *Crucial Decisions: Leadership in Policymaking and Crisis Management*
    (New York: Free Press).
Janis, I. L. and Mann, L. (1977), *Decisionmaking: A Psychological Analysis of
    Conflict, Choice, and Commitment* (New York: Free Press).
Lawrence, P. R. (1985), 'In defense of planning as a rational approach to change',
    in J. M. Pennings (ed.), *Organizational Strategy and Change* (San Francisco:
    Jossey-Bass), pp. 373–82.
Lebow, R. N. (1987), *Nuclear Crisis Management: A Dangerous Illusion* (Ithaca:
    Cornell University Press).
Lindblom, C. E. (1980), *The Policy-making Process* (2nd edn) (Englewood Cliffs,
    NJ: Prentice Hall).
Lipsky, M. M. (1978), 'Implementation on its head', in W. D. Burnham and
    M. W. Weinberg (eds.), *American Politics and Public Policy* (Cambridge,
    MA: MIT Press), pp. 390–402.
March, J. G. (1981), 'Decisions in organizations and theories of choice', in A. H.
    Van de Ven and W. F. Joyce (eds.), *Perspectives on Organization Design and
    Behavior* (New York: Wiley).
McLaughlin, M. (1976), 'Implementation as mutual adaptation', in W. Williams
    and R. Elmore (eds.), *Social Program Implementation* (New York: Academic
    Press).
Nakamura, R. T. and Smallwood, F. (1980), *The Politics of Policy Implemen-
    tation* (New York: St. Martin's).
Neustadt, R. E. and May, E. R. (1986), *Thinking In Time: The Uses of History for
    Decision Makers* (New York: Free Press).

Pressman, J. L. and Wildavsky, A. (1973), *Implementation* (Berkeley: University of California Press).

Radin, B. A. (1977), *Implementation, Change, and the Federal Bureaucracy* (New York: Teachers College Press).

Rein, M. and Rabinovitz, F. F. (1978), 'Implementation: a theoretical perspective', in W. D. Burnham and M. W. Weinberg (eds.), *American Politics and Public Policy* (Cambridge, MA: MIT Press).

Simon, H. A. (1976), *Administrative Behavior: A Study of Decision-making Processes in Administrative Organization* (3rd edn) (New York: Free Press).

Starbuck, W. H. (1983), 'Organizations as action generators', *American Sociological Review*, **48**, 91–102.

 (1985), 'Acting first and thinking later: theory versus reality in strategic change', in J. M. Pennings (ed.), *Organizational Strategy and Change* (San Francisco: Jossey-Bass), pp. 336–72.

Stein, J. G. and Tanter, R. (1980), *Rational Decision Making: Israel's Security Choices* (Columbus, OH: Ohio State University Press).

Van Meter, D. S. and Van Horn, C. E. (1975), 'The policy implementation process: a conceptual framework', *Administration and Society*, **6**, 447.

Wheeler, D. and Janis, I. L. (1980), *A Practical Guide for Making Decisions* (New York: Free Press).

3

STRESS AND EFFECTIVE LEADERSHIP
DECISIONS

FRED E. FIEDLER, EARL H. POTTER, III,
AND MARK A. MCGUIRE

ABSTRACT

This chapter discusses the role of the leader's intellectual abilities in organizational decision-making in situations which are marked by relatively stress-free or stressful relations with the immediate superior or boss. Data based on a field study and a laboratory experiment show that the leader's intellectual abilities are utilized primarily in situations in which the relationships between leader and boss are relatively free of stress. However, when these relations are stressful the more intelligent leaders make poorer decisions than do leaders with lower intelligence. Furthermore, stress most strongly affects the effective use of 'fluid' rather than 'crystallized' intelligence (Horn, 1968) in making sound decisions. These studies suggest that boss stress seriously interferes with the ability to deal with new problems and novel situations rather than with the ability to learn and use knowledge acquired from such sources as school and books. These findings have important implications for organizational leadership.

The consistently low relationship between leader intelligence or experience and performance has long been a puzzling problem for leadership theorists. One tends to think that the leader's intellectual abilities must surely play an important part in analysing the group's problems, planning and deciding on a course of action, communicating the decision and action strategies to the group, and evaluating and monitoring its implementation. It should be reasonable, therefore, to expect substantial correlations between leader intelligence and performance. It is thus difficult to understand why the median correlations between leader intelligence scores and various performance measures are generally no higher than 0.22 to 0.28 (Stogdill, 1948; Mann, 1959; Ghiselli, 1963; Bass, 1981). The counter-intuitive nature of these findings has led us to hypothesize that intelligence is related to performance only under some conditions but not others. This paper attempts to explain these counter-intuitive findings and attempts to identify more specifically the conditions under which intellectual ability contributes to effective performance.

The question of when leader intelligence, technical competence, and experience are effectively used is an important facet of Cognitive Resource Theory (Fiedler, 1986; Fiedler and Garcia, 1987). This theory, building on early work by Blades (Blades and Fiedler, 1976) supports a series of interrelated hypotheses which account for these findings. One hypothesis of this theory predicts that a moderate level of job stress resulting from, for example, a shortage of time or a complex problem, forces the leader to attend to the task. Thus, the more intelligent leader is more likely to perform well than the leader with relatively less intelligence. In contrast, interpersonal stress, and especially stress with one's superior, diverts the individual's focus from the task to the troubled relationship. The leader may then ruminate about the consequences of failure, the need to avoid the boss, or how to find another job. These thought processes divert the leader's intellectual effort from the task and thus lower the relationship between leader intelligence and task performance.

That boss stress has a greater effect on the effective use of leader intelligence than does job stress was suggested in our previous research (e.g., Fiedler, Potter, Zais, and Knowlton, 1979; Fiedler and Leister, 1977). These studies showed that boss stress strongly affects the contribution of the leader's intellectual abilities to the task. This finding was further substantiated by a large field study of an army infantry division (Borden, 1980; cited in Fiedler and Garcia, 1987) which is here briefly summarized.

Borden (1980) collected data from a combat infantry division's officers and non-commissioned officers, i.e., 45 company commanders, 37 company executive officers, 106 platoon leaders, 42 first sergeants, and 163 platoon sergeants. These men completed various tests and questionnaires, including the Wonderlic Personnel Test (Wonderlic, 1977), a measure of intelligence substantially correlated with other tests of intellectual ability. A questionnaire also asked them to rate stress with their boss and stress created by the job, using an 11-point scale.

Performance of these leaders was rated by 3–5 superiors on a 61-item 5-point scale developed by Bons (Bons and Fiedler, 1976) which asked to what extent the particular leader exceeded, met, or failed to meet various standards of performance, e.g., 'the way he handles his job when demands are extra heavy', or '… when he finds himself under severe pressure'. Split-half reliability of the scale was 0.95, interrater agreement for two raters was 0.65.

The data were analysed by (a) dividing the leaders within each job (company commander, company executive officer, first sergeant, platoon leader, platoon sergeant) as nearly as possible at the 33rd and 67th percentile of the boss and job stress scales, and (b) correlating the leader's intelligence with rated performance under the relatively low, moderate, and high-stress conditions. As expected, the trend in correlations was from a high positive correlation under conditions of low boss stress to a near zero correlation when stress with the boss was high ($r = 0.44$, $N = 129$, $p < 0.001$ for low stress; $r = 0.31$, $N = 116$, $p < 0.01$ for moderate stress; $r = -0.02$, $N = 110$, $p = NS$ for high stress). These correlations were lower and the difference between correlations under low stress and high stress conditions was less when the groups were divided on the basis of low, moderate, and high job stress ($- 0.02$, $N = 131$; -0.06, $N = 123$; 0.54, $N = 114$, $p < 0.01$).

There is then considerable evidence that the correlation between the intellectual ability of managers and the performance of the groups they supervise is moderated by stress. The next question is how does stress inhibit the performance of managers. Mintzberg (1973) describes three clusters of managerial roles – decisional roles, informational roles, and interpersonal roles. This suggests three alternative explanations for the influence of stress upon managerial performance:

(a) Stress may divert the leader's intellectual effort from the decision-making task. This explanation is supported by Sarason's (1984) and Spielberger and Katzenmeyer's (1959) findings that evaluation anxiety leads to rumination and worry about self-efficacy with the consequence that the leader cannot pay attention to the task.
(b) Stress may affect the ability of the leader to communicate clearly. This is evidenced, for example, by the many people who stammer and sound confused when stress is high, or the common experience of stage fright, or freezing up in an oral examination.
(c) Stress may interfere with the leader's ability to control and supervise the group process that leads to the implementation of the leader's plans and action strategies. Some leaders become so distracted and disorganized under stress that they do not pay attention to the management of their group.

COAST GUARD STAFF OFFICERS

Potter and Fiedler (1981) shed some light on the differential impact of stress on managerial functions. They conducted a study of 130 Coast Guard officers and petty officers who occupied responsible staff positions in a large headquarters organization. Almost all subjects headed offices or staff sections. These men were asked to indicate how much of their time and effort was devoted to each of ten important staff functions that had been identified, and independent judges from the Coast Guard rated the degree to which each of the ten functions was intellectually demanding. The functions, ranked by intellectual demand characteristics, were: (1) advising seniors or preparing information for decisions made by a senior, (2) project engineering, (3) evaluating field units, (4) decision-making, (5) providing logistic/administrative support for staff or field units, (6) attending staff meetings, (7) supervising subordinates, (8) training field units, (9) public representation, and (10) routine paperwork.

Thirty-four subjects reported that a major proportion of their time was devoted to decision-making; fifty-seven reported that a major proportion of their time was devoted to advising on policy issues, a function highly related to decision-making. We shall compare these two functions with various others that involve communication but relatively little decision-making, namely, routine paper work and training subordinates according to a detailed work plan. Also included are data on public representation (public relations) which, of course, requires communication skills. Finally, we include data on officers performing design engineering work, a function demanding a high degree of intellectual effort but relatively less of decision-making and communications functions. We asked each of the officers to report stress with his boss and job stress. The boss stress measure was based on a 6-item, 7-point scale defined by factor analysis with items loading 0.56 to 0.72. The items asked how much stress each person felt as a result of his boss behaving in a certain way (e.g., 'He acts unfriendly and unapproachable', 'He does not inform me what he expects of me').

Job stress was measured by a single item, 7-point scale asking subjects to rate how much stress their present job places on them (no stress to extreme stress). The correlation between the boss stress scale and job stress was 0.15 ($N = 102$).

The staff officers' and petty officers' immediate superiors were asked to rate their performance with a previously used 16-item scale developed by Bons (1974) which had a split-half reliability of 0.86. The scale asked the superior officer to rate the subject 'in comparison to all other persons you know in a similar position', e.g., 'His consistency in setting high standards of performance'. The correlation between stress with boss and bosses' performance ratings of subordinates was −0.07; the correlation between job stress and performance was 0.09 ($N = 102$). The absence of a direct relationship between stress and performance permits consideration of boss stress in a moderating variable by computing the correlations between the management functions performed by Coast Guard staff personnel and intelligence under two different stress conditions.

The results of table 3.1 differ in one important respect from those of the Borden (1980) study. In the latter, the correlations between intelligence of line personnel and their performance under conditions of low stress

Table 3.1. *Correlations between intelligence and performance in decision and supervisory functions of Coast Guard personnel with high and low boss and job stress*

	Boss stress		Job stress	
	Low	High	Low	High
Decision-making				
Making decisions	0.11 (21)	−0.47 (13)	0.06 (24)	−0.24 (23)
Policy advising	0.27 (30)	−0.46* (22)	0.15 (25)	−0.19 (23)
Communicating and executing orders				
Supervising subs.	0.07 (29)	0.04 (18)	0.15 (23)	−0.01 (24)
Training	0.11 (26)	−0.17 (21)	0.03 (16)	−0.12 (24)
Public representation	0.04 (26)	−0.36 (16)	−0.09 (19)	−0.04 (13)
Administration				
Paper work	0.01 (25)	−0.25 (21)	−0.03 (25)	−0.16 (21)
Project engineering	0.38 (20)	−0.16 (21)	0.27 (22)	−0.05 (19)

Notes: Figures in brackets are numbers in the sample.
* $= p < 0.5$.

tended to be relatively high and positive. In the Coast Guard study of staff personnel, intelligence was essentially uncorrelated with performance under low stress. However, we find significant negative correlations between intelligence and decision-making performance under high boss stress conditions; stress had relatively little effect on the correlations between intelligence and performance on jobs requiring supervising or training of subordinates, or communicating with the public.

In other words, boss stress appeared to affect the contribution of intelligence to decision-making rather than to the communication and the execution of orders, public relations work, or performance of routine tasks. These results suggest that interpersonal stress diverts the intellectual abilities from decision-making tasks rather than interfering either with communications functions or with the execution of plans and supervision of subordinates. As in the Borden (1980) study, job stress had no significant impact on the relationship between intelligence and performance.

The Coast Guard study raised several questions. The first is why the correlations between intelligence and performance under low boss stress were substantially lower than corresponding correlations obtained in the infantry division study. We suggest that the typical staff job in the Coast Guard as in most large organizations does not allow for much discretion. Hence, such intellectual abilities as original thinking and creativity are not highly valued, nor do they contribute highly to organizational success.

Who, for example, would want a district supply officer who sets up his own method of accounting for equipment, or filing records? On the other hand, everyone is familiar with the complaint that 'They never notice me unless I make a mistake.' While the opportunity to distinguish oneself in a staff assignment may be limited, the 'opportunity' for notorious error still exists.

A second question is why job stress seemed to affect the contribution of intelligence less than did boss stress. In the absence of sufficient data we hypothesized that the logical way to cope with job stress (lack of time, complex problems) is by putting one's mind to the task. However, there is no logical way of coping with *boss stress*. The very nature of boss stress as defined by Potter and Fiedler (1981) is that of a 'double-bind'. The boss exerts pressure for performance but does not provide needed support or direction on how to meet his demands. Not surprisingly, boss stress is likely to lead to unfocussed anxiety or rumination about one's problem, and hence diverts attention from the task.

Third, are certain intellectual abilities more vulnerable to stress than others? Specifically, does stress affect the application of intellectual abilities that reflect the ability to learn from existing materials, as in school subjects (i.e., Horn's (1968) crystallized intelligence), or does it affect the ability to think in analytic and original fashion (fluid intelligence)?

Fourth, does stress with the boss interfere with the ability of bright managers to use their intellectual resources effectively, or are the brighter managers, who recognize that they are not doing well, more likely to experience a greater degree of stress with their boss? A laboratory experiment sought to address these problems.

THE IN-BASKET STUDY

In attempting to answer these questions, McGuire (1987) conducted a laboratory experiment with thirty-four ROTC cadets which used the in-basket exercise from the Army's leadership assessment programme. The subject played the role of a new Second Lieutenant who has just returned to duty after having been on assignment elsewhere for several weeks. He finds twenty-one separate letters, memos, and messages on his desk to which he must respond in a thirty minute period.

This version of this particular in-basket exercise has been used extensively by the Army in its officer assessment programme. It is a carefully constructed task that evaluates nine specific leader behaviours and skills, shown on table 3.2. Three of these behaviours are identified as decision-making functions. The tasks identified as administrative skills correspond closely to those functions associated with Mintzberg's (1973) informational roles, while communication, personal/motivational, and inter-

Table 3.2. *Leadership dimensions used in the Army in-basket exercise*

Decision-making skills:

　　Problem analysis – The skill required to identify a problem, secure information relevant to the problem, relate problem data from different sources, and determine possible causes of problems.

　　Judgement – The ability to develop alternative courses of action based on logical assumptions that reflect factual information.

　　Decisiveness – The readiness to make decisions, render judgements, take action, or commit oneself.

Administrative skills:

　　Planning and organizing – The ability to establish a course of action for self or others to accomplish a specific goal; planning proper assignments of personnel and appropriate allocation of resources.

　　Delegation – The ability to use subordinates effectively; the allocation of decision-making and other responsibilities to the appropriate subordinates.

　　Administrative control – The ability to establish procedures for monitoring and regulating processes, tasks, or activities of subordinates, and job activities and responsibilities; to monitor actively the results of delegated assignments or projects.

Communications skills:

　　Written communication – The skill required to express ideas clearly, in writing, using good grammatical form.

Personal/motivational behaviour:

　　Initiative – The discipline that requires attempting to influence events to achieve goals beyond those called for; originating action; self-starting rather than passive acceptance.

Interpersonal behaviour:

　　Sensitivity – Those actions that indicate a consideration for the feeling and needs of others.

---

personal behaviours are clearly associated with Mintzberg's interpersonal roles. A manual is available for identifying and scoring the various behaviours. The effectiveness scores provided in the manual are based on the structured judgements of expert judges.

　　The thirty-four cadets were given the Horn (1968) scales of crystallized and fluid intelligence. The former (measured with vocabulary items) is related to formal education and seems to measure what a person learns over time. It is thus correlated with school performance. Fluid intelligence, measured by letter or number series items (A B, A C, A –?) is related to speed of learning in novel situations. It measures how an individual will utilize past learning and concepts in being resourceful and in dealing with novel situations. The effective contribution of intelligence is defined by the correlation between the intelligence score and the various leader behaviours.

　　The cadets were randomly assigned to work under one of two conditions. In the 'high stress' condition, the exercise was administered in a

Table 3.3. *Mean perceived stress for subjects with high and low test anxiety under high and low stress conditions*

| | | Test anxiety | |
		high	low
Stress	high	4.88 (8)	2.50 (6)
	low	2.45 (11)	2.56 (9)

Notes: Stress: $F (1,33) = 6.98, p < 0.05$,
Test anxiety: $F (1,33) = 3.30, p < 0.10$,
Stress × test anx.: $F (1,33) = 5.88, p < 0.05$.

very formal and relatively threatening military atmosphere. Military officers proctored the exercise, walking around, looking unfriendly, and peering over the cadets' shoulders. These cadets were also told that they might have to justify their test responses to their battalion commander. In the 'low stress' condition the atmosphere was relaxed, and was monitored by a non-military proctor who remained seated throughout the test, and the cadets were not told that they might have to justify their responses.

In our previous work boss stress has been defined as the stress the leader perceives in the relationship with his or her boss. A cursory examination of the data quickly reveals that individuals differ widely in the amount of stress they perceive in any one situation. Some people are easily stressed, others seem almost immune to stress. This means that only some individuals will feel stress or anxiety in experimentally induced stress conditions. Since the manipulation in this study was designed to evoke evaluation apprehension, a measure of evaluation or test anxiety was chosen as the predictor of perceived stress.

Overall results of a post-test questionnaire showed that the stress manipulation was successful. Table 3.3 shows the results of the manipulation for subjects with high and low test anxiety. These results clearly show that the predisposition to experience stress and the objective circumstances are necessary conditions for perceived stress.

When subjects are divided at the median of perceived stress, the results show that perceived stress strongly affects the role of fluid intelligence in decision-making. Under low stress, cadets with high fluid intelligence were more effective in analysing problems, planning, and organizing, and being decisive than under high stress. In the latter condition, the leaders with high fluid intelligence showed relatively poorer judgement and made poorer decisions than those with lower fluid intelligence (table 3.4).

Crystallized intelligence had very little effect on leader behaviours

Table 3.4. *Correlations between fluid intelligence and in-basket dimensions under low and high stress*

	Perceived stress condition		
	Low (N = 19)	High (N = 15)	Fisher's significance
Decision-making			
Problem analysis	0.537***	−0.130	0.056
Judgement	0.120	−0.561**	0.048
Decisiveness	0.427**	−0.583**	0.004
Administrative behaviours			
Planning and organizing	0.475**	−0.331	0.024
Delegation	0.398**	−0.334	0.040
Administrative control	−0.203	−0.374	NS
Personal/motivational behaviour			
Initiative	0.353	−0.072	NS
Interpersonal behaviour			
Sensitivity	0.223	−0.282	NS
Communication skills			
Written communication	0.223	0.236	NS

Notes: ** = p < 0.10.
*** = p < 0.05.

either under stress or low stress conditions (table 3.5). The study also throws light on our third question: communication skills (at least as evidenced in writing) were not affected by stress. The findings suggest, therefore, that stress affects the individual's intellectual abilities to deal with new and original problems rather than routine problems, and that the main impediment to effective performance under stress is its effect on the decision-making process rather than on the communication process or the plans for executing the leader's plans (table 3.5).

DISCUSSION

The studies which have here been presented make two main points. First, the most likely reasons for the low correlation between the intelligence of managers and their performance is that the intelligence of the manager correlates positively with performance ratings under low stress while it correlates negatively with performance under high stress. Second, the interference of stress in the management process tends to occur primarily in the planning and decision-making phase rather than in the communication or execution of the plans. Third, the stress that appears most detrimental to the effective utilization of intellectual abilities is stress

Table 3.5. *Correlations* *between crystallized intelligence and in-basket
dimensions under low and high stress*

	Low (N = 19)	High (N = 15)	Fisher's significance of difference
Decision-making			
Problem analysis	0.200	0.403	P = NS
Judgement	0.154	0.194	P = NS
Decisiveness	0.324	−0.155	P = NS
Administrative behaviours			
Planning and organizing	0.150	−0.127	P = NS
Delegation	0.061	−0.056	P = NS
Administrative control	−0.015	−0.096	P = NS
Personal motivational behaviour			
Initiative	0.119	0.268	P = NS
Interpersonal behaviour			
Sensitivity	0.092	−0.147	P = NS
Communication skills			
Written communication	0.242	0.496	P = NS

Note: $* = p < 0.05$; $** = p < 0.01$.

generated by the boss (and perhaps also by other interpersonal sources) rather than by the job itself.

Cognitive resource theory attempts to identify the role of intellectual abilities and job-relevant knowledge in determining leadership and group performance and it thus provides a more comprehensive understanding of the leadership process. The theory specifies the conditions in which these cognitive resources contribute to performance. We have here related cognitive resource theory to the managerial decision-making process.

While our data strongly suggest that the more intellectually able leaders tend to make better decisions than less intelligent leaders when stress with the superior is relatively low, it is far from obvious why the more intelligent leaders should make poorer decisions than less intelligent leaders under conditions of interpersonal stress. Research is currently under way to examine several alternative answers to this question.

One possible explanation is that the more intelligent leader has higher expectations, and therefore attempts riskier solutions to the problem in order to impress his or her boss. A second hypothesis is that the brighter leader under stress does not focus on the main problem and thus becomes diverted from the task. Third, the more intelligent leader, under stress, may work on different problems than the less intelligent, and perhaps also than the less cognitively complex leader, and that these other problems are not those the organization deems valuable.

A few words of caution are in order. The leader's intellectual abilities obviously are not the only factors that determine effective decision-making. Some decisions require tact and sensitivity rather than intellectual ability, and our data suggest that it is experience rather than intelligence that counts in stressful situations (Fiedler and Garcia, 1987). Our studies clearly show that we need to determine more specifically the conditions under which specific cognitive resources contribute maximally to effective decision-making in organizations (Fiedler and Garcia, 1987).

REFERENCES

Bass, B. M. (1981), *Stogdill's Handbook of Leadership* (New York: Free Press).
Blades, J. W. and Fiedler, F. W. (1976), 'The influence of intelligence, task ability and motivation on group performance', Organizational Research Tech. Rep. 76–8, University of Washington, Seattle.
Bons, P. M. (1974), 'The effect of changes in leadership environment on the behavior of relationship and task-motivated leaders', Doctoral dissertation, University of Washington, Seattle.
Bons, P. M. and Fiedler, F. E. (1976), 'The effects of changes in command environment on the behavior of relationship- and task-motivated leaders', *Administrative Science Quarterly*, 21, 453–73.
Borden, D. F. (1980), 'Leader-boss stress, personality, job satisfaction and performance: another look at the inter-relationship of some old constructs in the modern large bureaucracy', Doctoral dissertation, University of Washington, Seattle.
Fiedler, F. E. (1986), 'The contribution of cognitive resources and leader behavior to organizational performance', *Journal of Applied Social Psychology*, 16(6), 532–48.
Fiedler, F. E. and Garcia, J. E. (1987), *New Approaches to Effective Leadership: Cognitive Resources and Organizational Performance* (New York: Wiley).
Fiedler, F. E. and Leister, A. F. (1977), 'Leader intelligence and task performance: a test of a multiple screen model', *Organizational Behavior and Human Performance*, 21, 1–14.
Fiedler, F. E., Potter, E. H., III, Zais, M. M., and Knowlton, W. A., Jr. (1979), 'Organizational stress and the use and misuse of managerial intelligence and experience', *Journal of Applied Psychology*, 64, 635–47.
Ghiselli, E. E. (1963), 'Intelligence and managerial success', *Psychological Reports*, 12, 898.
Horn, J. L. (1968), 'Organization of abilities and the development of intelligence', *Psychological Review*, 75, 242–59.
Mann, R. D. (1959), 'A review of the relationships between personality and performance in small groups', *Psychological Bulletin*, 56, 241–70.
McGuire, M. A. (1987), 'The contribution of intelligence to leadership performance

on an in-basket test', unpublished master's thesis, University of Washington, Seattle.

Mintzberg, H. (1973), *The Nature of Managerial Work* (New York: Harper & Row).

Potter, E. H. and Fiedler, F. E. (1981), 'The utilization of staff member intelligence and experience under high and low stress', *Academy of Management Journal*, **24**(2), 361–76.

Sarason, I. G. (1984), 'Stress, anxiety and cognitive interference: reactions to tests', *Journal of Personality and Social Psychology*, **46**, 929–38.

Spielberger, C. D. and Katzenmeyer, W. G. (1959), 'Manifest anxiety, intelligence, and college grades', *Journal of Consulting Psychology*, **22**, 278.

Stogdill, R. M. (1948), 'Personal factors associated with leadership: a survey of the literature', *Journal of Psychology*, **25**, 35–71.

Wonderlic, E. F. (1977), *Wonderlic Personnel Test* (Northfield, IL: Wonderlic).

Zajonc, R. B. (1965), 'Social facilitation', *Science*, **149** (3681), 269–74.

4

DURATION AND COMPLEXITY IN STRATEGIC DECISION-MAKING

PIETER J. D. DRENTH AND PAUL L. KOOPMAN

ABSTRACT

In this chapter two aspects of strategic decisions are discussed: their duration and complexity in many cases being both caused by and leading to conflict of interest. Complexity is further determined by uncertainty of information and the serious consequences this has for personnel and organization. Both aspects make the control and coordination of such decisions difficult. Partly based on the results of an international comparative study, it is shown that a proper conceptual structuring of the decision-making process and a careful consideration of interests are essential prerequisites for good decision-making.

I INTRODUCTION

Much of the current organizational literature focusses on strategic decision-making and strategic management (Hickson *et al.*, 1986; Bass, 1983). One aspect which has repeatedly been singled out is that many managers, in industry as well as in government, are not really capable of reacting adequately to a changing environment. Another criticism is that some managers have insufficient negotiating skills to allow them to function effectively in situations in which strongly opposed interests exist or emerge. A possible explanation may be the fact that, in the past, managers were primarily selected on the basis of their skills in purely operational management.

The present chapter will focus on a number of characteristics which distinguish strategic decision-making from operational decision-making: namely duration, conflict, and uncertainty. The extended duration, the great uncertainty about which information elements are relevant, and the severity of the consequences for personnel and organization make it more difficult to coordinate and control strategic decisions. It is our view that a carefully devised phase structure of the decision-making process and a meticulous consideration of interests are important steps on the way to better decision-making.

2 CHARACTERISTICS OF STRATEGIC DECISION-MAKING

Three main issues can be distinguished in the many problems, which management has to face:

(a) The coordination of interaction between organization and environment; that is to say external coordination. This includes the definition of goals and the selection of ways to achieve these goals.
(b) The coordination of the activities of individual members and groups within the organization, as well as the interaction between technology and organization members; this is internal coordination and it comprises the definition and control of the production process.
(c) The development of a structure, or a framework in which means can be generated and coordinated to achieve the organizational objectives. Designing an organization structure implies the division of work, the distribution of decision-making powers, and the choice of certain forms of coordination.

There is another characteristic which is typical for managerial decision-making, and that is the level of abstraction and, related to this, the time perspective of the decisions with which management has to deal. A distinction can be made between operational, fairly short-time decisions on the one hand and complex, medium- or long-term decisions that have strategic and policy implications on the other. The former type of decisions occur more frequently and are concerned with operations which can be found lower in the organizations. The latter occur less frequently, have a medium- or long-time perspective, and concern issues which are located higher in the organization.

These complex medium- and long-term decisions are often relatively unstructured, do not always have precise precedents, and operate under conditions of uncertainty and ambiguity. Furthermore they often entail risks. These are the types of decisions that are the primary responsibility of middle and top management. The complex decisions can be further divided into *strategic* decisions (having direct relevance for the continuity of the organization; see Bacharach and Aiken, 1976; Mintzberg, Raisinghani, and Théorêt, 1976) and *tactical* decisions (more related to the control systems with respect to personnel, or to an adequate execution of the work; see Child, 1972).

A more or less related classification is that of Katz and Kahn (1978, p. 436). These authors distinguished three basic types of leadership behaviour:

'origination': the formulation of policy and the creation and change of structures (especially at the top level);

'interpolation': the development of ways of carrying out policy (especially middle management);

'administration': making use of the existing structure and the application of procedures and regulations (especially lower echelons).

In our study *Decisions in Organizations* (Heller *et al.*, 1988) this distinction required a distinct framework and methodology for the research on short-term operational decisions on the one hand and medium- and long-term tactical and strategic decisions on the other. In this chapter special attention will be paid to a number of characteristics of strategic decisions, which have important consequences for the behaviour of both the decision-makers themselves and the managers who are supposed to direct and control such complex decision-making processes. The first characteristic is the *complexity* as well as the incompleteness of the information with which the decision-maker is generally confronted. It was primarily on this point that Herbert Simon criticized as early as 1947 the suppositions that lay at the basis of the classic rational decision-making model:

there is one clear goal;
this goal can be described in quantitative terms;
the decision-maker knows the possible ways to reaching this goal; these ways are limited in number;
the decision-maker's aim is always to achieve a maximum of utility (Harrison, 1981).

As opposed to the 'economic man', who has thorough insight of all possible alternatives and rationally chooses the best alternative, Simon (1947), postulated the 'administrative man', who has only a limited knowledge of the possible alternatives, and can only evaluate a few of these simultaneously. Instead of the 'objective rationality' in the classic decision-making theories, Simon introduced the concept of 'bounded rationality'. The 'administrative man' chooses the alternative that gives him just enough satisfaction for his level of aspiration: he looks with a simplified model of reality and exhibits 'satisficing' rather than 'maximizing behaviour'.

In some strategic decisions the irrationality is further reinforced; for example in the case of decisions pertaining to reduction of production and the workforce and the layoff of personnel. The fear that the apparent failure of the organization will be ascribed to poor management – promotes a great deal of irrational behaviour on the part of management. It may react too late, or not at all. The significance of warning signals is often incorrectly interpreted. The search for relevant information is half-hearted and poorly conducted. 'Wishful thinking' predominates over sober analysis. Janis and Mann (1977) termed this 'defensive avoidance'. By lingering, passing the buck, and picking the alternative which is the least unpleasant at first sight, one tries to avoid the threatening situation.

A second characteristic of strategic decisions involves *conflict*. It relates to the strong interests of personnel and organization which are generally at stake. Decisions to change or reduce the organization or production may have serious negative consequences for part of the personnel. Innovative decisions can offer the prospect of a better future. The gravity of the possible consequences makes it understandable that the groups involved may come to stand in fierce opposition. Group interests may dominate the decision-making.

This is further strengthened by the fact that the necessary information is often ambiguous, as was described in the preceding paragraphs. As the interests become stronger and the ambiguity increases, objective views are replaced by subjective goals and interests, and rational decisions are replaced by bargaining, group pressures, and power relations. Conflicts become normal phenomena and conflict regulation requires a good deal of the manager's time and attention.

The third characteristic of strategic decisions is their *duration*. They often have a lead time extending over weeks, months, or even years. They frequently require discussions among organization members on several hierarchical levels and are influenced by a variety of internal and environmental factors. Sometimes the process of consulting of persons or groups is a deliberate choice of management, sometimes it is enforced by strong opposition or by law. In the Netherlands, for instance it is obligatory to consult the works' councils on important reorganization plans.

In the next section we will try to interpret some empirical material from our own and other studies to further analyse the time dimension and the strategic-conflict dimension in strategic decision-making.

3 TIME DIMENSION AND PHASING

The long time axis of strategic decisions and the need to build-up and keep sufficient support among those directly involved are both reasons for management to structure the decision-making process into several distinct phases. An advantage of classifying a lengthy process into easily recognizable steps is that it can be made clear to the groups involved what contributions are expected of them and when. This at least creates some clarity for those involved in a period of great uncertainty. It means that their fears about the consequences can be somewhat allayed as well. Several phase models for decision-making can be found in the literature. A typical example is the model of Brim *et al.* (1962), with the following steps: (1) identifying the problem, (2) seeking information, (3) generating possible solutions, (4) evaluating the alternatives, (5) selection, and (6) implementation of the decision. Other authors work with a somewhat simpler classification, since the distinctions between steps 2 and 3 and between steps 4 and 5 are often difficult to discern in practice (see e.g. Witte, 1972). Mintzberg *et al.* (1976) studied twenty-five strategic decisions and found three central phases: 'identification', 'development', and 'selection'.

Our own study was based on a four phase model: 'start, development, finalization, and implementation' (Heller *et al.*, 1988). This research involved 217 complex decision-making processes in the three countries Netherlands, United Kingdom, and Yugoslavia. In general, the empirical data supported the correctness of the phases hypothesized. But the decision steps did not always occur in this orderly fashion. Many major decisions were divided into several sub-decisions, in which the activities of search, development, evaluation, and selection were repeated again. The nature of these decision-making processes was therefore more circular than sequential.

Assuming these four phases (start, development, finalization, implementation), the question is how they should be interpreted in terms of influence and power relations. Two contrasting views can be brought forward. The first is that of Sfez (1978), who views decision-making as an integration process of knowledge and power. In his view, the first and the third phases are primarily characterized by power processes, while knowledge aspects are predominant in the second and the fourth phases. The second point of view is that of Enderud (1980), who assumes, like Sfez, that the power game is an essential part of strategic decisions. Their opinions differ as to the stage in which the power struggle is concentrated. According to Enderud, it is as early as the second phase, generally within a small group operating behind closed doors. The primary function of the third phase then becomes the official legitimation of the decision. This entails approval by the proper persons and the creation of support among those directly involved.

There is much to be said for both views on *a priori* grounds: it is difficult to decide which is a better representation of reality. Furthermore, the question which model is more correct might well depend on particular circumstances, such as the nature of the issue at stake, and the degree to which the decision-making process is formalized. In the democratized decision-making structure at Dutch universities and colleges during the 1970s, faculty and university councils, in which all scientific staff, administrative and technical personnel, and students were represented, had quite effective control of important decisions. This was primarily due

Table 4.1. *Influence scores (scale 1–5) of workers (A) and works'
council (Q) for phases (1, 2, 3, 4) of the decision-making process
across countries (medium- and long-term decisions)*

Level	Phase	UK (N = 80)	NL (N = 55)	YU (N = 82)
Workers	1	1.8	1.7	2.8
	2	1.7	2.1	2.1
	3	1.7	1.6	3.4
	4	2.0	2.7	2.1
Works' council	1	2.4	1.6	2.5
	2	2.6	2.2	2.4
	3	2.7	2.0	2.7
	4	2.4	2.0	2.0

Notes: 1 = no or minimal information,
2 = information only,
3 = opportunity to give advice,   Influence
4 = advice taken into consideration,   scores
5 = joint decision-making.   scale 1–5

to their influential participation in the first and the third phases: the
definition of the problem and the choice of the ultimate solution. But since
the 1980s decisions relate to cutbacks rather than expansion and the
importance of the second phase has increased: more and more, solutions
are prepared fairly minutely in informal and/or confidential circles in
which a prominent role is played by small groups of experts and
professional administrators. Research of the cutback decision in industry
points in the same direction: in crisis situations the power of management
increases. The official discussion of the plans with the works' councils has
the function of legitimation, but it seldom leads us to serious alteration
(Koopman, 1983). In such a situation, Enderud's model seems more in
accordance with reality than that of Sfez.

Our study of complex decisions in seven English, Yugoslavian, and
Dutch companies (Heller *et al.*, 1988) illustrates a variety of influence
sharing arrangements (see table 4.1). In the Dutch and the English
companies the lowest degree of influence by workers and works' councils
was found in the first and the third phases, the highest in the second and
the fourth.

In Yugoslavia the opposite was the case: the greatest amount of
participation and influence was found in the first and the third phases and
the lowest in the second and fourth.

This may suggest that when decision-making is more formalized, more
public, and less controversial (Dutch universities in the seventies, and
Yugoslavian companies), the workers' influence is concentrated more in

Table 4.2. *Mean influence-power scores of hierarchical groups for the four phases of the decision-making process, across two types of decisions*

Level	Phase	Long-term decisions	Medium-term decisions
Workers	1	1.9	2.4
	2	1.8	2.1
	3	2.6	2.0
	4	2.1	2.1
Middle management	1	3.2	3.2
	2	3.4	3.6
	3	3.2	3.5
	4	3.6	3.8
Top management	1	4.4	3.5
	2	4.5	3.7
	3	4.5	4.2
	4	4.4	3.4
Staff members	1	3.5	2.5
	2	3.9	3.0
	3	3.2	2.5
	4	3.9	2.8
Works' council	1	1.9	2.5
	2	2.1	2.7
	3	2.1	2.8
	4	2.1	2.2

Notes: The scores in this table, as in table 4.1, derive from an Influence-Power-Continuum with five positions:
1 = no or minimal information,
2 = information only,
3 = opportunity to give advice,
4 = advice taken into consideration,
5 = joint decision-making.

the 'power phases' (Sfez), possibly because this offers a better guarantee of the legitimation of the process. In regular strategic decision-making in the Netherlands and Great Britain the highest influence of workers and works' councils is found in the 'knowledge phases' 2 and 4. According to Sfez this would indicate an advisory, consulting type of influence, whereas in the view of Enderud this could indicate real power.

Further evidence on the importance of the distinction of decision phases is presented in table 4.2. It presents the amount of influence/power in long-term and medium-term decisions for: workers, middle management, top management, staff members, and works' councils in the four decision phases: initiation (1), development (2), finalization (3), and implementation (4). In this table the relevance of both the distinction in type of complex decisions and the phase of decision-making is clearly illustrated. More specifically the results suggest the following interpretations (see also Heller *et al.*, 1988, pp. 125–7):

1 Workers' score of involvement is highest within the first phase of medium-term decision-making, while in long-term decision-making it is highest in the third stage. This means that workers have much more opportunity to initiate those issues which refer to people oriented medium-term matters, than to those which refer to long-term decisions.

2 The pattern of participation exercised by top management on medium- and long-term decision-making activity reverses the patterns of participation for workers. Top management is not substantially involved in the first phase of medium-term decisions, but it is able to control the whole process through greater involvement in the strategic third phase. On the other hand, top management is intensively involved in all four phases of long-term decision-making.

3 Staff advisers are more involved in all phases of long-term than in medium-term decision-making. The pattern of participation for representative bodies is the opposite: representative bodies are more involved in all phases of medium-term decisions than in long-term decisions.

These phase patterns show that the domination of staff advisers and top management over decision-making in an organization is even greater than one can conclude by comparing only aggregate or cross-sectional indicators. It is clear that strategic issues and strategic steps of decision-making are in most cases strongly controlled by these two groups.

We assume that this is a fairly general picture in contemporary economic organizations. Previous research by ignoring phases could only come to conclusions about a simplified overall picture. For instance a recent twelve country comparative research (IDE, 1981) found that, in all countries, influence and power among managers was substantially greater in long-term decision-making activity than in medium- and short-term decision-making activity, while the opposite was found for workers and representative bodies.

4 CONFLICT OF INTERESTS AS AN ASPECT OF COMPLEXITY

As a result of the combination of unclear information and the seriousness of the consequences for those involved, many groups try to advance their own preferences and interests, thus creating uncertainty and complexity. An essential characteristic of many strategic decisions is therefore a blend of factual, rational decision-making and a promotion of the interests of those involved. The art of good decision-making requires the timely

Table 4.3. *Mean conflict scores across countries*

	UK	NL	YU
Frequency of operational conflicts[1]	1.6	1.4	2.1
Frequency of perceptual conflicts[2]	1.9	1.8	2.1
Frequency of all conflicts[3]	2.4	1.9	2.8
Intensity of conflicts[1]	1.9	2.0	2.1
Resolution method[4]	2.2	2.6	2.2

Notes: [1] scale: 1–3;
[2] differences about how an operation should be carried out; scale: 1–3;
[3] different perceptions of events; scale: 1–3;
[4] the higher the score the more frequently open facing was used and the less frequently forcing of smoothing.
Source: Derived from Lawrence and Lorsch, 1976.

creation of sufficient support among the parties which are most closely involved, and the avoidance of a clash of interests which would jeopardize rational as well as social considerations.

On the basis of our study of the 217 complex decision-making processes in Yugoslavia, England, and the Netherlands, some conclusions can be formulated about (1) the nature and the magnitude of conflicts and (2) the relationship between the participation strategy chosen and the final outcome of the decision-making process (see table 4.3).

First of all, conflicts indeed took place in the large majority of strategic decisions. However, it should be observed that the decisions studied generally offered a positive perspective for those involved: they were decisions about new investments, starting a new product, allocations, etc. It must be assumed that the conflict intensity will generally be higher in retrenchment and reallocation decisions. The Yugoslavian companies turned out to have the most conflict, although there were considerable differences in the degree of conflict among organizations in every country. The organizations with the highest frequency of both operational and perceptual conflicts were the organizations with the highest total amount of participation in organizations ($r = 0.29$ and 0.24). It seems that the number of disagreements or conflicts in organizations is compatible with influence sharing styles of decision-making. This finding has been confirmed elsewhere (IDE, 1981).

The greatest number of conflicts occurred in the second and third phases. This once again indicates that the transition from the second to the third phase must be regarded as strategically very important. Often the decision-making process turns out to be a series of negotiating processes at different levels in the organization, in which objective judgement is under strong pressure from group interests. And yet there are forces that prevent conflict management, the constructive forms such as 'open facing' or some degree of 'smoothing' were predominant (Lawrence and Lorsch, 1976). Approaches with more destructive effects on the integration of the organization, such as forcing a decision or eliminating the opponent, were used less frequently. However, the degree of forcing may be related to the nature of the decisions studied. A study by Koopman *et al.* (1983), showed that retrenchment and reallocation decisions do generate harder conflict management methods.

Of course, a central question still has to be answered: what decision-making strategy offers the best chance of success? In our study success refers to the degree to which the set goals were reached (effectiveness), the price that had to be paid for this (efficiency), and the degree of acceptance of the outcome by the organization members.

Decision-making strategy refers to the question which hierarchical groups participated in which phases and to what extent. The chief conclusion was that – generally speaking – no consistent relation existed between decision-making strategy and results.

In the first column of table 4.4 the results of an analysis of this relationship for the fifty-six Dutch complex decisions are presented (Koopman, 1980). One sees little systematic relationship for the total unspecified sets of decisions. But specification of conditions of conflict in which the decisions were taken does reveal an interesting picture (see columns 2 and 3). Conflict seems to be an important contingent variable. A high level of conflict is found only in situations where there are positive correlations between participation and a better use of capacities and skills and more satisfaction with decision-making.

With a low level of conflict there even seems to be a consistent negative relationship between participation on the one hand and efficiency, satisfaction, and the use of skill on the other.

Finally it is interesting to analyse the relationship of conflict variables (intensity and frequency) with other contingent and outcome variables. Space does not allow us to illustrate this extensively with empirical data (we have to refer to the relevant publications (Heller *et al.*, 1988; Drenth and Koopman, 1984)). A summary of these findings can be formulated as follows: conflictuousness is negatively related to trust, clarity of goals, acceptability, feasibility, satisfaction with outcomes, and skill utilization.

Even if conflicts are not very strong they create uncertainty within the decision-making system. In the first section of this paper, ambiguity and uncertainty were described as important characteristics of strategic decisions. It seems that conflicts are important ingredients of ambiguity and uncertainty within the decision process.

Table 4.4. *Kendal tau correlations (×100) between influence scores IPC (for workers) and dependent variables for the total set (col. 1) and for the decisions under high and low conflict conditions (N = 56)*

Dependent variables: IPC-A	Total set of conflict	High level of conflict IPC-A	Low level IPC-A
Rating of success	−02	−05	−03
Rating of efficiency	−08	03	−34
Satisfaction with process	12	27*	−38
Satisfaction with outcome	14	21	−13
Satisfaction after implementation	21*	27*	00
Use of capacities	28	24*	−31
Time used	09	11	16

Notes: * $p < 0.05$.
IPC is the Influence-Power-Continuum described in tables 4.1 and 4.2.

At the same time a positive correlation was found between conflicts and the participation/influence score of the work force. One possible explanation may be that, in case of much disagreement or conflict, a participative strategy is selected by management, which would then lead to effective and well-accepted decisions. This suggestion could be in line with the finding that participation is more effective under conditions of conflict, whereas the reverse seems to be the case in non-conflictuous circumstances (table 4.4).

Another hypothetical explanation may be based upon the distinction between genuine and pseudo participation. The latter type of participation describes consultation and information dissemination designed to reduce resistance to change and to persuade people, rather than to give them real influence or to make use of their knowledge and skills. Harmony may be achieved, but effectiveness and quality of decision-making may not be improved. Genuine participation, however, opens up the possibilities for alternative solutions, deviating proposals, and disagreements. Such disagreements and different views may lead to improvement of the quality of the final decision outcome.

5 SUMMARY

In this chapter some logical and empirical evidence was provided for the importance of two characteristics of strategic decision-making: their extension over time and their complexity. Complexity is related to a conflict of interests and to a high level of ambiguity and uncertainty about information. It was shown that for a further understanding of the nature and mechanics of the decision-making process it is useful to make a distinction between at least four phases of the decision cycle: start, development, finalization, implementation. Various patterns of influence and power for different hierarchical groups in the organization were found, and differential effects of participation in the different phases could be shown. Uncertainty, the other important characteristic, is enhanced by disagreement and contentiousness of the decisions. The conflictuous character of decisions is negatively related to a number of contextual (trust, clarity, and goal) and outcome variables (effectiveness, satisfaction with outcomes). At the same time, the occurrence of conflicts is positively related to participation and influence of the employees. Neither of the two hypothetical explanations (conflicts call for participation and (genuine) participation creates disagreement) were in conflict with the empirical data.

NOTE

This paper is based on an international comparative study, in which in addition to the authors also Dr F. A. Heller (London) and Dr V. Rus (Ljubljana) participated. Their (indirect) contribution to this paper is gratefully acknowledged.

REFERENCES

Bacharach, S. B. and Aiken, N. (1976), 'Structural and process constraints on influence in organizations: a lead-specific analysis', *Administrative Science Quarterly*, 21, 623–42.

Bass, B. M. (1983), *Organizational Decision Making* (Homewood, Ill.: Irwin).

Brim, O., Glass, D. C., Larvin, D. E., and Goodman, N. E. (1962), *Personality and Decision Process* (Stanford, CA: Stanford University Press).

Child, J. (1972), 'Organization structure and strategies of control: a replication of the Aston study', *Administrative Science Quarterly*, 17, 163–77.

Drenth, P. J. D. and Koopman, P. L. (1984), 'A contingency approach to participative leadership: how good?', in J. G. Hunt, D. M. Hosking, Ch. A. Schriesheim, and R. Stewart (eds.), *Leaders and Managers: International Perspectives on Managerial Behavior and Leadership* (New York: Pergamon Press), pp. 303–15.

Enderud, H. (1980), 'Administrative leadership in organized anarchies', *International Journal of Management in Higher Education*, 235–53.

Harrison, E. F. (1981), *The Managerial Decision-making Process* (Boston: Houghton-Mifflin).

Heller, F. A., Drenth, P. J. D., Koopman, P. L., and Rus, V. (1988), *Decisions in Organizations: A Three-Country Comparative Study* (London: Sage).

Hickson, D., Butler, R., Cray, D., Mallory, G., and Wilson, D. (1986), *Top Decisions: Strategic Decision Making in Organizations* (Oxford: Blackwell).

IDE, International Research Group (1981), *Industrial Democracy in Europe* (Oxford University Press).

Janis, I. L. (1972), *Victims of Groupthink* (Boston: Houghton Mifflin).

Janis, I. L. and Mann, L. (1977), *Decision Making* (New York: The Free Press).

Katz, D. and Kahn, R. L. (1978), *The Social Psychology of Organizations* (New York: Wiley).

Koopman, P. L. (1980), *Besluitvorming in organisaties* (Decision-Making in Organizations) (Assen: Van Gorcum).

   (1983), 'Management strategies in organisational reduction', First North-West European conference on the psychology of work and organisations, Nijmegen, 28–30 March.

Koopman, P. L., Kroese, H. A. F. M., and Drenth, P. J. D. (1983), 'Complex decision making: rationality or inspiration?', International Workshop: Future Prospectives of Economic and Industrial Psychology, Dubrovnik.

Lawrence, P. R. and Lorsch, J. W. (1976), 'Organization and environment: managing differentiation and integration', Graduate School of Business Administration, Harvard University, Boston.

Mintzberg, H. (1983), *Power In and Around Organizations* (Englewood Cliffs: Prentice-Hall).

Mintzberg, H., Raisinghani, D., and Théorêt, A. (1976), 'The structure of unstructured decision processes', *Administrative Science Quarterly*, **21**, 246–75.

Sfez, L. (1978), 'Existe-t-il des decisions democratiques?', *Dialectiques*, **22**, 59–72.

Simon, H. A. (1947), *Administrative Behavior* (New York: Free Press).

Witte, E. (1972), 'Field research on complex decision-making processes: the phase theorem', *International Studies of Management and Organization*, **2**, 156–82.

5

DECISION-MAKING AND THE UTILIZATION OF COMPETENCE

FRANK HELLER

ABSTRACT

A considerable literature discusses the extent to which power and influence is shared in managerial decision-making. A critical question is whether influence and power sharing (IPS) has positive consequences for the organization. For example, are organizations which practise high levels of IPS more productive or profitable? And, if they are, why?

The thesis of this chapter is that, other things being equal, IPS does increase organizational efficiency. It achieves this result through three related processes: first it makes better use of organizational members' existing competence (experience and skill), secondly it helps develop new competence, and thirdly it liberates dormant motivation. The theoretical framework to describe these relationships is called the Motivated Competence model, which also suggests that attempts to use IPS when relevant experience and skill are absent results in inauthentic or manipulative participation.

INTRODUCTION

This chapter will analyse the role of competence as one of the conditions which operates both as a constraint and an opportunity in the process of IPS.

There is a large social science literature investigating different influence-sharing methods of decision-making (DM) or styles of leadership (for instance Allport, 1945; Stogdill and Coons, 1957; Blake and Mouton, 1964; Likert, 1967; Heller and Yukl, 1969; Vroom and Yetton, 1973; Misumi, 1985). The extensive attention given to this topic in several areas of social science, including organizational behaviour, theories of change, and leadership, is often commented on (Macy *et al.*, 1989) and has led to a proliferation of terms used to describe the influence-power-sharing (IPS) process, including: participation, initiating structure versus consideration, industrial democracy, involvement, power equalization, co-

71

determination, performance-maintenance behaviour, empowering, and decentralized leadership.

IPS covers a wider range of leadership styles than participation. It starts with access to the decision-making process through sharing information and goes beyond consultation and consensus decision-making to delegation or autonomy. Nevertheless, because the term participation is so widely used in the literature, it will also be used in this chapter.

Most researchers share the assumption that IPS has some identifiable advantage over more centralized decision methods, at least in some circumstances. The advantages of IPS are frequently based on values and ideologies (Strauss, 1963) as much as on practical considerations, like economic efficiency (Warner, 1984), and analogies are drawn between political and organizational democratic systems (Pateman, 1983) which may be inappropriate. Critical assessment of IPS can also be influenced by politically informed beliefs (Locke and Schweiger, 1979).

The emphasis on ideology has had positive and negative effects. On the positive side, it has undoubtedly led to a greater volume of research and experimentation (much of it of high quality) than would otherwise have occurred. On the negative side, apart from poorly designed investigations, there has been a tendency to assume that the appropriate antecedent and consequential conditions that most people accept as legitimate for political democracy can be translated into organizational life without much adaptation. The similarities and differences between political and organizational democracy have not received sufficient conceptual and empirical attention (Pusic, 1984), and since it is as difficult to argue against motherhood as against democracy, academics have been reluctant to probe sufficiently into the limiting and contingency factors which distinguish between feasible and non-feasible applications of IPS. These value positions are not easily substituted by more analytically based rational approaches, but it is hoped that a model of DM which pays special attention to the role of experience and skill and its relation to IPS will clarify many of the issues that at the moment rely on little more than good sense and personal values.

This chapter will analyse the role of competence as one of the conditions which operates both as a constraint and an opportunity in the process of participative decision-making.

EVIDENCE ABOUT SKILL JUDGEMENTS AND PARTICIPATION

One of the earliest pieces of evidence about the relationship between competence and participative DM comes from the fourteen country study of Haire *et al.* (1966). They found that in their sample of 3,600 managers there was a consistent tendency for managers to have little faith in the competence of other managers, while at the same time they approved of participative DM. The authors were conscious that this finding drew attention to a major inconsistency in attitudes, since participation only made sense if one could assume that there was sufficient experience and skill among participating members to improve the quality of decisions.

A few years earlier, Miles (1964) had found a similar negative assessment by managers of their lower level employees: 'although managers have few doubts about their own abilities, they have serious reservations concerning the abilities of those below them' (p. 78). Nevertheless, 'the typical manager generally endorses participative policies, whether or not he has faith in the capacities of those below him' (p. 89). The managers' judgements about their subordinates' capabilities may, of course, be wrong. In our own research on senior management in eight countries, we used different instruments from Haire *et al.* (1966) and Miles (1964), but again found that, on average, senior managers thought that their immediate subordinates, who were also senior managers, had substantially lower skills and would take a very long time to reach the level of competence of the next higher level (Heller and Wilpert, 1981). However, we also had objective measures of experience and qualifications and these objective indices showed that the subordinates were, on average, equal to their superiors and in some dimensions, like formal education, scored higher. We used a method called Group Feed-back Analysis (GFA) to confront our groups of managers with their own judgements and asked them to elaborate on them. It then emerged that, on reflection, most groups felt some discomfort about their negative assessment of subordinates. Since our research involved both levels with identical questions and procedures, we felt confident that in reality, the difference in competence between the two senior levels was very small. For instance, it emerged that, in a large number of cases, the senior managers travelled extensively through the year and, during such absences, the subordinate made all relevant decisions. In each case, the decisions were accepted as satisfactory.

While judgements about competence may be quite incorrect, they are nevertheless likely to influence behaviour. In Miles' early work he found a small but statistically significant relationship 'between managers' attitudes towards participation with subordinates and attitudes towards their subordinates' abilities' (Miles, 1964, p. 88). Attitudes towards participation were more favourable as the perceived skill gap between the manager and his subordinates decreased. Since then we have evidence that this relationship is not confined to attitudes, but affects leadership behaviour, particularly in relation to the methods used for making decisions.

Frank Heller

CONTRASTING MODELS OF THINKING

A study of decision-making of 260 top managers in fifteen large American companies used a list of twelve specific tasks to describe the decision behaviour by two interlocking boss-subordinate pairs of managers (Heller, 1971). At both levels each member of the dyad was asked to give scaled judgements of the minimum skills required for their own job and separately for the job on the other level. Later, managers on both levels described how each of the twelve decisions was taken. The findings show 'that senior managers are willing to share more influence and power with subordinates whose skills they perceive to be similar to their own' (p. 107).

Ten years later, an eight country study of 1,600 senior managers in 129 large companies (Heller and Wilpert, 1981) extended the inquiry, but retained the same measurements of skill judgements and decision-making with a larger and more diverse sample. The research again came to the conclusion that judgements about competence significantly affect managerial behaviour.[1]

The early work by Miles (1964) and Haire *et al.* (1966) required a reassessment of the theoretical model used to describe the participative process. Miles came to the conclusion that the starkly inconsistent managerial attitudes reflected genuine alternative models of thinking. One model expresses a manager's judgement about himself, the other refers to lower levels of the hierarchy. The model that describes how managers conceptualize the reaction of subordinates has been called the human relations model (HREL). It is the result of a movement away from the classical theories of 'scientific management' championed by Frederick Winslow Taylor and his followers, who advocated a highly centralized autocratic style. Taylor's writings (Taylor, 1911) show that he had a very low opinion of the ordinary employee and devised a system which sought to accumulate all competence at higher levels. Managers were expected to give orders and to be obeyed without question. The human relations philosophy, influenced by the work of Elton Mayo and others (Trahair, 1984) revolted against autocracy and viewed employees in more humanistic terms. Employees should be given information about management plans and have opportunities to feel that they participate in a common endeavour. Participation is a way of softening the effect of centralized structures by building cooperative work teams that will not resist managerial initiatives. Participation, in this model, is thought to be an effective way of increasing work motivation and satisfaction. The emphasis is on oiling the wheels and getting decisions accepted, not on producing a better mechanism and improving the quality of DM.

In contrast, the human resources (HRES) model, as described by Miles

(1965), starts from a different set of assumptions. Employees are seen as having a substantial reservoir of untapped resources which they are eager to make available to the organization. Not being involved in the decision process is then seen as a frustration as well as a loss of potential. The untapped resources include a wide spectrum of experience and skill, including creativity and the ability to work responsibly for the good of the organization, rather than narrowly in the pursuit of self-interest. The basic value underlying this model, is that people at all levels of the hierarchy want to fulfil themselves by realizing their potential through the process of DM.

The research mentioned earlier in fifteen American companies (Heller, 1971) as well as the larger comparative research (Heller and Wilpert, 1981) found extensive evidence to support both the HRES and HREL models. Senior managers consistently judged their competence levels to be substantially higher than that of their immediate subordinates, although our evidence, and their own admission later, showed this perceptual skill gap to be unrealistic and, in practical terms, also unworkable. For instance, the senior level believed that their most experienced subordinate would need twenty-one months to acquire the minimum skills necessary for the senior position. During feed-back discussion it was widely accepted that this would, in most cases, lead to inefficiency and frequently to bankruptcy. Despite their negative judgements on subordinates, they claimed to support a philosophy of participation and in this way demonstrated their adherence to the HREL model.

However, other parts of the same study supported the HRES model. Managers at both levels were asked to rank in order of importance five reasons for using participative DM. The results are shown in table 5.1.

With very few exceptions, managers at both levels and in nearly all countries gave as the most important reason for participation, the improvement of the technical quality of the decision. The two motives attributed to the HREL philosophy: increasing satisfaction and facilitating change were given much lower priority. Increasing satisfaction came third or fourth, and facilitating change came last at both organizational levels in nearly all countries. These results support the HRES model. Further evidence to support the HRES philosophy came through their judgements on the utilization of competence. The 1,600 managers in the 1981 study were asked how much of their current job-relevant experience and skill they were unable to use in their organization. The average under-utilization of their competence was about 20 per cent at both levels (Heller and Wilpert, 1981, p. 117). This figure varied significantly in the eight industrial sectors covered by the study, reaching 27 per cent in public transport (p. 118). More importantly, high under-utilization reached 52 per cent among the most qualified senior managers and nearly 62 per cent

Table 5.1. *Reasons for using participation rank orders of senior and subordinate levels in eight countries*

	Countries								
	US	GB	NL	D	F	S	IS	E	All
Level 1									
To increase satisfaction	2	3	2	3	4	3	3	3	3
To improve technical quality of decision	1	1	1	1	3	1	1	1	1
To train subordinates	4	4	5	4	2	4	4	4	4
To improve communications	3	2	3	2	1	2	2	2	2
To facilitate change	5	5	4	5	5	5	5	5	5
Level 2									
To increase satisfaction	3	3	3	3	4	3	4	3	3
To improve technical quality of decision	1	1	2	1	2	1	1	1	1
To train subordinates	4	4	4	4	3	5	3	4	4
To improve communications	2	2	1	2	1	2	2	2	2
To facilitate change	5	5	5	5	5	4	5	5	5

Notes: US = USA, GB = Britain, NL = Netherlands, D = Germany, F = France, S = Sweden, IS = Israel, E = Spain, All = average of eight countries.

among those under forty years of age (p. 121). There was clearly a very substantial loss of perceived competence in the 129 companies of our sample. Similar results come from O'Brien (1986, p. 26) who describes an extensive study of Australian employees who reported under-utilization varying from 29 per cent to 45 per cent.

Managers at both organizational levels answered some questions eliciting values and others describing specific decision behaviour. The inconsistency of their answers applied to values as well as to behaviour description. These inconsistencies could explain why participative practices are often contrived and inauthentic.

LONGITUDINAL RESEARCH

Most studies of decision-making, leadership, and participation are cross-sectional. This makes it impossible to come to any firm conclusions about cause and effect. Is skill utilization an antecedent to IPS or a consequence, or does it play a role in both directions? A four-year longitudinal research in three countries tried to address itself to this issue and concentrated on tracing the decision process over time with 217 specific tactical and strategic issues (Heller *et al.*, 1988). Some aspects of this study are described in the chapter by Drenth and Koopman.

We made the assumption that all strategic and tactical decisions can be traced through a cycle of events from start-up through development and finalization to implementation. During this progress, various people exert influence as long as they have access to the DM process. What we have called IPS (influence and power sharing) can be assessed on a continuum with six positions from no or minimal information being given to potential participants, via opportunity to give advice and joint decision-making, to delegation or complete control. We assessed the antecedent conditions to the IPS process and its consequences. Skill utilization was one of five postulated consequences of the IPS–DM process. The others were satisfaction, efficiency, achievement, and duration of the cycle.[2]

The results support a model in which skill utilization is an outcome of IPS. In particular, it could be shown that the utilization of experience and skill was significantly predicted by the way influence was distributed between senior management and lower levels of the organization. When top management exercised a very high degree of influence and prevented the participation of lower levels and reduced the influence of the works council, then the existing reservoir of experience in the organization was under-utilized (see Heller *et al.*, 1988, figure VII.2, p. 220 for a summary of results). The ethnographic material based on being present during committee meetings and individual discussions with staff at all levels, supported the statistical analysis. In the twelve month cycle of budget forecasting, for instance, senior management relied extensively on quantified predictions by chiefs of division, but failed to solicit inputs from lower levels that were more closely in touch with the customer. Substantial error in forecasting could be traced to this non-participative process (Heller *et al.*, 1988, pp. 165–78).

The failure to obtain lower level inputs into budget forecasts is further evidence to support the contention that the HREL philosophy is alive and well and the inconsistency in attitudes and behaviour is as noticeable today as it was four decades ago.

The HREL model lends itself to manipulation because it is content with creating a 'feeling of participation' rather than the reality. Many writers have observed this; Etzioni (1969) calls it inauthentic participation, Pateman (1970) talks of pseudo participation, which she describes as creating an impression of involvement when in reality no influence is shared. 'It is used to persuade employees to accept decisions that have already been made by management' (Pateman, 1970, p. 68). Hopwood (1976, p. 77) describes situations where managers induce a 'feeling of participation in situations which provide little freedom'; Heller (1971, pp. 97–9) came to the conclusion that 'participatory techniques were frequently used manipulatively' and in particular when managers described their behaviour as 'prior consultation', it frequently turned out that it would have been more accurate to call it 'post facto' participation.

Pseudo or manipulative participation would make no sense to people who genuinely espoused the HRES way of thinking, because involving people without using their experience and skills, would not contribute to the main objective, which is to achieve superior overall results based on the use of all available resources.

What makes people adopt two very different and inconsistent ways of thinking? Is it possible that the contrast between these models is too great, that there are other factors not accounted for and that the complexity of the situation is substantially greater than the models suggest? Is it possible that the human relations model takes too gloomy a view of human nature while the human resources model portrays an unrealistic ideal?

What follows is a tentative attempt to reassess the evidence we have reviewed and to suggest the need for amendments to the human resources model (HRES).

THE COMPETENCE MODEL

The strength of the HRES model is its stress on the under-utilization of available skills, but its weakness is in the assumption that most people have a very extensive portfolio of experiences and abilities, including creativity and an understanding of the substantial complexities of modern organizations. This idealistic assumption which underpins the HRES model is not supported by sufficient evidence. There are occasions when this competence is present, but there are at least as many when it is not. The literature on participation is replete with idealistic values showing, as Strauss noted: 'the earmarks of its academic origin' (Strauss, 1963, pp. 48–9). Mulder (1971) made a similar analysis.

Two recent examples will illustrate the need for an adaptation of the model to bring it closer to reality. They both come from Germany: one from the advanced economy of the Federal Republic in the west, and the other from the technologically less advanced German Democratic Republic, before their merger in 1990. A three-year research in the Federal Republic covered twelve companies using computer-aided production planning and control. The report describes in detail the difficulty trade unions and works' councils have in taking an active and useful part in the decision process of these organizations (Hildebrandt, 1989). Although management gave prompt and extensive information, the author concludes that, due to a lack of relevant competence, 'the works' councils have little to show for their activity, even in plants with a high degree of organization in an area where unions are strong' (p. 194). He also observed that many works' councils were not interested in taking part in technical aspects of decision-making, although they had important consequences for their members. This lack of motivation is underlined by the fact that the unions did not make use of their legal rights under the Works Constitution Act, to use the advisory services of experts, even though the cost of such advice would have been borne by management.

The research in East German companies using information technology came to similar conclusions (Meier, 1989). The qualifications of their labour force are said to be high. Only 15 per cent have no formal vocational training and 20 per cent are professionals with diplomas or degrees. Nevertheless, the opportunities for effective participation did not exist. Meier concludes that 'for democratic control of new technologies, two types of knowledge are indispensable: general job competence, including the necessary level of skills, experience and education ... and specialized information on prerequisites, strategy' (p. 201). More generally, Meier claims that, 'without competence based on knowledge which can be used for specific purposes, it seems impossible to turn potential opportunities for participation into real influence' (p. 204).

It should not be thought that this problem is confined to high technology companies. It exists over a wide range of activities but has received inadequate research attention. Mulder's (1971) well-known contribution to the participation literature cites evidence, mainly from Dutch research, that works' council members were not very interested in taking an active part in decision-making unless the subject fell within their personal sphere of interest. He also cites evidence from Yugoslavia, which had the most highly structured and legally supported scheme of self-management, to show that employees without special skills make very little contribution to council discussions and, in general, motivation to contribute, even to problems of very great importance, is low. Mulder's laboratory research supports the hypothesis that, when there are large differences in expert power between people, an increase in participation will increase the difference in power rather than reduce it. Much earlier, in experiments with teachers and students, Asch (1951) had shown that participation did not improve performance when the teacher rather than the students had the required skills. Calvin *et al.* (1957) found from laboratory studies that participative decision-making was successful in increasing productivity with competent students, but unsuccessful when competence was absent.

THE DUAL ROLE OF COMPETENCE

It seems that in analysing the relationship between influence and power sharing (IPS) in the decision-making (DM) process we have to distinguish two distinct roles for competence. In the first place as an antecedent, and in the second place as an outcome (see figure 5.1). As an antecedent to the IPS–DM process, competence is a prerequisite for genuine rather than pseudo participation. Without the relevant experience and skill, people

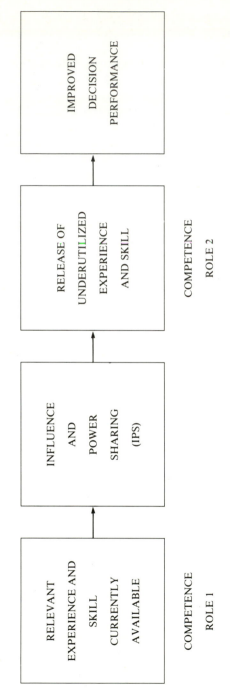

Figure 5.1   The two roles of competence

are neither motivated nor able to make a contribution to the DM process. However, there are circumstances when pseudo participation succeeds in giving people a feeling of being involved and this can lead to increases in satisfaction.

We do not know how long this induced satisfaction lasts, though there is some evidence that subordinates become aware of the inauthentic nature of IPS and then react against it (Heller, 1971, pp. 98–9).

There is a third position between IPS based on competence and inauthentic participation. This occurs when people take part in committees or other participative arrangements as a way of acquiring experience and skill which would subsequently allow them to switch to IPS based on competence. There is no systematic information about the use of this learning motivated form of participation, but it can play an important part in the total cycle of events (see figure 5.2). Where IPS is used as a learning experience, the subsequently acquired competence (Box 3) like the liberated competence (Box 2) would result in improved decision performance (Box 4). The competence released or created as a result of IPS then becomes the antecedents for further useful IPS. This is illustrated in the feed-back loop of figure 5.2.

We have seen that the limitation of the HRES model is due to its unrealistic assumption about people's experience and abilities. Many research projects have shown that employees are motivated to participate on subjects with which they have direct experience, but are reluctant or unwilling to take part or to assume responsibility over issues that are outside their competence (Mulder, 1971; Hespe and Wall, 1976; IDE, 1981; Drenth and Koopman, 1984). It would follow that, where people are expected or persuaded to be present in discussions on subjects outside their experience, they would take as little active part as possible (Obradovic, 1970) and would show little satisfaction. The important consequence of omitting competence as a necessary precondition for meaningful participation has been to encourage manipulative IPS and to neglect the critical role of training.

The literature on participation has paid almost no attention to the creation of experience and skill as a prerequisite to influence sharing and there are several well-documented examples where this neglect probably played a decisive role in the failure of major attempts by industry to involve inexperienced people in high-level decision-making (Brannen *et al.*, 1976; Batstone *et al.*, 1983). It seems likely that similar problems have occurred at the national level when legislation prescribed an active and important role for workers without giving them the necessary experience and training. The failure of self-management in Yugoslavia could be a consequence of this (Lydall, 1989). On the other hand, there is evidence that, where competence creation was taken seriously, influence sharing

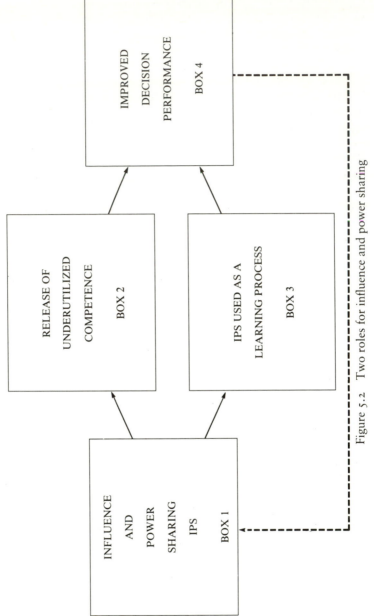

Figure 5.2 Two roles for influence and power sharing

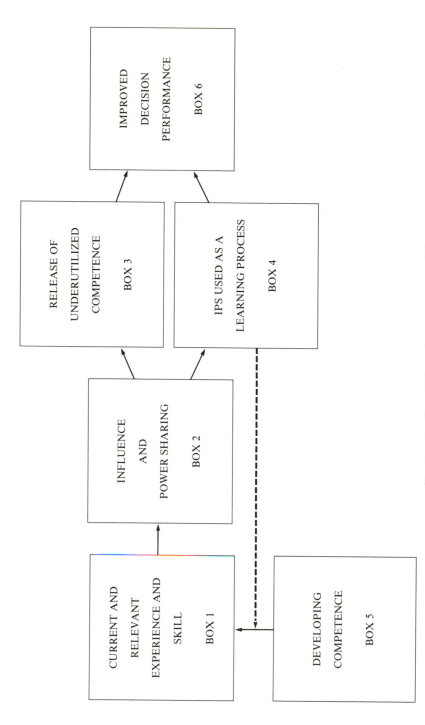

Figure 5.3   The motivated competence model

can be effective and satisfying. This is the lesson of the successful cooperative movement in the Basque country (Aurrezkia, 1986; Bradley and Gelb, 1981; Whyte *et al.*, 1983) and is probably the reason why semi-autonomous group work and its related quality circle movement in Japan has scored some successes (O'Brien, 1986, p. 277; Mohr and Mohr, 1983; Trist, 1981).

I have argued that there is a need to extend and amend the HRES model to include competence creation as well as competence utilization and to distinguish between IPS as a release of experience and skill and as a deliberate learning experience. These conditions are incorporated in the motivated competence model (MCM) (figure 5.3). The term 'motivated' is used on the assumption that merely providing opportunities for being involved in DM without relevant experience and skill is not enough. There is plenty of evidence that, as McCarthy (1989) shows, 'a major problem is that many employees when offered the responsibility of participation, choose not to become involved' (p. 115).

It is, of course, quite likely that, even if all the conditions of the MCM are met, some people will prefer to stay outside the DM process, but I believe that the number who will choose this option will be reduced.

HOW TO ASSESS OUTCOMES

Given the bewildering array of research approaches and ideologies, it is not surprising that global evaluation studies find it difficult to come to clear conclusions (Wagner and Gooding, 1987; Macy *et al.*, 1989). I want to mention three problems that explain the diversity of results. One is the choice of the outcome variable. Productivity and efficiency measures can usually be influenced by changes in a variety of circumstances apart from IPS. The output of a work unit producing soft drinks, for instance, will be decisively determined by changes in demand consequent on variations in weather rather than by participative work design. This may be an extreme case, but the principle holds. Secondly, we have seen that changes in IPS may leave employees unmotivated for a variety of reasons or may increase their job satisfaction without affecting other output measures. Thirdly, very few experiments apart from those described by O'Brien (1986) have taken account of changes in skill utilization which would explain changes in outcome according to the HRES model. Even fewer studies have taken note of the extent to which IPS is preceded by or requires skill development in its execution as demanded by the MCM.

Strauss (1982) realizes the limitations of some of the most widely used outcome measures and implicitly accepts the MCM when he argues that it is hardly surprising 'that the totally untrained workers in Peru and Algeria proved unequal to the demands of worker participation in management'

(p. 50). Strauss puts forward the view that IPS should be assessed by the effect it has on the wider society outside the factory gate, rather than on the narrow criterion of productivity and worker satisfaction (p. 174). For those who are content only with hard measures of success or failure, such a global approach would cause problems.

One alternative is to confine research to outcome measures that are largely or entirely controlled by IPS decision behaviour. Skill utilization would be an obvious candidate. One could put forward the view analogous with the engineer's concept of machine utilization that – other things being equal – better utilization of human competence should improve the quality of DM and ultimately the effectiveness of the operation. With this in mind, the three-country longitudinal research used two other outcome measures: efficiency (as an input/output measure of the decision process) and achievement (measuring the extent to which expected goals, objectives, and desired outcomes of the DM process were achieved). Efficiency was predicted by skill utilization and achievement by IPS variables (Heller *et al.*, 1988, pp. 149–60. See also the evidence reviewed by O'Brien, 1986, p. 65).

Although a great deal more evidence will have to accumulate, the MCM shown in figure 5.3 is a reasonable representation of the data currently available and the hypothesized relationships derived from the conceptual analysis presented in this chapter.

SUMMARY AND CONCLUSIONS

This chapter is concerned with leadership and decision-making processes and the use of influence and power. Influence and power sharing (IPS) has antecedents and consequences and I have isolated competence (experience and skill) as a major factor in the before and after events of decision-making (DM). It is, however, necessary to distinguish between situations where competence is present and where it is not.

It has been shown that, when people have the appropriate experience and skills, they are often prevented from using them. Excessively centralized, non-participative DM is largely responsible for the resulting wastage of human resources and consequent inferior decisions. This evidence supports the human resources (HRES) model. The previous human relations (HREL) model saw the main function of IPS as increasing job satisfaction and in this way, boosting organizational performance. By omitting competence, the human relations (HREL) model lends itself to manipulative behaviour. It allows, or even encourages, people to have a 'feeling' of being involved in the DM process, when in fact they have little or no influence over events.

We have seen that managerial beliefs oscillate between these two models of thinking; they apply the HRES model to themselves, because in their judgement they have the necessary competence and want to be genuinely involved in the DM process. At the same time, they prefer the ideas of the HREL model for lower levels of the organization because they have great doubts about the competence of their subordinates.

The weakness of the HRES model is that it makes unrealistic assumptions about competence and therefore neglects the need to develop further experience and skill resources. At all levels of organization there are potential or actual limits to the experience and skill currently available. While this has always been true, it has shown up more clearly in recent decades because of the enormous speed of technological change.

Influence and power sharing can be used as one method among many for creating relevant experience and skills, but the people designing and taking part in IPS with this objective have to be aware of what is happening. In many circumstances, more formal methods of training will be necessary to create the competence that would allow genuine IPS and achieve improved decision outcomes.

In this analysis, competence plays two distinct roles. One is as an antecedent to IPS behaviour. As an antecedent one has to make sure that the relevant experience and skill is currently available or is being developed through training. If the antecedent conditions are met, then IPS will draw on these resources of competence and this should enable the quality of decisions and organizational performance to improve. If the antecedent conditions are not fulfilled, IPS will fail to achieve improved performance, even if, at least for a time, job satisfaction may improve.

The dual role of competence requires an extension of the HRES model which I have called the motivated competence model (MCM) illustrated in figure 5.3 above. Some evidence in support of this model has been given, but more research is needed to test its main assumptions.

ACKNOWLEDGEMENTS

The material used in this chapter owes a great deal to the extensive financial support of the Economic and Social Research Council of Britain on two cross-national studies. In addition to the author, Professors Pieter Drenth, Paul Koopman, Veljko Rus and Bernhard Wilpert participated in some aspects of the various research studies.

I am grateful to Professors George Strauss and Raymond Miles for useful critical comments on previous drafts relating to the evidence on under-utilization of competence.

NOTES

1 Although the statistics used were based on concurrent correlations which do not allow one to interpret directional effects, the interpretation is based on tape recorded and content-analysed data from Group Feed-back Analysis.
2 For definition of these variables and detailed analysis and statistical results, see Heller *et al.* (1988).

REFERENCES

Allport, Gordon (1945), 'The psychology of participation', *Psychological Review*, 53, 117–32.

Asch, M. J. (1951), 'Non-directive teaching in psychology: an experimental study', *Psychological Monographs*, 65, 4.

Aurrezkia, Lan Kide (1986), *The Mondragon Experiment*, Caja Laboral Popular.

Batstone, E., Ferner, A., and Terry, M. (1983), *Unions on the Board* (Oxford: Blackwell).

Blake, R. and Mouton, J. (1964), *The Managerial Grid* (Houston, Texas: Gulf Publishing Co).

Bradley, K. and Gelb, A. (1981), 'Motivation and control in the Mondragon experiment', *British Journal of Industrial Relations*, 19, 2.

Brannen, P., Batstone, E., Fatchett, D., and White, P. (1976), *The Worker Directors: A Sociology of Participation* (London: Hutchinson).

Calvin, A. D., Hoffman, F. K., and Hardin, E. E. (1957), 'The effect of intelligence and social atmosphere on group problem solving behaviour', *Journal of Social Psychology*, 45, 61–74.

Drenth, Pieter and Koopman, Paul (1984), 'A contingency approach to participative leadership: how good?', in James Hunt, Dian-Marie Hosking, Chester Schjriesheim, and Rosemary Stewart (eds.), *Leaders and Managers: International Perspectives on Managerial Behavior and Leadership* (New York: Pergamon Press).

Etzioni, A. (1969), 'Man and society: the inauthentic condition', *Human Relations*, 22, 325–32.

Haire, M., Ghiselli, E., and Porter, L. (1966), *Managerial Thinking* (New York: Wiley).

Heller, F. A. (1971), *Managerial Decision-Making: A Study of Leadership and Power Sharing among Senior Managers*, (London: Tavistock Publications).

Heller, Frank and Wilpert, Bernhard (1981), *Competence and Power in Managerial Decision Making: A Study of Senior Levels of Organization in Eight Countries* (Chichester: Wiley).

Heller, F. A., Drenth, P., Koopman, Paul, and Rus, Veljko (1988), *Decisions in Organizations: A Longitudinal Study of Routine, Tactical and Strategic Decisions* (London and Beverly Hills: Sage).

Heller, F. A. and Yukl, G. (1969), 'Participation and managerial decision-making as a function of situational variables', *Organizational Behavior and Human Performance*, 4, 227–41. Also in Ervin Williams (ed.), *Participative Management: Concepts, Theory and Implementation* (Georgia State University, 1976).

Hespe, G. and Wall, T. (1976), 'The demand for participation among employees', *Human Relations*, 29, 411–28.

Hildebrandt, Eckart (1989), 'From codetermination to comanagement: the dilemma confronting works councils in the introduction of new technologies in the machine building industry', in Cornelis Lammers and Gyorgy Szell (eds.), *International Handbook of Participation in Organizations*, vol. I (Oxford University Press).

Hopwood, Anthony (1976), *Accounting and Human Behaviour* (Englewood Cliffs, New Jersey: Prentice-Hall).

IDE (Industrial Democracy in Europe Research Group) (1981), *Industrial Democracy in Europe* (Oxford University Press).

Likert, R. (1967), *The Human Organization* (New York: McGraw-Hill).

Locke, Edwin and Schweiger, David (1979), 'Participation in decision making: one more look', in Barry Staw (ed.), *Research in Organizational Behavior* (Greenwich, Connecticut: JAI Press).

Lydall, Harold (1989), *Yugoslavia in Crisis* (Oxford: Clarendon Press).

Macy, Barry, Peterson, Mark, and Norton, Larry (1989), 'A test of participation theory in a work re-design field setting: degree of participation and comparison site contrasts', *Human Relations*, 42, 1095–165.

McCarthy, Sharon (1989), 'The dilemma of non-participation', in Cornelis Lammers and Gyorgy Szell (eds.), *International Handbook of Participation in Organizations*, vol. I (Oxford University Press).

Meier, Artur (1989), 'In search of workers' participation: implementation of new technologies in GDR firms', in Cornelis Lammers and Gyorgy Szell (eds.), *International Handbook of Participation in Organizations*, vol. I (Oxford University Press).

Miles, R. E. (1964), 'Conflicting elements in managerial ideologies', *Industrial Relations*, 4 (1), 77–91.

Miles, R. E. (1965), 'Human relations or human resources?', *Harvard Business Review*, 43, 148–63.

Misumi, Jyuji (1985), *The Behavioral Science of Leadership: An Interdisciplinary Japanese Research Program* (Ann Arbor: The University of Michigan Press).

Mohr, William and Mohr, Harriet (1983), *Quality Circles: Changing Images of People at Work* (London: Addison-Wesley).

Mulder, Mauk (1971), 'Power equalization through participation', *Administrative Science Quarterly*, 16, 31–8.

Obradovic, Josip (1970), 'Participation and work attitudes in Yugoslavia', *Industrial Relations*, 9, 161–9.

O'Brien, Gordon (1986), *Psychology of Work and Unemployment* (Chichester: Wiley).

Pateman, Carole (1970), *Participation and Democratic Theory* (Cambridge University Press).

  (1983), 'Some reflections on participation and democratic theory', in Colin Crouch and Frank Heller (eds.), *International Yearbook of Organizational Democracy*, vol. I (Chichester: Wiley).

Pusic, Eugen (1984), 'The political impact of organizational democracy', in Bernhard Wilpert and Arndt Sorge (eds.), *International Yearbook of Organizational Democracy*, vol. II (Chichester: Wiley).

Stogdill, R. M. and Coons, A. E. (1957), *Leadership Behavior: Its Description and Measurement* (Columbus: Ohio State University, Bureau of Business Research).

Strauss, George (1963), 'Some notes on power equalization', in H. J. Leavitt (ed.), *The Social Science of Organizations* (Englewood Cliffs, NJ: Prentice-Hall).

Strauss, George (1982), 'Worker participation in management', in *Research in Organizational Behavior*, vol. IV, (JAI Press).

Taylor, F. W. (1911), *The Principles of Scientific Management* (New York: Harper).

Trahair, R. C. S. (1984), *The Humanist Temper: The Life and Work of Elton Mayo* (New Brunswick, NJ: Transaction).

Trist, Eric (1981), 'The evolution of socio-technical systems: a conceptual framework and an action research programme', *Issues in the Quality of Work Life*, No. 2, June, Ontario Ministry of Labour.

Vroom, Victor and Yetton, Philip (1973), *Leadership and Decision-Making* (University of Pittsburgh Press).

Wagner, John A. and Gooding, Richard (1987), 'Effects of societal trends on participation research', *Administrative Science Quarterly*, 32, 241–62.

Warner, Malcolm (1984), 'Organizational democracy: the history of an idea', in Bernhard Wilpert and Arndt Sorge (eds.), *International Yearbook of Organizational Democracy*, vol. II (Chichester: Wiley).

Whyte, William Foote, Hammer, Tove Helland, Meek, Reed Nelson, and Stern, Robert N. (1983), *Worker Participation and Ownership: Cooperative Strategies for Strengthening Local Economies* (Ithaca, NY: ILR Press).

6

REASSESSMENT OF PARTICIPATIVE
DECISION-MAKING: A CASE OF TOO MUCH
PARTICIPATION

PHILIP YETTON AND MIKE CRAWFORD

ABSTRACT

The widespread belief in the importance of management skills and management development has, for many, come to be associated with a belief in high participation in decision-making. A substantial 'industry' has grown up to service this perceived need in business.

Opportunities to examine the effectiveness of this 'industry' are rare but important. Such an opportunity was provided by the CEO of PTV, who instituted a change strategy for his firm involving both reorganization and team building. Very detailed data about the organization and its managers were collected before and after the intervention.

An extensive team building programme, based on the managerial grid, was instituted. Management teams at every level of the organization spent substantial time in activities intended to build their skills as team members and/or leaders.

After the treatment, managers at PTV expressed a strong preference for a highly participative management style but acted much like the typical Australian manager. The gap between expectations and behaviour also occurred in terms of other aspects of managerial behaviour (e.g. warmth, support conflict legitimacy, and responsibility). This gap between their strongly held expectations and their own behaviour was an emergent but unrecognized problem. It was manifest in dissatisfaction throughout the organization.

Before and after the intervention there were substantial differences between parts of the firm in manager style. These can be explained in terms of differences in task environment for various parts of the firm and the consequent *typical problem distribution* of roles. This typical problem distribution strongly influences the manager's actual leadership behaviour.

It follows that effective management training programmes need to be tailored to match role circumstances and this is likely to require prior unit or role context analysis. The case demonstrates why training programmes that meet one group's need may not be effective for others. In addition, the study highlights why leadership behaviours learned by a manager in one situation may prove unsuccessful if he moves to another context.

INTRODUCTION

The experience of a company which had invested in a major management development programme to increase commitment to group decision-making, provides a rare opportunity to assess the contribution of that intervention strategy to increasing organizational effectiveness. All such development programmes have implicit, if not explicit, underlying theories which specify how the participants' intended behavioural changes are linked to improvements in organizational performance. It would seem therefore that these programmes, which are legion, should be powerful 'laboratories' in which to test and develop organizational theory. In practice, this has not generally been the case (Mirvis, 1983). This is often because the intended changes are not achieved or the programme is prematurely aborted. These failures have generated considerable interest and theory development about the design of effective interventions and change strategies, but have provided few opportunities to test theories linking changes in behaviour to organizational outcomes.

This chapter explores an instance in which the objectives of the behavioural intervention were achieved, and, therefore, focusses attention on the consequences of the change strategy. The central issue then is the extent to which the strategy of increased participative decision-making was itself successful in achieving the organization's objectives, rather than alternative methods of implementing the intended changes. Here, accepting Lewin's famous words that 'There is nothing so practical as a good theory' (Lewin, 1945), we observe practice to test whether the underlying theory is a 'good' one.

OVERVIEW

Although the management development programme had met its primary objective in creating a strong shared belief in group decision-making, managerial dissatisfaction was unexpectedly high. It was this dissatisfaction which motivated the CEO to commission a review. The analysis revealed that a gap existed between managers' preferences for participation and their actual behaviour. It further showed that managers were responding more directly to requirements of specific jobs and the structure of the business than to their preferences for participative decision-making. This 'test' of the theory strongly supported a contingent framework for decision-making at both the individual manager and organizational levels of analysis, with important implications for improving decision-making in organizations (Locke, Schweiger, and Latham, 1986; Schweiger and Leana, 1986; Powell and Posner, 1980).

The presentation here is that of an empirical essay. It combines the breadth of coverage of a clinical case study, with its emphasis on completeness and integration of all findings within a single story, and a quantitative analysis, with its claims for rigour and external comparability of results. The database contains variables from the Vroom and Yetton (1973) model of decision-making, as well as organization and managerial behaviour indices. These include pre- and post-intervention measures of inter-unit dependence, and intra-unit measures of cooperation, conflict style, and quality of communication. For a comparable breadth of intra- and inter-unit data, see Van de Ven and Ferry (1980). The study is therefore somewhat unusual in the organization development literature, being both complex and quantitative.

In analysing the specific change intervention as a test of its underlying theories, this chapter addresses four broader issues. First, it evaluates a non-contingent theory of leadership decision-making relative to a contingent one. This analysis suggests an extension to the contingent theory, specifically, the development of a conceptual framework which links management decision-making style to organization structure. Second, it illustrates the potentially adverse consequences of an OD intervention which creates shifts in preferred decision-making styles which are not compatible with the organization's other authority and control systems. Third, it argues for context sensitivity, essentially for a contingent needs analysis, in the design and selection of training programme and OD interventions (Powell and Posner, 1980). Finally, it demonstrates the application of an extensive set of quantitative measures of management decision-making style, organizational context, and performance in order to assess the intervention in a theoretically relevant way. It is the integration across these different measures which gives the analysis its power.

THE FIRM AND ITS CHANGE STRATEGY

The firm, which employed about 700 people, was geographically dispersed across Australia. Each of the five branches offered essentially the same product range to its local market, and manufactured the bulk of what it sold. Product movement between branches was rare, with only a few specialized lines not produced at all locations. Partly as a function of Australia's demographic pattern, which means these branches were more than 1,000 kilometres apart, and partly because the products were typically high in bulk and weight, there were major barriers to any centralization and rationalization of production and distribution. Cross supplying occurred only when unanticipated fluctuations in demand or production exigencies created a product shortfall in some local market.

Pre change, each branch was identically organized, with a functional structure headed by a branch manager. The corporate head office was also functionally organized in a fashion that mirrored the structure at branch level. The heads of the corporate functional units were responsible for the policies governing the operation of the corresponding branch functional units, and, through these, exercised a strong reporting oversight, as well as some degree of influence on day-to-day branch activities.

This level of direct control exerted by head office over functional elements within the branches was a major source of dissatisfaction at branch level. Branches saw this as a significant intrusion into their activities. Conversely, and not surprisingly, the corporate office claimed that it failed to receive from the branches the information it regarded as important.

At the time of the initial study, PTV was enjoying market success. This was reflected in the usual financial indicators and in the assessments that the firm's managers made about its sales volume, market share, and profitability. While at that stage the CEO was pleased with PTV's market and financial performance, he was concerned to remedy what he perceived as deficiencies in the way the firm managed and used its staff.

His efforts had two thrusts, which he expected to be mutually reinforcing. One was increased participation in decision-making. The other involved structural decentralization.

The first thrust was to improve both the quality and acceptance of decision-making, so that the staff would be committed to working together and getting the job done. For that purpose, an extensive and continuing team-building programme was instituted. This was guided by an external consultant (not the authors). It involved management teams at every level of the organization. Each team spent substantial time attending class presentations and participating in experiential exercises to gain both a conceptual framework about, and experience of, greater team involvement and effectiveness in decision-making. As new people joined the firm, they were involved in a variant of this, so that there was an ongoing effort to maintain the culture of high participation in decision-making. The programme was based on the managerial grid (Blake and Mouton, 1978) and made extensive use of experiential learning.

The second element of the intervention was fundamentally a decoupling between corporate and branch functional units in those cases where the previous degree of interdependence was seen by the CEO as unnecessary, messy, and made it difficult to hold anyone accountable. This restructuring combined two of the corporate units and redefined responsibilities across the remaining corporate units and between them and the branches. Implicitly, this was a strategy of reducing internal complexity in order to minimize the cost of managing that complexity (Galbraith, 1973). Rather than committing resources to increasing integration (Lawrence and Lorsch, 1967), the approach was to reduce the required level of integration by reducing inter-unit task dependence.

EVIDENCE SUPPORTING THE CHANGE STRATEGY

The effectiveness of participation in decision-making has been the subject of many reviews. Generally, changes in supervisory style which increase the use of participation, through retraining or redeployment of roles, have been found to enhance organizational productivity. This includes improved quantity, quality, and cost effectiveness; reduced disruptions in terms of accidents and strikes; and reduced withdrawal, in forms such as absenteeism and labour turnover (Guzzo, Jette, and Katzell, 1985; Katzell and Guzzo, 1983).

Spector's (1986) review found that employee participation in decision-making and feelings of perceived control were consistently related to greater overall job satisfaction, and, specifically, with supervision and growth satisfaction; organizational commitment and job involvement; job performance and motivation; and reduced role conflict and ambiguity and absenteeism and labour turnover. Similarly, Cotton, Vollrath, Froggart, Lengnick-Hall, and Jennings' (1988) review found that participative structures that are formal, direct, long term, with high influence and about the work itself enhanced performance. Informal participation through face-to-face relationships and direct influence (as in the case of PTV) was associated with productivity, job satisfaction, satisfaction with work and supervisor, and less role ambiguity, conflict, and tension.

So, based on the evidence, it would have appeared reasonable for the CEO to encourage participation in decision-making through team-building and to develop more formal, direct, long-term high access structures through decoupling corporate and branch functional units. However, a closer inspection of the empirical evidence shows that the results are generally weak in magnitude, especially for informal participation in decision-making (Wagner and Gooding, 1987; Cotton *et al.*, 1988; Miller and Monge, 1986; Spector, 1986) and retraining of supervisors (Guzzo *et al.*, 1985; Katzell and Guzzo, 1983).

More importantly, contingency factors frequently moderated the impact of participation on performance and satisfaction, including the task relevant maturity of subordinates (Vecchio, 1987), the characteristics of the problems faced (Cotton *et al.*, 1988; Schweiger and Leana, 1986), and the nature of the task (Van Fleet and Yukl, 1986). For example, autocratic and *laissez-faire* leadership have been shown to be effective in certain situations (Van Fleet and Yukl, 1986). Hence Schweiger and Leana's (1986) review of laboratory and field studies concluded that moderator effects (such as employee knowledge, the nature of the decision) moderated the impact of participation in decision-making on performance. In a similar vein, the two components of the managerial grid, supportive and directive leadership behaviour, have been found by reviewers to be generally effective (Fisher and Edwards, 1988), but the effectiveness with respect to performance varied substantially according to the task's structure, scope, and repetitiveness (Idvik, 1986). In particular, Idvik reported the seemingly counter-intuitive findings that directive leadership resulted in greater performance with highly, but not lowly structured tasks.

These caveats for weak, contingent, and sometimes counter-intuitive effects therefore provide warnings that participation is only effective when matched with the nature of subordinates, the nature of the task, and the nature of the decision problems faced. If these contingencies are not heeded, the generally positive effects of participation may not occur. Hence reviewers (e.g. Locke, Schweiger, and Latham, 1986, and Schweiger and Leana, 1986) have concluded that because contextual variables moderate the relationships, it is simplistic to propose that participation enhances performance. Combined with the difficulty in developing the leadership skills for participative decision-making (Miner, 1980), the implementation of participative decision-making as a panacea for organizational problems must be approached with more caution than was the case here.

THE PRE- AND POST-CHANGE PROFILES

The 'quasi experiment'

The initial study that this chapter describes preceded and was 'independent' of the change intervention. Instead, it formed part of a separate, larger organization structure field study. PTV was approached and agreed to be one of more than twenty such research sites (see Crawford, 1984, for a complete description). 'Independent' is qualified because, at the time of commissioning the post-change review, the CEO said that the feedback from the initial study had influenced the restructuring leg of his strategy. The post-change review was commissioned directly by the CEO. It repeated the coverage of the initial study, and extended it to analyse the managerial decision-making style at PTV.

In the initial study a sample of in-depth interviews was undertaken among the top managers at PTV, and questionnaires were distributed to

112 of the senior staff throughout the organization. Data were collected on inter-unit relations, unit context, behaviour, and performance.[1] A cover letter signed by both the CEO and the researcher
accompanied the questionnaires. This explained the purpose of the
research, and emphasized the confidentiality of the individual
responses. Participants were invited to return their questionnaires direct
to the researcher.

The post-change review repeated the above survey for 119 of the staff.
The questionnaire was extended to include leadership and climate
measures. The latter was a modification of the Litwin and Stringer (1968)
questionnaire (see Crouch, 1982, for a detailed description). For the
former, the top twenty-six managers in this group completed the Vroom
and Yetton (1973) Problem Set which asks managers which of five
decision-making styles (levels of participation) they would use in each of
thirty cases. Again, respondents were given assurance of confidentiality
and their responses were returned direct to the researchers. On that
occasion, the cover letter explained that the survey was part of a
consultancy study commissioned by the CEO. The response rate was over
90 per cent in both surveys.

The structure: pre- and post-change

The initial organization assessment showed that branch functions were
quite strongly dependent on the equivalent corporate head function:
manufacturing – average; commercial – moderately high; and sales –
high. Specifically, manufacturing branch function's score for dependence
on corporate technical services fell in the sixth decile when compared with
scores for Australian managers in general. That is, the score fell in the
range between the fiftieth and the sixtieth percentiles for Australian
managers evaluating the dependence of their sub-unit on another sub-unit
in the same organization.[2] The dependence of commercial and sales on
corporate technical services was in the seventh and eighth deciles
respectively.

Not surprisingly, the branches' judgements about the adequacy of the
autonomy allowed to them by the relevant head office function were low
for manufacturing (third decile) and very low for sales and commercial
(second decile). To increase their autonomy, the branch units tended to
withhold information from the centre. This created high strain for
corporate functions, especially for finance which saw itself as totally
dependent on the branch commercial function for information (tenth
decile). It would appear then that the CEO's view that the organization
could restructure to decouple the branches and corporate head office was
correct.

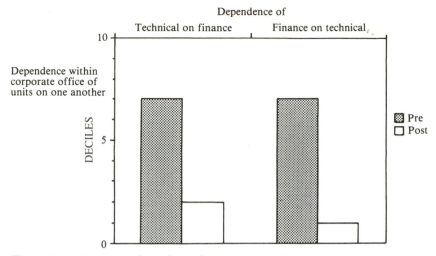

Figure 6.1a   Inter-unit dependence for corporate office

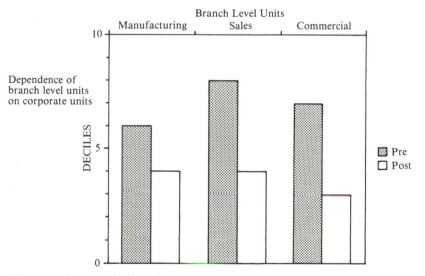

Figure 6.1b   Branch dependence on corporate office

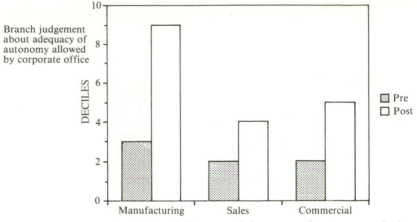

Note: Values depicted are decile scores relative to scores from many organizations

Figure 6.2   Branch judgements about the adequacy of the autonomy allowed by corporate office

Assessment of structural change programme

Post change, the intended decoupling of units had largely occurred, as figure 6.1 illustrates. Both within the corporate office and between that office and the branches, the level of interdependence had dropped. For example, the moderately high dependence of technical services and finance on each other (seventh deciles) had declined to a very low level (second and first deciles, respectively); and the dependence of branch functions on their corporate counterparts had decreased at least two deciles (see figures 6.1a and 6.1b). Consistent with the latter, branch autonomy had risen commensurately (see figure 6.2). The data strongly supported the CEO's view that this leg of the intervention had been a success.

Decision-making style

Prior to the change intervention, PTV's ranking on characteristics related to decision-making style was comparable with the average organization, rather than strongly participative. The levels of communication, cooperation, and participation were about average, and the frequency with which collaboration was used to resolve conflict was also average. In all cases the average score for PTV managers was in the fifth or sixth decile (between the fortieth and sixtieth percentiles) (table 6.1). While use of collaboration and forcing to resolve conflict were unchanged after three years of team-building activity, levels of cooperation, communication,

Table 6.1. *Conflict and decision-making behaviour*

	PTV average	
	Pre-change	Post-change
Cooperation	6*	7
Communication	6	7
Participation	6	7
Collaboration	6	6
Forcing	5	5

Note: * Deciles: 1 – lowest 10%; 10 – highest 10%.

and participation had moved up to the seventh decile (table 6.1), in keeping with the general thrust of the evidence for participation (Miller and Monge, 1986; Spector, 1986).

Together the unexceptional initial levels on participative dimensions, and the slight subsequent improvement in three of them, confirmed the CEO's pre-change view that the culture about participative decision-making could be strengthened.

However, although the immediate objectives of the behavioural intervention appeared to have been achieved, the CEO commissioned a review because he thought the overall impact of the training programme had been unsatisfactory. In doing so, he stressed that, while the programme seemed to have been carried through effectively, he sensed that the state of the organization was not what he was aiming for. Surprisingly, dissatisfaction was widespread. The CEO was conscious of morale problems, but not able to identify their basis.

In part, the explanation for this state of affairs lay in the managers' failure to act out their 'learnt' highly participative espoused decision-making style. The responses of the top twenty-six managers on the thirty cases in the Vroom–Yetton Problem Set illustrated that for themselves individually, and implicitly for others, PTV managers espoused high levels of participation. Recall, managers were asked to indicate which of five styles (level of participation) they would use on each of thirty cases. As shown in figure 6.3, the average level of participation across the thirty cases for the median manager at PTV was in the highest decile for managers in general. Indeed, only 3 per cent of managers in the comparison database were more participative in the Problem Set than the average senior manager at PTV (figure 6.3).

In contrast, the average level of actual participation within PTV was in the seventh decile (table 6.1, earlier). While this was above the mean for Australian organizations, it was nonetheless well short of the espoused level of PTV's senior managers (figure 6.3). This is consistent with the evidence which shows that managers' espoused Blake and Mouton styles

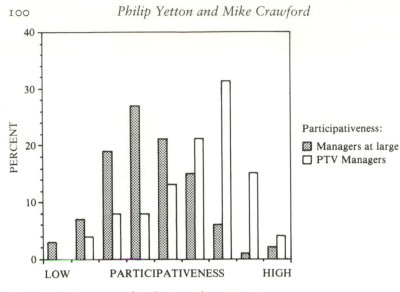

Figure 6.3   Frequency distribution of participativeness

are frequently a highly biased overestimate of their behaviour (Blake and Mouton, 1978). Thus, there was a substantial disparity between aspirations and expectations about participation and the actual level of participation. Perhaps more importantly, within the firm there was substantial variation in the extent of actual participation, an issue which is analysed in the next section.

The gap between expectations and behaviour is also clearly illustrated by the organizational climate data presented in table 6.2. The perceived management team climate profile was typical of management teams in general with the exception of the high conflict legitimacy (ninth decile). Managers were not inhibited in voicing their opinions, including criticisms of the CEO. However, while in general the perceived team climate was typical, the preferred climate was highly atypical. The managers would have preferred to work in an environment that was extremely high in warmth, support, conflict legitimacy, and responsibility – rather different from the one in which they currently worked.

Assessment of behaviour change programme

If the goal of the team-building programme was to create an espoused norm supporting a high level of group decision-making, it was undoubtedly a success. If, on the other hand, the intent was to change managers' behaviour, its success was limited. In contrast, experience elsewhere suggests that 'human relations' skills training improves the

Table 6.2. *Group climate: post change*

Group climate dimensions	Perceived group climate	Preferred group climate
Responsibility	6*	10
Warmth	4	9
Support	5	10
Conflict legitimacy	9	10

Note: Deciles: 1 – lowest 10%; 10 – highest 10%.

learning of new and relevant leader attitudes and results in improved performance (Burke and Day, 1986). Together, tables 6.1 and 6.2 show a coherent picture in which perceived team climate was consistent with the managers' current behaviour, whereas the preferred (extreme) climate profile would have been well matched to their espoused leadership style. The emergent but unrecognized problem was this gap between their strongly held expectations and their own behaviour (Rice, McFarlin, and Bennett, 1989).

Consequences of misfit between espoused and actual style

If the managers were committed to their espoused highly participative leadership style, why did they not act it out? Certainly, during unstructured interviews most managers in PTV claimed to believe that all problems both could and should be solved participatively. Of course, this was the central message of the experiential training programme. The programme notes actually offered some guidance on conditional use of participation, but this was neither a central theme of the training nor the message that participants absorbed. However, such an extreme style is unrealistic, for two reasons which were as pertinent to PTV as to most enterprises. One is that the cost of such a style in management time spent attending meetings would be prohibitive. The other is that such a style assumes that when subordinates do not share the organization's goals, as embedded in their manager's formal role responsibilities, the manager would still confidently share influence with his subordinates, trusting them to set aside their own interests in favour of the organization's goals.

The managers' espoused leadership style on the Vroom–Yetton Problem Set provided specific data on the second issue: namely, their violation rate for the Goal Congruence Rule. This rule is intended to protect managers against the risk in giving their subordinates responsibility for decisions where the managers' interests and the subordinates' interests are not compatible (Vroom and Yetton, 1973, p. 33). In such cases, while managers may appropriately consult their subordinates, they should not let them make the decision. The average PTV manager's violation rate for this rule across the cases in the Problem Set was over three times that of a typical manager. So, in an unconstrained world, such as the cases posed for them in the Problem Set, the PTV managers chose responses that revealed a preference for high participativeness. However, constrained by the reality of the organization's authority structure and the performance demands of the control systems, the managers acted much like other managers.

How would typical managers 'resolve' this major inconsistency between their espoused leadership style and actual behaviour? They are committed to the desired 'new order' (high participation) as advocated by the team-building intervention but act out, at best, only a slight 'improvement' on previous behaviour (see table 6.1). The failure to implement behaviour in which the managers believe and which the organization espouses is likely to result in frustration. This, in turn, is likely to lead to the assignment of blame to others for this failure to implement the 'new order'. After all, the managers know they are not to blame – they are committed to being highly participative. Instead, blame is likely to be assigned to either, or both, their boss and subordinates and, in particular, to 'the boss', namely the CEO. The level of blame assigned to the CEO in this case was indicated by managers coding their satisfaction with his supervision as measured by the Job Diagnostic Survey (Hackman and Oldham, 1976) in the second lowest decile. Not surprisingly, for someone who had championed participation and involvement, this level of rejection was hard for the CEO to confront.

Differences across operating units within PTV

The preceding analysis deals with PTV managers' average behaviour. Implicitly, it assumes that the contexts in which these managers and their teams work are similar, or alternatively, that team behaviour and its effectiveness are not contingent on any differences that do exist. This assumption of homogeneity is a very powerful simplifying assumption and obscures important contingencies which were revealed by a comparison across operating units.

Post change, PTV could be modelled as five operating groups – two at the corporate level (technical and finance) and three at the branch level (manufacturing, sales, and commercial). Each group at the branch level consisted of five separate units performing the same function independently of one another. One branch was located in each of the five mainland states, New South Wales, Victoria, Queensland, Western Australia, and South Australia. Table 6.3 shows that there were significant

Table 6.3. *Conflict and decision-making behaviour for operating groups*

	Pre-change						Post-change					
	Corporate tech. fin.*		Branches manf. sales comm.			PTV avg.	Corporate tech. fin.		Branches manf. sales comm.			PTV avg.
Cooperation	8**	8	2	7	6	6	10	10	2	10	3	7
Communication	7	8	2	7	6	6	10	10	2	8	3	7
Participation	6	7	4	7	7	6	10	10	5	10	1	7
Collaboration	10	9	2	7	4	6	10	10	3	8	1	6
Forcing	4	3	9	3	5	5	1	1	8	3	10	5

Notes: * Unit abbreviations: Tech. – Technical; Fin. – Finance; Manf. – Manufacturing; Comm. – Commercial.
** Values shown are decile score: 1 – lowest, 10 – highest.

differences in both the ways the five groups operated pre change, and the effect of the intervention on them.

Technical and finance (corporate level) were very similar to each other and sales (branch level) was also similar to these two units. Initially, these three groups were participative, cooperative, communicative, and disposed to a collaborative style of resolving potential conflicts. Over the change period, these characteristics were reinforced and increased to a high level consistent with the espoused participation decision style. The finding was in keeping with the general evidence on participation in decision-making (Cotton *et al.*, 1988; Miller and Monge, 1986; Spector, 1986), and that specifically for effects on communication, participation, and cooperation (Miller and Monge, 1986).

The profile for manufacturing was quite different, both before and after the intervention. Unlike the previous groups, there had been little change over the period. While actual participation was about average, communication and cooperation were low (second decile). In addition, a forcing style of conflict resolution (eighth decile post change) was used rather than collaboration (third decile).

Finally, post change, the branch commercial units were similar to manufacturing in most respects. The exception was that participation was very low (first decile) in commercial rather than average. The data in table 6.3 indicate that post change the branch commercial units had become internally less cooperative, participative, and communicative. The level of collaborative behaviour had declined while forcing had increased.

So it appears that after three years of the team-building intervention, the units that were originally disposed to collaborative and participative behaviour had had that tendency strengthened. The units which were least like that pre change (e.g. manufacturing) had scarcely changed. Finally, the commercial units had actually become less participative and collaborative. Rather than helping to develop a common participative style, the OD intervention had increased differences in style across the units.

Process and context

Now recall, from the previous section, that PTV managers had an extreme preferred climate and reported that they would act very participatively in the Problem Set. There was little variance in these aspirations within the firm. So, were the differences reported above simply perverse behaviour on the part of managers and supervisors in manufacturing and commercial, or was there some other reason for their apparent 'resistance' to the intervention? Examination of the task environments for the five groups suggested an alternative explanation which was consistent with the proposition that behaviour is a function of role and organizational pressures as well as preferences, beliefs, and ability. The data showed that the roles of managers and the pressures to which they were subject differed substantially between units.

Table 6.4 indicates that sales and the two corporate units faced fairly uncertain environments (high novelty and complexity), where participation and collaboration may be important for effective problem solving. In contrast, manufacturing and commercial had little uncertainty in their environments, so there were few new problems to which collaboration and participation might provide valuable solutions. In addition, both faced environments where immediacy was high, i.e., quick responses were required, and where participation and collaboration may simply have wasted valuable time. Finally, far more than any of the other units, manufacturing faced a hostile environment (i.e., one where it was easy to make costly errors, e.g., spoiling a batch of product, dangerous accidents, and provoking industrial relations disputes). Added to that, its staff had low skill levels, while most of the other units had highly skilled staff. The Vroom–Yetton normative leadership theory prescribes low levels of participation for problems where the nature of the problem is clear, supervisors know how to deal with the problem, subordinates are unlikely to add additional information and insight, and subordinates will accept and implement supervisors' decisions. Note, the evidence for Vroom–Yetton (Schweiger and Leana, 1986) shows that application of the model results in greater productivity and satisfaction with supervision.

The manufacturing and commercial units in PTV were ones where most problems had these characteristics. Consequently, the relatively low levels of participation in manufacturing seem appropriate. Inviting low skilled staff to participate in finding new solutions in a hostile environment that demands quick responses makes little sense. This is particularly

Table 6.4. *Unit task environment: post change*

	Corporate		Branches		
	Tech.	Fin.	Manf.	Sale	Comm.
Dynamism	4	9	1	4	1
Novelty	10	10	3	8	1
Complexity	9	10	2	4	1
Immediacy	1	4	10	8	8
Hostility	4	2	9	1	1
Task interdependence	1	7	9	3	6
Skill of staff	10	10	1	10	9

Notes: Values shown are decile score: 1 – lowest; 10 – highest.
Unit abbreviations: Tech. – Technical; Fin. – Financial; Manf. – Manufacturing; Sale – Sales; Comm. – Commercial.

true when acceptable answers already exist to most of the problems which are routine for the managers concerned. For similar reasons, the mode of operation in branch commercial units also appears appropriate.

The nature of these results is consistent with findings that directive leadership is best for performance with high, but not low structured tasks (Idvik, 1986). Furthermore, a recent study by Courtright, Fairhurst, and Rogers (1989) showed that organic and mechanistic structures involve qualitatively different interactions with organic structures having more problem-solving interactions, while mechanistic structures had more interactions based on authority and order giving. Overall, the impact of the nature of the task and its environment on the choice of how much participation to use is in keeping with the literature (Idvik, 1986; Schweiger and Leana, 1986; Van Fleet and Yukl, 1986). Certainly participation isn't good in all situations, as shown by the Vroom–Yetton model and House's Path–Goal theory (Fiedler and House, 1988) and Hersey and Blanchard's Situational Leadership approach (Vecchio, 1987).

These contextual and process differences between units were the source of a potential validity threat to our earlier explanation of the inconsistency between espoused and actual participation. That interpretation implicitly assumed an organization-wide shared gap between values and behaviour. As an alternative, might the dissatisfaction with the CEO be explained by the respondents' membership of different units? In particular, were the most dissatisfied managers members of the 'non-participative' units? If so, then the dissatisfaction observed would not be attributable to a general climate of unreal expectations. Rather, it would reflect a gap between espoused and actual behaviour in only some units.

In fact the evidence did not support this alternative interpretation. The in-depth interviews showed that the managers in the corporate technical and finance areas blamed the CEO for too many meetings, with no one feeling responsible for anything or able to act without first having a committee meeting. So, they were trying to act out the espoused behaviour and blaming the CEO for its inappropriateness as a universal style of decision-making. They scored the CEO in the third decile on satisfaction with supervision.

In contrast to the corporate managers, the branch managers claimed that after three years of training nothing had changed. 'We've all had to work hard to cover for those on the courses and it's the same as it was.' The intervention was – 'all a manipulation by the CEO to get us to cooperate with him rather than the other way round'. They scored him in the second decile on satisfaction with supervision. So, for different reasons, but consistent with contingency theories such as Vroom and Yetton, the CEO lost out with both the high- and low-participation managers.

DISCUSSION

Having explained the quasi-experiment investigated in this study, the first stage of the analysis examined the intervention and its outcomes within the less restrictive Vroom–Yetton analytical framework, rather than the Managerial Grid framework from which the intervention was derived. This analysis explained the dysfunctional and unanticipated consequences of the team-building intervention. Most important for the CEO, the blame put on him was found to be an outcome of a misspecified intervention rather than indicative of poor line management.

The second step was to examine the differences in outcome across the various functional areas – specifically across corporate/branch and sales/commercial/manufacturing. This revealed that the managers' actual (as opposed to preferred) responses to both the process (team-building) and structural (decoupling) interventions were contingent upon the unit in the organization to which they belonged.

Theory development

This final section presents a theoretical exploration of the interactions between these levels of analysis and discusses its implications for organization development and training.

A case study typically offers a specific solution to a specific problem. Often the particular problem can be solved without providing a general solution for the class of such problems. That is the case here. There is no accepted theory which links team-building and business unit structure.

However, as shown above, it is possible by 'inspection' of data from different paradigms to derive conclusions for this specific case. The next step is to attempt a more general integration. What is needed is a construct which provides a theoretical link between the two levels of analysis.

Consider the following speculative argument. The Vroom–Yetton model makes style contingent on problem characteristics such as level of conflict among the subordinates, and the degree of task structure (Vroom and Yetton, 1973). These are implicitly treated as a function of an autonomous environment in which the manager acts. Furthermore, each problem is assumed to be independent of the other problems confronted by the manager. In practice, the problems experienced by managers are a function of their roles. Differences between units in part reflect role differences. It then follows that a role based construct could provide the link between the two levels. More specifically, the 'Typical Problem Distribution' of a role, defined as the mix of problems experienced by the typical manager in such a role, would be simultaneously a function of the unit structure and environment, and a determinant of both the manager's normative and descriptive leadership behaviour. Thus, inter-unit and inter-manager behaviour differences would be two aspects of a single underlying situation. In that case, the different behaviours in the various units reported above could be both normatively appropriate and descriptively predictable.

This can be illustrated by comparing managers in the technical unit (corporate level) and the manufacturing units (branch level). The data in table 6.4 indicate that the former typically faced novel and complex problems, for which prior experience did not provide the answers. Any one manager was unlikely therefore to have good quality, readily available answers to many of these problems. Further, since the skill of staff in the unit was high, they were likely to be capable of making a positive contribution to the solution of such problems. Finally, since issues that arose were not the ones that required immediate responses, there was time for discussion and joint consideration. The Vroom–Yetton normative model prescribes group decision-making for such problems.

In contrast, the manufacturing units faced low novelty and complexity. The managers were experienced and had seen most problems and their effective solutions before. Furthermore, since complexity was low, they were readily able to recognize particular problem types and link them with previous solutions. Indeed, the low novelty allowed many of these problems and their solutions to be codified into acceptable procedures or job manuals. In addition, because the skill level of staff was low, their capacity to make a worthwhile contribution if invited to participate in decision-making would have been small. Finally, the environment was hostile, rapid responses were required, and the cost of poor or slow decisions was high. In this context, poor decisions were likely if much reliance were placed on participation. So, consistent with the Vroom–Yetton normative model, in this context the distribution of problem characteristics was such that the typical problem was appropriately handled in a non-participative way.

Application

The preceding analysis implies that the 'right' strategy for team-building, particularly relating to group decision-making, is contingent upon the specific circumstances of individual units within an organization. The implications for training are critical. Crouch and Yetton (1987) have shown that the typical manager does not possess all the skills necessary to enact the Vroom–Yetton normative model consistently. As a general principle, it would be possible to train managers both in the Vroom–Yetton leadership diagnostic (when to use which style) and the behavioural skills to act out each style in any context. However, the needs for and hence the payoffs from the full range of these skills would vary across units. Furthermore, learning new skills for participation in decision-making, such as coping with conflict, is time consuming and therefore expensive. For this reason, a training programme in which all participants receive similar training would be inefficient.

It follows that a training programme which is both efficient and effective would require, as a prerequisite, the type of unit or role context analysis presented here. Tailoring such programmes to match role circumstances depends on establishing the theoretical links between the two levels of analysis. Certainly, this case demonstrates why a training programme that meets one group's needs may not be effective if made available to other units in the same organization, let alone to another organization. For PTV, this analysis provides a basis on which to design differential skill training programmes linked to the specific needs of each unit. Thus a tight fit could be achieved between the organization structure and teams' management styles. This type of analysis is just one element in the strategic needs analysis that should always be undertaken as a matter of course before implementing a management development programme.

In addition the study highlights the reason why decision-making behaviours learned by managers in one situation may prove unsuccessful if they move into a different context. This may be the case with either lateral shifts or hierarchical progression. Retraining, or at least resensitising to the different responses called for by the 'typical problem distribution', is likely to be beneficial to the relocated or promoted manager.

CONCLUSIONS

The breadth of data collected in this study, and their interpretation, support three propositions.

1 Managers' behaviours are a function of individual preferences, role abilities, task structures, group climate, unit membership, and organizational reporting relationships.

An intervention which 'manipulates' only one or two of these factors while leaving the others unconstrained may have unintended consequences. Here, all these factors are measured. The managers and their teams are considered within the context of their units and the relevance of the attempted change and its impact are examined in relation to the task and environment context.

2 Performance is a function of behaviour and context.

Few behaviours are universally effective in the sense that they generate high performance in contexts as different as the assembly line and the body design shop of an automobile firm, and against objectives as different as minimizing unit cost through volume and standardization and being first to market with the next generation memory chips. However, many development programmes train all managers in a firm to adopt the same style and, at least implicitly, violate this assumption.

3 Satisfaction is a function of outcomes relative to preferences.

This assumption underlies most needs based theories of job satisfaction (Locke, 1976). Thus managers' satisfaction with their own behaviour and that of others will be a function of both the actual behaviour and preferences about it. Interventions that change managers' preferences, but do not alter organization functions that prevent those new preferences from being acted out, are likely to generate frustration and to result in the scapegoating of others. Indeed, dissatisfaction with such a gap between espoused and actual behaviour was one of the significant features in this case and was in fact the reason the CEO requested the post-intervention review.

NOTE

We would like to thank Jane Craig, Lex Donaldson, Boris Kabanoff, Maria Stafford, and Phyllis Tharenou for their comments on earlier drafts. In addition, we would like to acknowledge the contribution made by the managers, and particularly, the CEO, of PTV Ltd.

NOTES

1 The variables are seven and nine point Likert scales which satisfy the typical α coefficient and generalizability coefficient levels of reliability. The authors will provide more information on request.

2 Comparisons implicit in descriptions used here, such as 'average' and 'sixth decile' are between the scores obtained by units or managers in this study and the distribution of scores on those same variables for over 2,000 Australian managers in more than 100 functional units, from more than twenty organizations.

REFERENCES

Blake, R. R. and Mouton, J. S. (1978), *The Managerial Grid* (Houston: Gulf Publishing Co.).

Burke, M. J. and Day, R. R. (1986), 'A cumulative study of the effectiveness of managerial training', *Journal of Applied Psychology*, **71**, 232–45.

Cotton, J. L., Vollrath, K. L., Froggart, M. L., Lengnick-Hall, M. L., and Jennings, K. R. (1988), 'Employee participation: diverse forms and different outcomes', *Academy of Management Review*, **13**, 8–22.

Courtright, John A., Fairhurst, Gail T., and Rogers, Edna L. (1989), 'Interaction patterns in organic and mechanistic systems', *Academy of Management Journal*, **4**, 773–802.

Crawford, Michael (1984), 'The character, determinants and performance effects of inter-unit interactions within organisations: a disaggregated systems approach', unpublished Ph.D. thesis, Australian Graduate School of Management, University of New South Wales.

Crouch, A. G. D. (1982), 'Psychological climate, behaviour, satisfaction and individual differences in managerial work group', unpublished doctoral dissertation, Australian Graduate School of Management, University of New South Wales.

Crouch, A. and Yetton, P. (1987), 'Manager behaviour, leadership style and subordinate performance: an empirical extension of the Vroom–Yetton conflict rule', *Organization Behaviour and Human Decision Processes*, **39**, 384–96.

Dienesch, R. M. and Liden, R. C. (1986), 'Leader-member exchange model of leadership', *Academy of Management Review*, **11**, 618–35.

Fiedler, F. and House, R. J. (1988), 'Leadership theory and research: a report of progress', in C. L. Cooper and I. T. Robertson (eds.), *International Review of Industrial and Organisational Psychology* (New York: Wiley), pp. 73–92.

Field, R. A. (1979), 'A critique of the Vroom Yetton Contingency model of leadership behaviour', *Academy of Management Review*, **4**, 249–57.

Fisher, B. M. and Edwards, J. E. (1988), 'Consideration and initiating structure and their relationships with leadership effectiveness', in F. Hoy (ed.), *Academy of Management Best Paper Proceedings*, 48th Annual Meeting, pp. 201–5.

Galbraith, J. R. (1973), *Designing Complex Organizations* (Reading, MA: Addison-Wesley).

Guzzo, R. A., Jette, R. D., and Katzell, R. A. (1985), 'The effects of psychologically based intervention programs on worker productivity: a meta-analysis', *Personnel Psychology*, 38, 275–92.

Hackman, J. R. and Oldham, G. R. (1976), 'Motivation through the design of work: test of a theory', *Organization Behaviour and Human Performance*, 16, 250–79.

Indvik, J. A. (1986), 'Path goal theory of leadership: a meta-analysis', in J. A. Pearce II and R. B. Robinson Jr (eds.), *Academy of Management Best Paper Proceedings*, 46th Annual Meeting, pp. 189–92.

Katzell, R. A. and Guzzo, R. A. (1983), 'Psychological approaches to productivity improvements', *American Psychologist*, 4, 468–72.

Lawrence, P. R. and Lorsch, J. W. (1967), *Organization and Environment: Managing Differentiation and Integration* (Homewood, Ill.: Irwin).

Lewin, K. (1945), 'The research center for group dynamics at Massachusetts Institute of Technology', *Sociometry*, 8, 126–35.

Locke, Edwin A., Schweiger, David M., and Latham, Gary P. (1986), 'Participation in decision making: when should it be used?', *Organization Dynamics*, 14, 65–79.

Miller, K. I. and Monge, P. R. (1986), 'Participation, satisfaction, and productivity: a meta-analytic review', *Academy of Management Journal*, 29, 727–53.

Miner, J. B. (1980), *Theories of Organizational Behaviour* (Hinsdale, Illinois: Dryden).

Mirvis, Philip H. (1983), 'Measuring program implementation, adoption, and intermediate goal attainment: missing links in OD program evaluations', in S. Seashore, E. Lawler, P. Mirvis, and C. Cammann (eds.), *Assessing Organizational Change* (New York: Wiley).

Powell, Gary N. and Posner, Barry Z. (1980), 'Managing change: attitudes, targets, problems, and strategies', *Group and Organization Studies*, 5, 310–23.

Rice, Robert W., McFarlin, Dean B., and Bennett, Debbie E. (1989), 'Standards of comparison and job satisfaction', *Journal of Applied Psychology*, 74, 591–98.

Schweiger, D. M. and Leana, C. R. (1986), 'Participation in decision-making', in E. A. Locke (ed.), *Generalizing from Laboratory to Field Settings* (Lexington, MA: Lexington Books), pp. 147–66.

Sims, H. P. and Manz, C. C. (1984), 'Observing leader verbal behaviour: reciprocal determinism in leadership theory', *Journal of Applied Psychology*, 69, 222–32.

Spector, P. E. (1986), 'Perceived control by employees', *Human Relations*, 11, 1005–16.

Van de Ven, Andrew H. and Ferry, Diane L. (1980), *Measuring and Assessing Organizations* (New York: Wiley).

Van Fleet, D. D. and Yukl, G. A. (1986), 'A century of leadership research', in D. A. Wren and J. A. Pearce (eds.), *Papers Dedicated to the Development of Modern Management*, Academy of Management.

Vecchio, R. P. (1987), 'Situational leadership theory', *Journal of Applied Psychology*, 72, 444–51.

Vroom, W. H. and Yetton, P. W. (1973), *Leadership and Decision Making* (Pittsburgh: University of Pittsburgh Press).

Wagner, John A. III and Gooding, Richard Z. (1987), 'Shared influence and organizational behaviour: a meta-analysis of situational variables expected to moderate participation-outcome relationships', *Academy of Management Journal*, 30, 524–41.

7

CONCEPTS OF DECISIONS: MAKING AND IMPLEMENTING STRATEGIC DECISIONS IN ORGANIZATIONS

DAVID J. HICKSON AND SUSAN MILLER

ABSTRACT

This chapter gives some of the results so far of a programme of ongoing research on decisions in organizations. It deals first with the ways by which major decisions are reached 'at the top', and then with how they are implemented. The aim is to evolve concepts of process and of success with which differing cases can be compared.

Three typical patterns of decision-making processes are discerned: sporadic, fluid, and constricted. These are the 'pre-decision processes' from which ensue formally authorized decisions. 'Post-decision' processes of implementation are then examined and compared, and a partial answer given as to why some decisions are implemented more successfully than others.

Illustrative cases are taken from the case-based method of data collection.

Strategic decisions, their formulation, and their implementation, are the subject of this chapter. It reports the results of research on the *formulation* of decisions prior to the point of decision, and ideas that are emerging from ongoing current research on the *implementation* of decisions. To understand what happens both before a decision and afterwards, concepts are needed to enable comparison of case with case between organizations and within any one organization, and also as the basis of explanation. This chapter has this conceptualization and explanation as its primary aim.

The research has studied and is studying the making of the larger, least frequent, least programmed decisions by the senior managements of organizations, and their implementation. These are the decisions on investments, on takeovers, on new products or services, on main sites and buildings, on design of the principal control systems including computerization, on structure, and the like, which shape the future for years to come. We describe first how pre-decision formulation processes have been

113

conceptualized, and the ensuing typology, and then the more tentative concepts of decision implementation. We tell the stories of illustrative cases as well as define variables by which to compare them.

THE PRE-DECISION FORMULATION PROCESS

The conceptualization of something so elusive as a decision-making process is not an easy task. For it is not 'something' at all. It is a movement of events through time. Hage (1980) visualizes a decision following a 'trajectory' through time which bounces around like a molecule in a bubble chamber. Certainly the process can bounce around. This has been nowhere better revealed than by Mintzberg *et al.* (1976) who studied twenty-five cases of decision-making, one in each of a variety of Canadian organizations. They identified no less than seven kinds of processes, the most notable feature of which is the way they are fragmented and repeat themselves. In most cases there were 'sudden events that interrupted them and caused changes in pace or direction' (Mintzberg *et al.*, 1976), and all processes cycled and recycled, reassessing information and alternatives again and again.

The Bradford team widened the search for comparability to 150 cases (see Hickson *et al.*, 1986 and Cray *et al.*, 1988).[1] There were five in each of thirty British manufacturing and service organizations in both the public and private sectors. Information about each process was obtained through structured interviews with executives which included a narrative of the recalled process and events, together with open-ended questions plus some rating scales to reiterate and fill out the narrative. Six cases in three organizations were studied in greater depth by intensive case-study methods, three concurrently and three retrospectively. The outlines of three main types of pre-decision process were discerned. They are outlines of *sporadic processes*, *fluid processes*, and *constricted processes*. The three types are derived from analysis of a large number of process variables over 136 cases on which data in the required form were complete. These were reduced to ten variables for final analysis as follows:

1 'Expertise' is the number of internal and external sources, from staff experts to consultants or other organizations in the same field, from which information comes.
2 'Confidence disparity' is the variability in the quality of that information, as indicated by the differing confidence that management had in its sources.
3 'Effort' is how information was acquired, from merely having it on hand in people's personal experience and knowledge, to having it

accessible in records, to research to collect it, to creating it by meetings or other means that synthesized it from disparate sources.

4 'Formal interaction' is how many kinds of pre-arranged meetings were included in the process, such as boards, councils, committees, working parties, and project teams.

5 'Informal interaction' is how much discussion, toing and froing, or arguments took place (on a six point scale from none to a very great deal).

6 'Negotiation scope' is indicated on a scale of seven ordered categories. These run from the decision not being open to negotiation at all, for example, when a chief executive forces a conclusion and leaves little room for negotiation among the others interested, to so much negotiation that a decision is made when negotiation is still inconclusive and dissent persists.

7 'Disruption' is how far the process was interrupted by delays (on a four point scale from no delays to prolonged delays).

8 'Impedance' is indicated on a nine point scale running from least impediment, the matter for decision in effect having to wait in a queue of items demanding attention, through impediments in the form of search and problem-solving activities, to most impediment, resistance from a source external to the organization.

9 'Process time', the period of decision-making that was studied, runs from the first recalled action that started movement towards a decision to the decision itself.

10 'Authority level' is where the process ends in an authorized decision, following which implementation can legitimately proceed. The lowest level at which such a decision was authorized was a semi-autonomous division, the highest was at national or international headquarters, and in between were the chief executive and board levels or equivalent (complete definitions appear in Appendix C, Hickson *et al.*, 1986).

It had been apparent from personal familiarity with the case histories that some decisions were made in a more fluent way than others, but analysis beyond this general intuition was required to sort through this large number of cases, each described by a large number of process characteristics, to see whether a pattern could be discerned. Hierarchical statistical cluster analysis was used to work out a three-fold clustering or grouping of cases in terms of their mutual affinity on these ten process variables (full details of data analysis can be found in Cray *et al.*, 1988). The three are a balanced representation, for the cases divide evenly into clusters of 53, 42, and 41 processes. Thus about a third of all strategic decisions might be made in each way, that is either *sporadically, fluidly,* or *constrictedly.*

SPORADIC PROCESSES

The first of the three ways is through a *sporadic* type of process. By comparison with decisions reached by fluid or constricted processes, it will probably have shown higher impedance, higher disruption, more sources of expertise, and greater differences in the confidence placed in their information and views, more informal interaction, some negotiation, longer process time, and final authorization at a higher level.

This means that in a full third of the occasions when top managers or administrators enter upon a decision, they are likely to have begun on a twisting trail that will not end for a year or two, or even longer. As they make their way along it they will come up against all sorts of obstacles that delay direct movement towards a conclusion. They will have to turn aside whilst staff experts prepare fresh estimates or reassess capacity, they will have to pause until the time is judged right to move on, they will have to take time to negotiate among themselves and with outsiders such as banks or customers. They will find that not all the information they get can be relied upon, so they and their staff will have to sift out what they feel they can place confidence in, and what is better ignored. They will be drawn into bursts of activity in corridors and offices, in between the delays, when the matter is on everyone's mind and answers to questions are demanded there and then, until the excitement dies down as other things become even more pressing and demand attention. *In brief, a sporadic type of decision-making process is one that is informally spasmodic and protracted.* It usually ensues from a highly complex and politically charged matter for decision.

For example, it was a sporadic process that brought the management of a nationalized industrial firm to decide to buy a one third share in a company that was a large purchaser of its products. This decision was an attempt to ensure future sales in a situation where either other interested parties might take complete control of the company, or it might go out of business. Two multinational oil corporations, a multinational chemical corporation, and another very large nationalized industry were all involved as well as the prospective subsidiary which wanted assured funds for expansion, and all the other interests wanted to expand or at least to protect the firm's demand for their own products. The local government, on the other hand, resisted expansion on ecological grounds. The prospective subsidiary itself wished to ensure its own future.

The decision-making process in this nationalized firm moved in fits and starts. Spasms of work by departmental staff to produce forecasts of future output and costs, and estimates of the investment the subsidiary might make in new plant if capital were injected into it, and spasms of hectic toing and froing amongst senior managers, were broken by pauses whilst the reactions of the other powerful interests to reports and proposals were awaited. The financial grounds for injecting new capital by means of a takeover were very much in doubt. Time passed while successive reports and proposals were tossed backwards and forwards between the organizations concerned, and renegotiated to suit their differing interests, until after eighteen months an agreement was reached. The board of the nationalized industry made a commitment to take a one third share in its customer firm, along with one of the oil corporations and the other state owned industry, each of which also took one third. A difficult uneven process came to an end.

FLUID PROCESSES

Quite the opposite to sporadic processes in most ways (though not precisely so) are *fluid* processes. In terms of the empirical variables defined earlier, a fluid process is probably comparatively less disrupted, less impeded, has fewer sources of expertise with less of a gap between them in the confidence placed in them, passes through more kinds of committees, sees some negotiation, and in a shorter time reaches an outcome at a high level of authorization.

This means that almost a third of strategic decisions at the top flow along fairly fluently to quite a quick decision. In this type of process, managers and administrators attend a greater number of committees and kindred bodies, but far from getting in the way these formally arranged proceedings seem to facilitate a conclusion comparatively rapidly. Whilst any one meeting may be frustratingly fruitless, the arranging of meetings makes sure that things move along, if not during the meetings then in between them in anticipation of them. In these processes, there are fewer occasions when it is necessary to wait for the timing to be right, or for reports to be compiled, or for opposition to be reconciled. It is possible to move ahead comparatively steadily with at least a clear degree of confidence in the information gleaned, even if the level of confidence is less than desirable, and despite there being some scope for negotiation over the possible decision. *In brief, a fluid type of decision-making process is one that is steadily paced, formally channelled, and speedy.* It usually deals with a matter that is much less politically charged.

One fluidly processed decision was in a metropolitan municipality to venture into the realms of chance by launching a lottery to augment the normal funds from local tax payers and the national government. In not much more than a month, following the return of the Leader of the Council from a holiday, the proposal for a lottery was manoeuvred through a local government committee structure that was not prepared for it.

Another fluid process carried the management of a savings bank to the conclusion that they would try to upgrade it to the status of a cheque-issuing bank, competing with the established national banks across the full range of services, by applying for membership of the big banks' 'Clearing House'. This forms the basis of the cheque system, and therefore of credit banking, by clearing cheques between banks to arrive at the net balances owing from one to another. Essentially, the process of reaching the decision was very simple. It revolved around the deliberations of a special Working Committee of senior managers set up to consider the matter. This met constantly, steadily collating information with which to assess the cost of admission to the Clearing House and of competing in the wider and tougher market that would be opened up, and sounding out competitor banks and the Bank of England on the chances of admission. In about a year the main Board had accepted the Committee's recommendations to make this radical move which, if successful, would transform the business. Here again this was a smooth committee-focussed process ending at the highest level.

The contrast between fluid processes and sporadic processes shares something with that frequently made between 'rational' and 'political' decision-making, the rational flowing more evenly and the political more turbulently. Likewise, the types of processes put forward by Mintzberg *et al.* (1976) range from comparatively uninterrupted 'search' and 'design' kinds to those that are more 'blocked' and 'political'. We would resist any implication that sporadic processes are not guided by purported rationalities but, this having been said, the sporadic-fluid distinction fits a broad difference in the nature of decision-making that has often been intuitively assumed and alluded to.

CONSTRICTED PROCESSES

At first sight, the third type of process, *constricted*, seems sharply different from the fluid type and more akin to the sporadics. A constricted process can share some of the delays that sporadics encounter, more so than fluids at any rate, and also like the sporadics it draws on numerous sources for information and views, and is not so committee-focussed. However, it is as different from the sporadic type as it is from the fluid. It allows less scope for negotiation about the decision, and that decision is made at a level below the highest point – though still high in the hierarchy, of course, since it is a strategic decision. Thus it is a process less fluid than the fluids and less sporadic than the sporadics.

The unique character of a constricted process is that it tends to be more held in, more restrained, than either of the other two types. In the wording of the variables, it probably brings in expertise that can provide infor-

mation and views with no great effort, it does not give much scope for
negotiation nor figure much on the agendas of formal committees and the
like, and it can be made at a chief executive or similar level.

This means that almost another third of strategic decisions are likely to
be arrived at in a way that does not stir up so much activity as the other
types of processes do. The pertinent facts and figures are already in being
or can be easily put together, and to get hold of them it is only necessary to
pick up the phone and ask whomever has them at his or her fingertips, or
could calculate them more or less routinely. There is not much in this to
negotiate over, and the matter does not generate much coming and going
between offices, nor is there any reason to set up a special project team or
working party or sub-committee. It does not concern all the committees,
anyway, but can go through with just the approval of a local board or
whatever. Many of those in management are not closely involved, and the
process moves in well-worn channels under the control of the chief
executive, who takes the final decision. *In brief, a constricted type of
decision-making process is one that is narrowly channelled.* It usually
concerns something less complex than the sort of matter which triggers a
sporadic process.

A decision to modernize an insurance company was made in this way.
On the surface it was merely a commitment to updating and centralizing
the data processing for the main line of business, vehicle insurance, but as
with a number of the other cases its significance for those concerned was
in a wider context. The company had been taken over by a larger firm, and
despite assurances there was a risk of its business being absorbed into that
of the parent and the company being obliterated as a working organization. They realized that the best defence was for the parent's management to see its subsidiary as a profit earner too good to be disturbed. The
company was already in a leading position in its sector of the market, so
that the range of insurances offered and the sales approach were felt to be
as good as possible. Any move to ensure continued profitability and,
equally important, to sustain an image as a vigorous up-to-the-minute
enterprise had therefore to be in the direction of improving administration
and organization.

The decision process circled around the chief executive within whose
purview it legitimately came, never far out of his hands. There was no
committee work, not even a special task force or group to work out
details. Approval from the board of directors sitting as a board was not
needed, though individual directors knew what was in the wind. The
motor insurance department, the claims department, and other departments where appropriate, produced analyses of the existing system and
what would be required of any new system. Externally, IBM were quick to
offer their sales and advisory services, the insurance industry trade

association was contacted about experience elsewhere, and some of the larger brokers who handled business for the company confided what competitors were doing. In just a few months, with no real delays, it was decided that a reorganization of the administration based on centralized micro-film records ought both to raise earnings by improving the premium-to-expenses ratio, and improve efficiency in the field by speeding up the calculations of premiums and cover sent out to sales agents. This it was felt would go as far as anything else could to ensure company autonomy, as indeed it has done when last the company was contacted.

A constricted process may always be a possibility when there is a good base of information to start with, or at least one that can be assembled without too much effort. A corporate plan, for example, does not have to start from scratch but can begin where the previous one left off. It can proceed from the principal estimates on which the previous plan was constructed, projecting them forwards. Departments can simply be asked to update their forecasts, which they are well used to doing.

By so postulating variables of process, it has been possible to compare the similarities and differences between processes. Although the comparison is founded on a large number of cases it has also been possible to simplify conceptually by deriving from the underlying variables three overall characterizations of what processes are like. These give the flavour of events, characterizing an episode in the history of an organization much as periods in the histories of nations are characterized as stable or eventful or turbulent or whatever. In the same way the making of a decision can be called sporadic or fluid or constricted.

We do not have space here to go into how far it seems possible to *explain* the differences between the three types of process. Suffice it to say that the type of process which takes place can be largely explained as due primarily to the nature of the matter under decision, secondarily to the kind of organization in which the matter arises.

But, when a decision has been formulated and authorized, what happens next? The process does not stop there. The decision is supposed to be implemented.

THE POST-DECISION IMPLEMENTATION PROCESS

Will it be implemented, or will it not? There are many at all levels, who will be involved in this. There will be those who made the decision (the deciders or authorizers), there will be those who are affected by being 'implemented upon' (the implementees). Implementation is important to some if not all of these: they may want to know whether the effort to make a decision was worthwhile, whether it has the consequences intended, and whether they will gain or lose.

Once again the problem is to find concepts with which cases can be compared, and on the basis of which explanations can be constructed.

Cohen *et al.* (1972) have drawn attention to the symbolic aspects of decision-making, maintaining that it can be more important to take part in the process (and be seen to take part) than to make any particular choice. Indeed, since influences extraneous to the process of making a decision may shape that decision, it can – in a manner of speaking – be said to be partially uncoupled from the process by which it was arrived at (March, 1988), which may well mean that it is also partially uncoupled from its own implementation. In that case, pre-decision processes and post-decision implementation processes may not be linked in any meaningful way. In other words, what happens after a decision is taken may not have much to do with how it was arrived at.

Whether it does or whether it does not is a question we intend to examine when our empirical work has progressed further. To answer it, we have to define concepts with which cases of implementation can be compared. In this chapter we will move towards these via available published ideas and two suggestive cases.

WHAT IS IMPLEMENTATION?

How can what happens 'pre-decision' be separated from what happens 'post-decision'? Heller *et al.* (1988) see implementation as being part of the total decision process. They break this down into four phases, implementation being the fourth and final phase, covering 'the period between finalization and the final operation of the decision or its failure' (p. 4). So, while they see implementation as just a phase in a larger process, it is distinguishable. According to Heller *et al.* (1988), implementation starts when the decision has been made, and finishes when the decision is either working or is seen to be unworkable for whatever reasons.

So let us, for the moment, take the straightforward definition that to implement something is to put it into effect, to enact it. This includes not only actions directed to furthering implementation, but also any action or inaction which is directed towards thwarting implementation.

Much has been made of the *problems* of implementation in public administration, the so-called 'implementation gap' – the fact that there are significant problems in realizing some decisions. Pressman and Wildavsky (1973) were among the first to document these in their description of the difficulties faced by a local government agency in the US when trying to implement federal policy.

Barrett and Fudge (1981), Barrett and Hill (1983), Bardach (1977), and others studying public administration in Britain have similarly drawn attention to these problems. Barrett and her colleagues are particularly wary of a managerialist thesis which attempts to provide 'recipe book' answers to implementation problems. They maintain that it is necessary to take a more politically aware view. Many of the so-called problems encountered during the implementation process and the 'failures' of policy are explained, in their opinion, by recognizing the implementation process as a political process. Implementors may therefore act in a self-interested way which will confound the intentions of others in the organization.

Indeed, there is an essential *ambiguity* about implementation which leaves it open to political behaviour. Drawing on ideas about the 'garbage-can' nature of decision-making (Cohen *et al.*, 1972), Baier *et al.* (1986) note that policies are often ambiguous because of the very nature of the process of policy-making which relies on coalitions, negotiation, and other forms of 'horse-trading' in order to arrive at a conclusion. Not only may adopted policies be over-optimistic in order to win support, they may even be intentionally ambiguous. This allows for many interpretations, so that different interests can lend support for different reasons. Moreover, it obscures whether particular policies have been successfully implemented or not, the aims being so ambiguous that this cannot be clearly judged. So failures are not embarrassingly exposed.

COMPARING IMPLEMENTATION

The research at Bradford is not about public administration in particular, though it includes publicly owned institutions. It is an attempt to describe and to explain what occurs in a wider range of organizations. We are attempting to take a close look at the implementation process in a number of contrasting organizations in order both to provide some conceptualization of how 'implementation' takes place, and to see what factors make it easier or harder. What causes problems during implementation and under what circumstances, and what makes things go more smoothly?

Two strategic decisions in each of five organizations were studied, and a single decision in a sixth organization, making eleven cases in all. Of the organizations, two are public service organizations (a university and a water authority), two are in the private service sector (both mail order companies), and two are private manufacturers (in the chemicals industry). The research was carried out by extensive interviewing plus document searches. The aim was to interview a range of people in each organization – the decision-makers, the implementors, and those who were affected by the decision (the 'implementees'). In some instances these categories overlap. The final number of interviews (each of approximately an hour in duration) was in excess of 150. Interviewing began with those managers who were most closely concerned and then spread in a 'snowballing' fashion to as many significant others at all levels who were mentioned. An overall picture was gradually built up.

Vivid differences are found even in the implementing of identical kinds of decisions. This emerging finding contrasts with what happens beforehand when the decisions are being made. Hickson *et al.* (1986) argue that at that stage there is a strong probability that the process of deciding upon a similar matter in *different* organizations will be similar. But when it comes to implementation, things do not look that way at all. There is no evidence that if the same decisions are taken in two similar organizations, even at about the same time, they will be carried out in the same way. The personnel, the interests, the circumstances are likely to differ too much for that. The following cases of the managements of two companies, both in mail order, each deciding on the installation of a major computer system but finding the implementation of those decisions very different, demonstrate this forcefully.

If we may apply the terms coined by Hickson *et al.* (1986) to characterize pre-decision formulation processes to these instances of implementation processes, the first case was more 'sporadic', the second comparatively 'fluid'.

It should be appreciated that these decisions and their implementation were vital to both companies. In the mail order business, survival and success depend upon the speedy and accurate handling of the orders mailed in. Computerization of this is not merely a matter of changing a managerial support system. It is changing the core technology of the entire organization.

EASYSHOP FASHION COMPANY

The first decision took place in the 'Easyshop Fashion Company' (all names of companies and individuals are fictitious), a mail order company established in the 1890s and employing some 3,000 people, based in the north of England.

From the 1960s to the mid 1970s, Easyshop, in common with other mail order companies, was enjoying expansion and financial success. However, the business depended on extensive administrative arrangements in order to run its empire, which consisted of a large number of 'agents' – usually housewives who were sent the Easyshop catalogue, ordered goods for themselves and friends, and generally ran the paperwork side of things from their home. Since the company employed numerous clerks to receive and process the agents' orders, the whole business was extremely labour-intensive. By the 1970s labour-costs were rising and it was decided to install computerized systems to try and cut costs and increase efficiency.

In taking this step the company was one of the first in the industry. But such initiative also meant that Easyshop had little experience on which to plan such an exercise, and this, coupled with the fact that the computer industry itself was still in a learning stage, meant that there were many unknowns for the company to cope with. For reasons of safety and low-risk, managers decided to simply transfer all the manual routines straight on to the computer without reorganizing or rationalizing them. This eventually was to mean that they were burdened with over-complicated, over-detailed systems, which took up vast computer capacity and yet did not provide them with information in a readily accessible or usable form. As the Chief Executive remarked, they had a 'Rolls Royce system for a Ford operation', and they were becoming bogged down in the minutiae of their activities.

In the early 1980s the decision was made to start again and attempt to re-computerize Easyshop's systems. This was not a popular decision as much time and effort had already been invested in the existing system. A particular difficulty was to keep one system running while another was being developed. This was especially complex since all the different parts of the computer operation (the order-processing section, stock control, agency administration systems, etc.) interlinked with each other, which made it very awkward to try and separate one from another in order to upgrade one area at a time.

The other feature of this decision was the intense conflict between interests at a senior level which began during decision-making and continued into the implementation phase. Indeed, the antagonism was so damaging that implementation ceased almost completely at one point. This conflict centred around the Computer Director and the development staff who had spearheaded the existing system and were not in favour of another radical change. Even though re-writing the systems was put under the auspices of the Sales Administration Director, the Computer Director was able to delay implementation for nearly a year by withholding necessary information and resources.

Implementation was initially anticipated to take a year (although the Sales Systems Manager, who was writing the systems, privately forecast twice this). The internal conflict, and also the possibility of a takeover by another large company (whose computer systems were already running smoothly and would therefore be installing their own systems into Easyshop in the event of a successful bid) also caused long delays. In the event, the decision was still not fully implemented seven years later, although the arrival of a new Managing Director and the subsequent enforced departure of the contentious Computer Director gave new impetus to what was being done.

What are the features of this particular implementation process? It was certainly not an easy, straightforward one. Disagreements during the predecision process continued even when the decision had been taken by the Board to go ahead. There were delays due to internal conflicts, and to external eventualities. There were also the problems resulting from the unknowns of a new technology, and the inexperience and lack of expertise of organizational members. Meetings were held to try and hurry matters along, memos were written, management time was taken up. Political behaviour impeded progress, and because the disruption emanated from the top of the organization it both absorbed senior management's attention, and filtered downwards to hold up the work of those lower down.

In short, the process encountered impediments, both from conflict and from the occurrence of unforeseen external events. The result was that the decision was not implemented easily, it was not implemented completely, it was not implemented successfully, and matters did not go in the way the majority of the decision-makers had intended.

But it was not all negative. The decision did move, albeit slowly and haltingly, towards being implemented. What made this possible?

To begin with, although there was conflict between interest groups, there were more influential people in favour of going ahead than there were against it. Although the Computer Director was antagonistic, he only succeeded in delaying matters, not in stopping implementation altogether. Things did move along sporadically even while he was at Easyshop, and they moved along a great deal faster when he had left.

This was due to the decision being pragmatic and widely seen as necessary. Systems central to Easyshop's operation were not working satisfactorily and therefore something had to be done. Also, the seriousness of the firm's financial position made change urgent. If the company were to continue operating in the same way it seemed clear that it would not be operating for much longer. It could not compete.

But undoubtedly one of the major factors is that a new man came in at the top of the organization. The arrival of the new Managing Director gave the whole decision an added thrust. He was horrified at the length of time the implementation had taken and immediately insisted that it was a priority. It was this 'new broom sweeping clean' that really got things moving in the end.

By contrast, in the second case they moved along much more 'fluidly' from the start.

GREAT NORTHERN MAIL ORDER COMPANY

Again, the organization studied was a mail order company, Great Northern Mail Order, also based in the north of England.

In many ways the history of Great Northern is similar to that of Easyshop. Both did well in the 1960s while the industry was enjoying growth and expansion, and both suffered the consequences of a check in growth during the 1970s. Like Easyshop, the early 1980s saw Great Northern in a serious financial position. Lulled by past successes, management had failed to anticipate, and subsequently to respond to, changes in the retailing world. There was increased competition from other mail order companies and from high street shops. Tentative attempts at introducing some computerization had resulted in limited, uncoordinated systems which performed poorly. Debt recovery procedures in particular were inadequate and the company was losing money.

The need for a thorough up-dating of the company's systems was just as urgent as in Easyshop, the technical difficulties just as complex and interrelated. The problems which each company faced stemmed from similar causes, the solutions seemed obvious to each, and both companies made the decision to develop major new computer systems in the early 1980s. But while Easyshop was still battling to fully implement its decision at the end of the 1980s Great Northern had its systems up and running at the beginning of the decade. The implementation in Easyshop took more than seven years, in Great Northern it took six months. Why was this?

One of the essential features of Great Northern's success story is the fact that the decision was made and implemented by an almost completely new management team.

In 1981, while the company was still in the doldrums, the Chairman brought in a new Managing Director, David Jackson, who although young, had considerable experience in a larger, rival, mail order company. Jackson attracted with him a huge number of senior staff from his old company, in all over twenty people, most of whom were computer personnel. Many established Great Northern directors and senior managers lost their jobs and one department in the computer section was closed completely.

Because of his experience in the industry Jackson knew straightaway that the computer systems required major improvements, and this was his first big decision and his priority. In essence, the decision was unopposed. Firstly, because most of the old Great Northern personnel (directors and computing staff who might have been unhappy about such a radical change) were replaced by Jackson's people, who included three new directors in the computing area. Secondly, as in Easyshop, it was realized by the staff that the company was in a serious position and that radical remedies were necessary.

Another factor which made the implementation of this decision much easier was that Jackson had been involved with the installation of a new computer system at his previous company, which had worked success-fully. He and the Computing Director therefore already knew which computer firm and systems they wanted. Although these systems had to be modified to accommodate Great Northern's requirements, the fact that senior management were already familiar with them meant the company could start further along the learning curve and that fewer mistakes were likely to be made. Unlike Easyshop, they were not struggling with what to them were unknowns.

Of course it was not all plain sailing. The decision required a large capital investment, not an easy matter in a flagging company. And some of the staff who were left in the computer section were demoralized and frightened of losing their jobs. Yet it was these individuals to whom the task was given of compiling the new programs. They had to get used to new equipment and operating systems, had to learn a new, higher-level, computer language and then write programs in it. All this had to be done to a very strict deadline imposed by senior management.

Nevertheless, both old and new employees rose to the task. Implemen-tation was rushed along at a frenetic pace which was exhilarating but highly pressured. The deadline was a date in July and, by working evenings and weekends for six months, they made it. Implementation was complete, on time, and successful.

CONTRASTING CASES

What then can be learned from these two contrasting cases? What concepts can be derived to enable them to be compared, and to enable further comparisons? Easyshop and Great Northern were companies in the same industry, mail order, implementing the same kind of decision, to computerize. Yet their implementation processes differed sharply. Is it possible to begin to deduce from this some of the reasons why one was more successful than the other, reasons that may be generalized and applied to other cases?

But first, what might be some of the criteria of success? Most obvious is the time taken, the sheer *speed* of implementation, which was so much faster in Great Northern. There is then what might be broadly termed *ease* of implementation, the smoothness and absence of substantial impedi-ments which distinguished the Great Northern process from that at Easyshop. This faster, easier, process also took Great Northern to a greater *completion* of the computer installation and operation, Easyshop

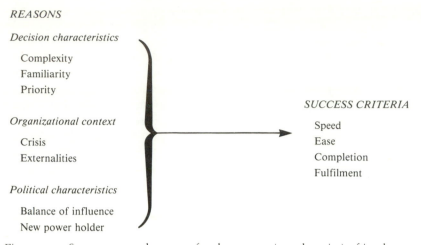

REASONS

Decision characteristics

   Complexity
   Familiarity
   Priority

                                                 SUCCESS CRITERIA

Organizational context

   Crisis
   Externalities

                                          Speed
                                          Ease
                                          Completion
                                          Fulfilment

Political characteristics

   Balance of influence
   New power holder

Figure 7.1   Some suggested reasons for the success (or otherwise) of implementation

being left with something less than a complete and functioning system. Finally, Great Northern's implementation represented a greater fulfilment of the intentions of its board when they gave the go ahead. These four criteria of successful implementation, speed, ease, completion, and fulfilment, are shown in figure 7.1.

However, whilst such criteria of success can readily be conceptualized, the researcher faces more difficult problems in defining them empirically. Different individuals in different departments and at different levels in an organization may have differing views of how successful implementation is. Typically, top management is likely to see it as easier and more complete than do the 'implementors', for example those middle managers who must make a new computer system work, or the 'implementees', for example any clerical staff whose jobs are degraded.

A conceptualization of some (certainly not all) of the reasons for success also appears in figure 7.1. We have discerned three kinds of reasons why the implementation of a decision should succeed (relatively speaking) rather than fail. First because of the sort of decision it is, second because of the organizational context in which it has to be implemented, third because of the political situation between those involved.

THE DECISION ITSELF

Firstly, the characteristics of the decision itself. The decisions in both the cases described were about new core technology. Thus they were both very *complex*, as the computer linked together central aspects of the functioning of the entire organization. But what simplified things for Great Northern was the fact that to their new personnel it had all been done before – the decision-makers were familiar with the kinds of problem they were facing and with potential solutions. This *familiarity* ensured that time and effort were not expended in pursuing costly and wasteful alternatives. Easyshop had no such experience to follow and consequently turned up many a wrong path.

In both firms the decision was given *priority* over other decisions. This was most true in Great Northern as the new management team there made it a number one priority, providing resources in terms of finance and manpower to ensure success. But in Easyshop whilst the majority of senior management appeared to recognize the necessity for such a decision, and resources were made available, the priority was nullified by competing interests.

THE ORGANIZATIONAL CONTEXT OF IMPLEMENTATION

The fact that both firms were in difficult financial straits made the implementation of the new computer systems that much more urgent. People were ready to accept that 'something had to be done'. So the awareness of overall *crisis* kept implementation moving, and made it more acceptable than it might have been otherwise. *Crisis* decision-making and implementation have already been documented by Dutton (1986), and Rosenthal (1986), among others.

Events external to the organization, beyond its control, are clearly critical. Easyshop's implementation process was impeded and seriously delayed by the threatened takeover bid from another competitor. Work on the new computer systems was virtually suspended whilst management faced this threat. It came out of the blue and was unforeseen at the time of making the decision. Great Northern suffered no such occurrence and was able to proceed without distraction or interruption. Whilst Easyshop's experience illustrates the delaying effect that such *externalities* may have, they could also speed up implementation.

THE POLITICS OF IMPLEMENTATION

Lastly the politics of implementation itself must be considered. At Easyshop implementation was characterized by conflict and lack of cooperation. At Great Northern, although the staff were rather wary and disillusioned to begin with, they had little choice but to cooperate (or leave!). The results were plain to see. Great Northern sped on and completed in six months, while Easyshop languished, held up by a Computer Director strong enough to stand in the way.

Perhaps most important of all for success, in both organizations it eventually took 'a new broom to sweep clean'. New management arrived in Great Northern who swept aside any opposition and imposed their solution. Although it took longer for this to happen in Easyshop, it was the arrival of a new Managing Director that got things moving again, and prised out the opposing Computer Director when his residual usefulness had expired.

Hence the *balance of influence* and more specifically a *new power-holder* can be crucial to the speed, ease, completion, and ultimate fulfilment of implementation.

CONCLUDING THOUGHTS

We have tried to show how we are attempting to study both pre-decision processes and post-decision processes. With the single exception of Heller *et al.* (1988) who focus upon influence and participation, the principal large-scale studies of the general processual characteristics of managerial decision-making have all stopped where the decision was taken. That is, they have studied the process only so far as official authorization, when the go-ahead for implementation was given (notably Mintzberg *et al.*, 1976; Nutt, 1984; Hickson *et al.*, 1986). We are going beyond that point to see what happens next, to see just how and how far implementation is carried through, and to link that with the decision and how it was arrived at.

To compare implementation processes, concepts are required in terms which facilitate useful comparisons. We have suggested some concepts which relate to the matter for decision, to the organizational context, and to the pertinent political situation, which may go towards the explanation of what happens; and four concepts (speed, ease, fulfilment, completion) which describe the successfulness or otherwise of implementation.

The political aspects of implementation, such as the balance of influence for and against, can be thought of in the same way as the 'politicality' of pre-decision processes described by Hickson *et al.* (1986). In this respect, decision-making and implementation processes can be treated in similar terms, as Heller *et al.* (1988) have demonstrated. It may also be possible to characterize the overall movement through time of post-decision processes as sporadic or fluid or constricted as we have characterized pre-decision processes.

But in other respects, pre- and post-decision cannot be thought of in the same way. Most obviously, pre-decision processes move towards a decision, whereas post-decision processes flow from it, even if not entirely since implementation can have begun before being formally authorized. Thus whereas pre-decision processes seem primarily a response to the matter in hand, the matter being decided, post-decision processes are largely a response to the decision that was made. Further, they ensue from what happened in the making, from the pre-decision process as well as from the decision. In the case of Easyshop described above, unresolved conflict over the decision surfaced again in resistance to its implementation.

So, as we said earlier, whilst in different organizations the process of deciding upon a similar matter is likely to be more similar than different, the implementing of even identical decisions can contrast sharply. The adage that making a decision is less than half the battle is borne out again.

NOTE

1 Here we draw upon the work of a team, in which David Hickson was a member, that included Richard Butler, David Cray, Geoffrey Mallory, and David Wilson, and earlier also Graham Astley.

REFERENCES

Baier, V. E., March, J. G., and Saetren, H. (1986), 'Implementation and ambiguity', *Scandinavian Journal of Management Studies*, May, 197–212.

Bardach, E. (1977), *The Implementation Game – What Happens After a Bill Becomes Law* (Cambridge, MA: MIT Press).

Barrett, S. and Fudge, C. (1981), *Policy and Action* (London: Methuen & Co.).

Barrett, S. and Hill, M. (1984), 'Policy, bargaining and structure in implementation theory – towards an integrated perspective', *Policy and Politics*, 12(3), 219–40.

Cohen, M. D., March, J. G., and Olsen, J. P. (1972), 'A garbage can model or organizational choice', *Administrative Science Quarterly*, 17, 1–25.

Cray, D., Mallory, G. R., Butler, R. J., Hickson, D. J., and Wilson, D. C. (1988), 'Sporadic, fluid and constricted processes: three types of strategic decision-making in organizations', *Journal of Management Studies*, 25(1), 13–39.

Dutton, J. E. (1986), 'The processing of crisis and non-crisis strategic issues', *Journal of Management Studies*, 23(5), May, 501–17.

Hage, Jerald (1980), *Theories of Organization: Form, Process and Transformation* (New York: Wiley).

Heller, F., Drenth, P., Koopman, P., and Rus, V. (1988), *Decisions in Organizations – A Three-Country Comparative Study* (London: Sage).

Hickson, D. J., Butler, R. J., Cray, D., Mallory, G. R., and Wilson, D. C. (1986), *Top Decisions: Strategic Decision Making in Organizations* (Oxford: Blackwell; San Francisco: Jossey-Bass).

March, J. G. (1988), *Decisions and Organizations* (Oxford: Blackwell).

Mintzberg, H., Raisinghani, D., and Theoret, A. (1976), 'The structure of unstructured decision processes', *Administrative Science Quarterly*, 21, 246–75.

Nutt, P. (1984), 'Types of organizational decision processes', *Administrative Science Quarterly*, 29(3), 414–50.

Pressman, J. L. and Wildavsky, A. B. (1973), *Implementation, How Great Expectations in Washington Are Dashed in Oakland, etc.* (Berkeley: University of California Press).

Rosenthal, U. (1986), 'Crisis decision-making in The Netherlands', *The Netherlands Journal of Sociology*, **22**(2).

8

STRESS AND LEADERSHIP

BERNARD M. BASS

ABSTRACT

The stress reaction arises in individuals, groups, and organizations when their well-being is threatened. Their decision-making is likely to suffer unless they are effectively led by transformational leaders who can help maintain the quality of their decisions. In dealing with disasters, panic will be prevented by leaders who create well-trained, well-organized credible systems, and advanced preparation. Prolonged stress will be better handled when leaders are able to transform personal concerns into efforts to achieve group goals.

Such transformational leadership is seen to reduce feelings of burnout and symptoms of stress in professionals. Confidence in such leadership is particularly salient in crisis situations as well. The transformational leaders themselves appear to be able to maintain extraordinary presence of mind in the face of such threats and crises.

Groups and organizations, confronted with threats to their steady states of well-being, will experience stress. In many instances, their leadership operating through the decision process makes the difference in the prevention or occurrence of stress and burnout. Thus, with professional county extension employees, job stress was found by Graham (1982) to be lower when their district programme leaders were described as higher on the Leadership Behaviour Description Questionnaire (LBDQ) in both initiation of structure and in consideration. At the same time, of course, leadership can be the source of increased stress. Abrasive leaders are known for their capacity to cause stress. Many studies have reported that for subordinates their immediate supervisor is the most stressful aspect of their work (e.g., Herzberg, 1966). The tyrannical boss is frequently mentioned as the source of stress.

Stress produces faulty decision-making. Instead of careful analysis and calculation or effective intuition by the expert based on learning and experience, the stressed individual will fall back on non-productive intuitive reactions which satisfy immediate personal emotional needs rather than the objective requirements of the situation. 'Lying, for example, is much more often the result of panic than of Machiavellian scheming' (Simon, 1987, p. 62). When Sorokin (1943) examined reports of the reactions of groups and communities to the calamities of famine, war, and revolution, he found that a calamity tended to greatly intensify emotional arousal, distort cognitive processes, focus attention upon the calamity and away from other features of the environment, hasten disintegration of the self, and decrease rationality of behaviour.

Our purpose here is to show the linkages between stress in followers and the kind and quality of their leaders, especially their leaders' decision-making.

A MODEL OF GROUP RESPONSES TO STRESS

Janis and Mann (1977) looked at responses under stress induced by conflict in the face of an impending threat and the risks and costs of taking action to avoid it. They argued that the completely rational approach to an authentic warning of impending danger would be a thorough examination of objectives, of values, and of alternative courses of action. Costs and risks would be weighed. A final choice would be based on a cost-benefit analysis. Included in the effective process would be development, careful implementation, and contingency planning. But such vigilance, along with thorough search, appraisal, and contingency planning are likely to be short-circuited as a consequence of emotional arousal and the socio-emotional phenomena generated by the impending threat. Various defective reactions to the danger warnings are likely to happen. These include fixed adherence to the status quo, too hasty change, defensive avoidance, or panic.

LEADERSHIP UNDER STRESS

Numerous causal relations can be used to describe the interplay between stress and leadership. For instance, in times of crisis, informal leadership and temporary groups are likely to emerge if the formal authorities and emergency services cannot deal with the crisis events (Mileti, Drabek, and Haas, 1975). The direct removal of the threats and obstacles that are the source of stress may be facilitated by such informal leadership. Drive and anxiety may be reduced by providing supportive leadership resulting in an increasing sense of security.

Leaders can help their groups in many other ways to cope with stress. Individuals, groups, and organizations frozen into inertial disbelief when they are seriously threatened may be aroused and alerted by influential leaders. Faced with hasty, poorly thought-out decisions, leaders may delay premature disclosure of options and call for reconsideration of proposals. When their followers are engaged in defensive avoidance, leaders may bring them back to reality. Panic can be reduced or avoided by strong leadership that points the way to safety. In general, groups with leaders are likely to cope better with stress than those without such leadership. More directiveness will be expected and desired from leaders by groups and organizations under stress. Moreover, whoever takes the role of leader, during times of social stress, will be expected to revise goals, define common objectives, restructure situations, and suggest solutions to deal with the sources of stress and conflict (Downton, 1973). But, as we shall also see, while directive leadership is most expected, desired, and successful when stress is high, it may not always be the most effective style.

Leadership may contribute to stress

Unfortunately, leadership may be the cause rather than the amelioration of stressful conditions that result in emotionally driven actions by the followers and poorer long-term outcomes. And the leaders who emerge are likely to be different from those in unstressed situations. They may actually contribute to the stress. Leaders can cause more stress among their followers, for instance by exciting a mob, which is already at fever pitch, to take too hasty actions. Political leaders manufacture crises to enhance their own power, to divert public attention from real problems, and to gain public support for their own arbitrary actions.

Those who are elected to office may be themselves more prone to stress. Sanders and Malkis (1982) manipulated problem importance, difficulty, and external incentives involving recognition of esteem and success. They found that Type A (stress-prone) personalities were nominated more often as leaders than Type B's. However, the fewer Type B's who were chosen as leaders tended to be more effective as individuals in the assigned task than were the Type A leaders.

Seltzer, Numerof, and Bass (1989) unexpectedly found that, when other factors were held constant, *intellectually stimulating* leaders increased the felt stress and job 'burnout' among their subordinates. Misumi (1985) reported the results of a series of experiments that showed that production-prodding leadership with instructions such as: 'work more quickly', 'work accurately', 'you could do more', 'hurry up, we haven't much time left', generated detectable physiological stress symptoms. Systolic and diastolic blood pressure increased in experimental subjects as did galvanic skin responses. In similar laboratory experiments, such production-oriented leadership caused feelings of hostility and anxiety about the experiment.

SUCCESSFUL BUT NOT NECESSARILY EFFECTIVE LEADERSHIP
IN STRESSFUL CONDITIONS

Directive leadership often succeeds when followers are under stress. That is, the followers are influenced by the directiveness. For instance, such leadership can point the way to escape from a panic. It would be effective in helping the followers to avoid disaster. Directive leadership can also influence followers to take actions in particular ways which may not be most *effective* in helping followers to reach their goals. Successful but ineffective leaders may cause faulty decisions to be made too hastily or defensive reactions among followers.

Stress, hasty decision-making, and directive leadership

Crisis provokes a centralization of authority (Hermann, 1963). Both government and industrial groups are more likely to accept leadership when the problem is urgent (Berkowitz, 1953). When followers are under stress, speedy decisions from directive, task-oriented, structuring leaders are likely to be readily accepted. But speedy decisions do not necessarily provide the best solutions to the problems facing the followers.

It is not the speed of the decision nor the leader directiveness that may result in inadequate solutions to the stressful circumstances. It is rapid decision-making without the opportunity in advance for careful structuring and support. For, as we shall see, generally rapid decision-making is sought in crisis and disasters and will be effective if the decisions are not hastily made at the last minute but are based on advanced warning, preparation, and organization, along with commitment and support.

As Janis and Mann (1977) noted, when threat is finally perceived, it generates the desire for prompt decisive action. Leadership becomes centred in one or in a few who gain increased power to decide for the group. The price for the rapid, arbitrary dictation is the cost in lost freedoms and abuses and corruption by placing power in the hands of the dictator. Hertzler (1940) examined thirty-five historical dictatorships and concluded that they arose during crises and when sudden change was desired. Additionally, Downton (1973) suggested that followers stressed by ambiguity become easily influenced by aggressive, powerful leaders who promise to reduce the ambiguity and restructure the situation.

Alwon (1980) argued that social agency administrators, even if it means a change in their leadership style, must adopt a strong, directive style during times of crisis to avoid dangers and to seize opportunities. In emergencies, when danger threatens, subordinates want to be told what to do, and in a hurry. They perceive that they have no time to consider alternatives. Rapid, decisive leadership is demanded (Hemphill, 1950).

Five hundred groups were described in questionnaires by members on a variety of dimensions formulated by Hemphill. The adequacy of various leadership behaviours was correlated with group characteristics. Hemphill concluded that, in frequently changing and emerging groups, leaders who failed to make decisions quickly would be judged as inadequate.

Considerable evidence is available to support the contention that leaders speed up their decision-making as a consequence of stress. Failure to do so leads to their rejection as leaders (Korten, 1962). Acceptance of their rapid, arbitrary decisions without consultation, negotiation, or participation is also increased. A leader who can react quickly in emergencies will be judged as better by followers than one who cannot.

Flanagan *et al.* (1952) found that, according to respondents, 'taking prompt action in emergency situations' was a critical behaviour, differentiating those judged to be better military officers from those judged as worse in performance. Large-scale surveys of the American soldier during the Second World War by Stouffer, Suchman, DeVinney, Star, and Williams (1949) confirmed (particularly at lower levels in the organization), that the military emphasized rapidity of response to orders from higher authority. This emphasis was despite the fact that most units seldom operated under battlefield conditions.

Where rapid decisions are called for, executives are likely to become more directive than participative (Lowin, 1986). Consistent with this, the more organizations wish to be prepared for emergency action, the more they are likely to stress a high degree of structure, attention to orders, and authoritarian direction. Foder (1976) demonstrated that industrial supervisors exposed to the stress of simulated, disturbing subordinates became more autocratic in dealing with the situation. College students did likewise (Fodor, 1973). From half to two-thirds of 181 airmen, asked for their opinions about missile teams, rescue teams, scientific teams, or other small crews facing emergencies, strongly agreed that they should respond to the orders of the commander with less question than under normal conditions. In an emergency, the commander was expected to 'check more closely to see that everyone is carrying out his responsibility'. A majority felt that 'the commander should not be "just one of the boys"' (Torrance, 1956/7).

In a survey of Dutch naval officers' performance by Mulder, deJong, Koppelaar, and Verhage (1986), the officers were more favourably evaluated by their superiors if they were seen to make more use of their formal power in crisis compared to non-crisis situations. In crisis conditions, both superiors and subordinates of the officers looked for more authoritative direction from the officers. At the same time, the officers were evaluated more favourably by their subordinates if they were seen to be more openly consultative in non-crisis compared to crisis situations.

In the same way, during the unstable period of a union's organization, as it goes from one emergency to the next, militant, decisive, aggressive leadership is demanded. Under stress, strength and activity take on more importance for leadership. After the struggle for survival is over and the union is recognized, the kind of leadership required changes. Now it must exhibit more willingness to compromise and to cooperate (Selekman, 1947).

One reversal of the call for rapid-decision leadership in crisis conditions was found by Streib, Folts, and LaGreca (1985) in thirty-six retirement communities. Most residents were satisfied ordinarily to let others make the decisions for them but they wanted the possibility of involvement in the decision-making if crises arose or the stability of the community was threatened.

Directive leadership and prolonged stress   When the stress is a chronic situation or one that is prolonged, the same tendencies towards directive leadership and acceptance of it are observed. During the Second World War, Japanese-American residents of California were subjected to isolation, loss of subsistence, threat to loved ones, enforced idleness, and physiological stress due to internment. As a consequence, the internees were apathetic and blindly obedient to influence (Leighton, 1945). Similarly, Fisher and Rubinstein (1956) reported that experimental participants deprived of sleep for forty-eight to fifty-four hours showed significantly greater shifts in autokinetic judgements indicating that they were more susceptible than normal to the social influence of their partners.

Hall and Mansfield (1971) studied the longer-term effects of stress and the response to it in three research and development organizations. The stress was caused by a sudden drop in available research funds. This resulted in strong internal pressures for reduced spending and the increased search for new funds. As would be expected, the response to the threat was to increase top management control and direction. There was a reduction in consultation with the researchers. Subsequently, the effect over two years on the researchers was to decrease their satisfaction and identification with the organization. However, their research performance was unaffected.

To conclude, directive leadership will be preferred and successful in influencing followers under stress. But such leadership may be counterproductive in the long run.

Leadership and defensive avoidance

As already noted, often it is the political leadership which contrives the threats, crises, and ambiguities. For centuries, political leaders have used real or imagined threat as the way to increase the cohesiveness among their followers and gain unquestioning support for their own dictates. The common scenario begins with economic weakness and dislocation, followed by international complications, appeals to nationalist revolution and/or civil war, and finally a breakdown of political institutions. The dictator organizes ready-made immediate solutions that soothe, flatter, and exalt the public. Defensive avoidance is promoted. Blame is directed elsewhere.

When business and government leaders are seen to consult and share decisions with subordinates in times of crises (Berkowitz, 1953), often it is because they seek support from their subordinates about the wisdom of their already chosen solutions. Also, they would like to spread the responsibility for the decision from themselves to their group.

STRESS AND EFFECTIVENESS AS A LEADER

House and Rizzo (1972) among others showed the importance of the leader in helping their groups effectively cope with conflict and stress. By leadership that is effective in coping with stress, we mean leadership that results in rationally defensible quality decisions, appropriate use of available information, skills, and resources, and enhanced performance of followers in reaching their goals despite the threats and obstacles to doing so.

Changing leadership

Groups, organizations, and communities under stressful conditions may remedy the inadequacies of their leadership by changing it. Thus, Lanzetta (1953) found that different leaders emerged in the same groups as more stressful conditions were imposed. In the same way, results obtained by Hamblin (1958b) indicated that members of experimental groups, when facing genuine crisis situations, tended to replace their old leaders with new ones if the old leaders were unable to cope with the crisis.

Combat conditions

High morale and less stress are found in soldiers, in combat, with confidence in their commanders (Gal and Jones, 1985). This confidence is based on the seen professional competence of the commander, on belief in his credibility, and on their perception of his caring about his troops. But, under continuing combat stress, professional competence becomes particularly important according to Kalay's (1983) study of Israeli soldiers in Lebanon in 1982.

Handling conflict

Among eighty-four randomly selected faculty members from twenty departments of two universities, R. Katz (1977) found that the amount of affective and substantive conflict in departments contributed to felt tension (0.49 and 0.47) and perceived lack of departmental effectiveness (−0.28 and −0.29). At the same time, for departments in conflict, leader initiation of structure correlated more highly with departmental effectiveness than when such conflict was absent. The correlation between leader initiation of structure in a department and its effectiveness was 0.63 when affective conflict was high and only 0.29 when affective conflict was low. The correlation between initiation and effectiveness was 0.51 when substantive conflict was high and 0.38 when substantive conflict was low. In an experiment to confirm these findings, participants were hired to perform routine tasks. For a routine coding task, initiating structure correlated 0.46 with productivity when conflict was high and −0.62 when conflict was absent. Less clear results materialized with a cross-checking task. Consistent with this, Katz, Phillips, and Cheston (1976) demonstrated that more directive, structured, preemptory 'forcing' may be more effective in resolving interpersonal conflicts than 'problem solving'.

Dealing with panic

The most effective leaders in helping groups to escape from panic conditions display performance-maintenance (PM) leadership; that is, high task and high relations-orientation. In a study reported in Misumi (1985) in which a panic situation had been simulated with 672 undergraduates in six-person groups and the percentage of successful escaping, the degree of jamming, and aggressiveness were measured, four styles of leadership were compared. The percentage of successful escaping was highest and aggression lowest in the PM condition when leaders both focussed on performance planning and maintenance of relationships in contrast to focussing on only one or the other, or neither. PM leadership behaviour was seen as most appropriate by the subjects. Additionally, Misumi and Sako (1982) found it was important to initially provide the support and encouragement, followed by the concentration on performance requirements, rather than vice versa.

Kugihara and Misumi (1984) compared subjects dealing with a maze under fearful and unfearful conditions. Consistent with the previously cited Japanese experiments of reaction to simulated panic, PM leadership generated the least fear, the largest amount of planning, and least unreasonable felt pressure from the leader. This was in contrast to the effects of performance leadership or maintenance leadership alone, or the absence of both.

A. L. Klein (1976) observed in an experimental study of the panic condition, of too many people trying to escape through the same door, that the stressed group preferred a strong leader rather than a leader who under low stress was elected and more highly acceptable. Acceptance and election, which under conditions of low stress gave the accepted legitimate leader control of the group's fate, was replaced under high stress by the group turning to a less legitimate but stronger leader, seen to be endowed with more competence.

Dealing with disaster

A body of observation, commentary, and research on coping with disasters points to the critical contributions of leadership and public management which is well-organized, well-prepared, and well-trained to provide both the needed instrumental and supporting leadership (Harman, 1984). At the mass populace and community level, this translates into leadership which provides credible warning systems and is prepared for when disasters actually strike. The absence of such effective leadership and management is marked by maladaptive coping defensiveness by the public and exacerbation of panic reactions. For organizations, Mitroff, Shrivastava, and Udwadia (1987) advocate both technical and behavioural preparation by the organizations for crises. Management needs early warning systems and high quality control and crisis command centres. Among other things, employees need training in security and detection as well as emotional preparation for emergencies.

Weinberg (1978) reviewed thirty cases of group behaviour in disaster situations: earthquakes, blizzards, accidents, and hurricanes. Trained judges examined each case history. Breakdown occurs in situations of high stress when there is an absence of appropriate leadership. Effective coping occurs with leadership that provides the needed support, structure, and preparations. For example, according to Hammerschlag and Astrachan (1971) in the Kennedy Airport 'snow-in' of February 1969, the assembled people became passive, compliant, helpless, and without initiative and indigenous leadership. Salvation was predicated on the arrival of some technical authority who could ensure deliverance – a 'leader', the 'omnipotent one' who would clear runways, facilitate departure, feed the hungry, and make everyone happy. The persons in the snow-in never became collaborating groups; there was no task that could have unified them. There developed a sense of abandonment which was internalized as a retribution for some fantasied wrongdoing. Food swindling and hoarding began to occur.

The need for structure Effective leadership is seen in the creation of the necessary structure by local administrators to deal with future stress. Tests of the Lawrence/Douglas County, Kansas emergency preparedness system demonstrated that the structure needs to be ready for future disasters along with a strong chain of command. Resources must be well organized and staff highly trained (Watson, 1984). City-wide drills for ambulance drivers were seen to have paid off in the handling of the Hyatt Regency disaster in Kansas City (Ross, 1982). Similar conclusions about emergency preparedness were reached in Alexandria, Virginia's dealing with disastrous flooding (Harman, 1984).

Available leadership at the time of crisis The need for structure and prepared response provides the reason for the public service agencies of local government, such as the local police, fire, ambulance services, and public works departments, to be the critical human resources whose effective utilization is paramount in the times of crisis (Kartez, 1984). Above and beyond this, the available leadership of these resources at the time of the crisis makes a difference in the effectiveness of the organized response to disaster. The most effective organizations maintain their own identity and do not depend on outside volunteer help. The least effective have an amorphous organizational structure.

TRANSFORMATIONAL LEADERSHIP NEEDED

Transformational leadership includes the factors of charisma, inspirational leadership, intellectual stimulation, and individualized consideration (Bass, 1985), and contributes to effective leadership under stress. To illustrate, charismatic transformational leaders tend to keep their 'cool' when faced with threats to their lives. Mahatma Gandhi, F. D. Roosevelt, Kemal Ataturk, Benito Mussolini, Kwame Nkrumah, and Ronald Reagan displayed composure and presence of mind when faced with attempts to assassinate them. They were not easily frightened, disconcerted, or thrown off balance. They remained calm and maintained their sense of humour in the face of danger or crisis (Willner, 1968). They were like medal-winning heroes of military combat. According to an analysis by Gal (1985) of seventy-seven Israeli medal winners in the Yom Kippur War contrasted with ordinary soldiers, the medal winners exhibited more leadership, perseverance under stress, decisiveness, devotion to duty, and emotional stability.

What transformational leaders can do

While transactional leadership can provide for structure and consideration, transformational leadership adds to it by helping the followers to transcend their own immediate self-interests, increasing their awareness of the larger issues, and by shifting the goals away from personal safety and security and towards achievement and self-actualization. The transformational leader may have the charisma to satisfy the frustrated identity needs and lack of social support felt by followers. Thus, in a study of fifty-seven communes over a four-year period, Bradley (1987) showed that the presence or absence of charisma in the commune's leader contributed to the commune's likelihood of survival. Communes were least likely to survive if their members were strongly seeking charismatic leadership which was not provided. Those with charismatic leaders were most likely to survive along with those communes which did not seek such leadership.

The transformational leader may reveal the individualized consideration to convert crises into developmental challenges. The transformational leader may provide the intellectual stimulation to promote subordinate's thoughtful, creative, adaptive solutions rather than hasty, defensive, maladaptive ones to the stressful conditions.

It should be kept in mind that transformational leadership does not replace transactional leadership. It adds to it (Waldman, Bass, and Yammarino, 1988). Transformational leadership augments transactional leadership as seen in initiation and consideration (Seltzer and Bass, 1986). It adds substantially to helping individuals, groups, and organizations under conflict and stress.

What transactional leadership alone fails to do

As already shown in the preceding section, a transactional leader can be influential in groups under stress. Such a leader can supply solutions for immediate member needs as perceived by them. There will be immediate satisfaction with such leadership but not necessarily long-term positive effectiveness. What is required is a transformational leader who can evoke higher-level needs, such as for the common good, who can move the group into a fully vigilant search for long-term solutions. Mulder, Ritsema van Eck, and deJong (1971) studied leadership patterns in a Dutch navy flotilla on active duty. The usual interpersonal and task-oriented factors emerged but what distinguished crisis from non-crisis leadership was intense, powerful, self-confident leadership that characterized the charismatic transformational leader. This was in contrast to the 'mild' person–leader relationship in non-crisis situations.

Evidence of the effects of transformational and transactional leadership

More direct evidence of the effects of transactional and transformational
leadership were accumulated by Seltzer, Numerof, and Bass (1989). A
total of 277 MBA students holding full-time jobs completed the Personal
Stress Symptom Assessment (Numerof, Cramer, and Shachar-Hendin,
1984), in which they indicated how often they experienced headaches,
fatigue, irritability, loss of appetite, insomnia, inability to relax, and so
on. They also completed the Gillespie-Numerof Burnout Inventory
(Numerof and Gillespie, 1984), responding to such items as: 'I'm fed up
with my job', and 'my job has me at the end of my rope'. Felt stress and
burnout correlated 0.58. The 277 respondents described their immediate
superior with the Multifactor Leadership Questionnaire (Bass and Avolio,
1990). Table 8.1 shows the first-order correlations of the transformational and transactional leadership scores of the superiors and the
felt stress and burnout of their subordinates. Seltzer, Numerof, and Bass
concluded that 14 per cent of the variance in reported symptoms of stress
and 34 per cent of the variance in feelings of burnout could be attributed
to the lack of transformational leadership and contingent rewarding and
more frequent management-by-exception.

Multiple regression analyses suggested that, if the other factors were held
constant, although reported stress was lessened if working under charismatic and individually considerate leaders it was raised somewhat when
working under intellectually stimulating leaders. As for transactional
leadership, contingent rewarding was modestly associated with less stress
and management-by-exception with more stress. The pattern was the
same for feelings of burnout but the relations with leadership were
stronger.

Why transformational leadership is needed

Rather than the autocratic, rapid decision-making demanded of the leader
by the ready-to-be-influenced group, effective leadership in stressful
situations organizes group efforts of followers in ways which will help to
promote vigilance, thorough search, thorough appraisal, and contingency
planning to avoid defective coping with threat. Bolstering can be mini-
mized by encouraging 'devil's advocates'. Heterogeneity rather than
homogeneity can be pursued in selecting members for the group so as to
promote harder-to-attain creativity rather than quick and easy decision-
making. Considering the distinctions between frustration, fear, anxiety,
and conflict (Bass, Hurder, and Ellis, 1954), to be effective under stress the
leader must be transformational – able to rise above what the group sees
as its immediate needs and appropriate reactions. The leader must arouse

Table 8.1. *First-order correlations of transactional and transformational leadership of superiors and the felt stress and burnout among their subordinates*

Leadership	Symptoms of stress $N = 285$	Felt burnout $N = 296$
Transformational		
Charisma	−0.17[**]	−0.53[**]
Individualized consideration	−0.18[**]	−0.47[**]
Intellectual stimulation	−0.11[**]	−0.36[**]
Transactional		
Contingent rewards	−0.09[**]	−0.43[**]
Management-by-exception	0.11[**]	0.22[**]

Notes: [**]$p < 0.01$, $r = 0.14$.
Source: Adapted from Seltzer, Numerof, and Bass (1989).

an inert group to the significance of threats and the group's lack of preparedness. The leader must alter the inert group's willingness to live with frustration rather than make efforts to deal more adequately with obstacles in its path to positive goals. Again, to be effective, instead of catering to the group's immediate needs and fears, a leader may need to calm the demands for hasty change. An effective leader may need to be transformational in identifying and publicizing the inadequacy of defensive pseudo-solutions. The effective leader is transformational in providing superordinate goals transcending self-interests for the hypervigilant group in a state of panic. Clear, confident direction is important for effective leadership when panic is imminent. While the transformational leader's vision for the future may set the stage for planning ahead, transactional leadership may also be important in planning.

Planning ahead

Crises can be prevented or their stressful effects mitigated by effective political leaders planning ahead (Yarmolinsky, 1987). Effective transactional leaders set up early warning mechanisms to avoid surprises produced in hasty ill-conceived responses. Active practice of management-by-exception can result in potential crises being recognized rationally. Appropriate searches for information can be instituted without hasty defensiveness. Nevertheless, it is the transformational leader who sounds and articulates the need for early warnings and mobilizes the organization to avoid the emergency or to prepare for it (Tichy and

Devanna, 1985). Such leaders devise strategies to avoid or defuse the crisis and persuade immediate subordinates and peers to accept the proposed strategies and mobilize support for them. In this regard, political leaders take on an important teaching function (Yarmolinsky, 1987).

In the same way, by planning ahead, by anticipating potential crises, and by preparing the group in advance for them, industrial supervisors will be more effective than if they only engage in dealing with immediate problems. Studies of leader behaviour in a public utility company, an insurance office, an automobile plant, and in heavy industry found that supervisors of groups with better production records more often exhibited long-range planning and anticipated future problems rather than limiting themselves to day-to-day operations (D. Katz, 1951).

Dealing with mergers

Schweiger, Ivancevich, and Power (1987) noted that, when a firm is acquired by another, the employees in the firm taken over are stressed by the loss of identity, purpose, and ego ideal. Shock, anger, disbelief, depression, and helplessness may occur among many of them. There is anxiety due to lack of information. The resignations and forced departure of others are seen as a loss of talent as well as a threat to one's own security. Survival in the reorganization becomes an obsession. Transformational leadership is needed to deal with the merging of the acquired firm's culture with that of the firm taking over. It may contribute to creating a new culture in the acquired firm or a new one transcending both firms. The contingent and reward system for the future needs to be clearly communicated as well as a feedback on how it is working. Again, support, consideration, and commitment at each level of supervision in the acquired firm is essential to cope with subordinates' stress. Particularly important, if possible to do so, are for those with leadership responsibilities in the acquired firm to:

get information about the acquiring firm for their subordinates; identify counterparts in the other firm and make contact and help subordinates to understand that their counterparts in the acquiring firm are not the 'bad guys' and, in many cases, are in a situation similar to their own. (p. 135)

At all levels in the firm, transformational leadership can help subordinates and colleagues in ending the previous attachments to the scene before the takeover. It can help reduce the tensions of disengagement, that is the disidentification with the old situation and disenchantment with the new which may produce disorientation without anchors to the past or the future. Leaders can help colleagues and subordinates to work through their denials and anger towards acceptance of the new situation (Tichy and Devanna, 1985).

Transforming crises into challenges

Effective transformational leaders can halt crises by disclosing opportunities, arousing courage, and stimulating enthusiasm. The key here, according to Nystrom and Starbuck (1984), is the need for the leaders to be intellectually stimulating, fostering unlearning, and eliminating fixation on old ways of doing things. When the cyanide-lacing of Tylenol struck Johnson and Johnson in 1982, the public relations department had no crisis emergency plans. The CEO rejected any half-way steps to gloss over the disaster and actually converted the marketing disaster into an opportunity to gain credit for good citizenship, regain the firm's market share by introducing a more tamper-proof Tylenol at a time of great public consciousness and publicity about the problem (Snyder, 1983).

Pines (1980) summarized the ways that leaders can provide support to make subordinates 'hardier', and maintain quality performance and decision-making despite the presence of stressful conditions. Dramatic changes can be presented as challenges, not as disturbances. Stress can become challenging if the subordinates who are selected by leaders in stressful conditions prefer a vigorous, fast-paced lifestyle, and have the knowledge, intelligence, and preparation to cope adequately with the stress. Subordinates' sense of fate control can be enhanced rather than their powerlessness. Subordinates' involvement and commitment can offset focussing on the deleterious effects of the stress. Rather than paying attention to the dangerous exposure seen looking down a vertical cliff face, focus is directed on the holds and grips available immediately in front of the exposed climber.

McCauley (1987) pointed to a number of transformational and transactional ways leaders can enhance performance by converting a potentially stressful situation into a challenging one. The leader needs to ensure that there will be positive outcomes and subordinates know what these are. Although they may be difficult, goals can be set which are clear and attainable. Interim rewards for progress can be given. More generally, taxing conditions can be converted into problems to be solved. Self-confidence can be increased along with greater tolerance for ambiguity, uncertainty, and working with new and unfamiliar conditions. Situations beyond one's control can be faced with the recognition that one may be unable to change an undesired state of affairs. The situation may need to be redefined, goals may need to be changed, and patience may be needed (seemingly insurmountable problems sometimes disappear when ignored).

Aside from their better effects on subordinates, leaders who view situations as challenges rather than crises, tend to be more open to ideas and suggestions from their subordinates which enables them to reach more effective decisions. This was shown by Tjosvold (1984) who conducted an experiment in which the focal 'managers' led confederates of the experimenter in dealing with an issue of job rotation which was either a crisis condition, a challenging condition, or of minor consequence. The 'managers' who thought they were in a crisis situation were most close-minded. They most felt in disagreement with their subordinates. At the same time, they were the least interested in hearing more from their subordinates and demonstrated less knowledge of their subordinates' arguments. They were least likely to change from their original position. On the contrary, those managers who thought they were in a challenging situation were most likely to explore and incorporate subordinates' views into their own. They most indicated the desire to hear more arguments. They tended to integrate their subordinates' opposing opinions into their own decisions.

Enhancing identification and social support

Felt stress is likely to be reduced if the individual can be made to feel part of a larger entity. The insecurity of feeling isolated is replaced by the security of a sense of belonging. Transforming leaders can create a sense of identity with a social network of support. Pines (1980) cited research which demonstrated that people with such social support as close friends, relatives, and group associations have lower mortality rates than those without them. During prolonged bombardments, the social support of children in kibbutzim made them less anxious than Israeli urban children. The loss of such social ties, ostracism, and isolation can be deadly among primitive peoples. Ganster, Fusilier, and Mayes (1986) reported for 326 employees of a large contracting firm that social support from their supervisors, co-workers, family, and friends, moderately buffered the experience of strain. The strains included somatic complaints, depression, role ambiguity, role conflict, and frustrating underutilization of skills. Again, Nelson (1978) surveyed the experiences of thirty child care workers dealing with child care crises. The crises were dealt with most effectively with leader supportiveness, respect, calmness, and confidence, clarification of the situation, and preparation for future crises. They were dealt with ineffectively by authoritarian attitudes and behaviour, lack of support, loss of control, and poor communicating.

Followers may be under their own intrapsychic tensions, feeling personally inadequate because of the gap between their self-perceived images of what they are and what they ideally should and would like to be. Stress

COMBAT STRESS AND TREATMENT

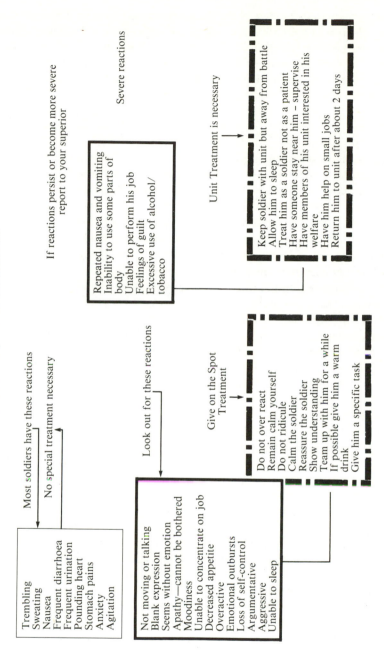

Figure 8.1   Stress in battle: a guide for NCOs and junior commanders. *Source:* The Army Personnel Research Establishment, UK.

will be increased if they feel they cannot reduce the gap. The frustration may result in aggression and feelings of dependency. To help followers cope with their frustration, self-aggrandizing leaders make themselves the object of identification for the followers (Downton, 1973) but socially directed leaders show their individualized consideration by providing opportunities for their followers to develop themselves (Levinson, 1980).

SUMMARY AND CONCLUSIONS

Stress situations can be categorized in a variety of ways, and emergent and effective leadership decision behaviour will vary accordingly. Groups may be frustrated by unattainable goals. They may be in fear of impending dangers. They may be anxious because of unclear and ambiguous demands. They may be in conflict over competing demands or with other groups. Groups may be in a state of inertia perceived as less risky and costly than actively responding to warnings of danger. They may be aroused to respond impulsively, defensively, or in panic. Threats to survival may be internal or external, substantive or interpersonal.

It is not the speed of decision nor the directiveness of leadership that is sought or commonly found during crises that is maladaptive, rather its inadequacy is due to its hastiness and lack of preparation and commitment to it. Such hasty directive leadership will be acceptable when followers must endure prolonged stress. In the same way, real or imagined threat will result in acceptance of leaders who encourage defensive avoidance. Again, panic will heighten the tendency for decisions that will be maladaptive.

The emergent leader will do what is immediately required to provide the group with ways of coping with the stress. Rapid direction, initiation of structure, and task-oriented leadership will make the leader more likely to succeed in these special circumstances and groups will be more susceptible to such influence.

Both demagogues and statesmen can exhibit such success as leaders in times of crisis. Transactional and transformational leadership can both be successful. The transactional demagogue can assure inactive followers that the warnings are unimportant and persuade impulsive followers that simple solutions are acceptable. He can convince defensive followers by bolstering and shifting responsibility and he can sway panicking followers with other worldly solutions. The demagogue can successfully lead the popular, easier search for internal subversion when complex external problems are paramount. The effective leader (who, of course, must also successfully influence followers) is a transforming statesman who addresses the inert followers by shaking them out of their torpor in the face of impending dangers or by rousing them to work towards what, at first, seemed to be unobtainable goals. The transforming statesman shows followers the inadequacies of simple solutions and defensive avoidance. Superordinate goals are provided for the hypervigilant, and motivation and initiation of structure are provided for adequate search, appraisal of alternatives, and contingency plans.

The survival of a group is dependent upon a type of leadership able to keep members and subgroups working together towards a common purpose, maintaining productivity at a level sufficient to sustain the group or to justify its existence, and satisfying member expectations regarding leader and group. Competent leadership is especially needed in times of crisis to unite the efforts of members and strengthen group cohesiveness around a common purpose. A group that desires to survive will prevent leaders of contending factions from destroying the legitimacy of the group.

Different types of stress call for different leadership behaviour. A measure of task-oriented structuring may be required in many stressful circumstances; the creation of supportive groups will be important for effectiveness in others. Ordinarily, both are important.

NOTE

This chapter is adapted from B. M. Bass, *Bass and Stogdill's Handbook of Leadership* (New York: Free Press, 1990) all rights reserved.

REFERENCES

Alwon, G. J. (1980), 'Response to agencywide crisis: a model for administrative action', *Child Welfare*, **59**, 335–46.

Bass, B. M. (1985), *Leadership and Performance Beyond Expectations* (New York: Free Press).

Bass, B. M. and Avolio, B. J. (1990), *The Multifactor Leadership Questionnaire* (Palto Alto, CA: Consulting Psychologists Press).

Bass, B. M., Hurder, W. P., and Ellis, N. (1954), *Human Stress Tolerance*, Final Technical Report, Baton Rouge, LA: Louisiana State University, USAF Aero-Medical Lab.

Berkowitz, L. (1953), 'Sharing leadership in small, decision-making groups', *Journal of Abnormal and Social Psychology*, **48**, 231–8.

Bradley, R. T. (1987), 'Charisma and social structure: A study of love and power', *Wholeness and Transformation* (New York: Paragon House).

Downton, J. V. (1973), *Rebel Leadership: Commitment and Charisma in the Revolutionary Process* (New York: Free Press).

Fisher, S. and Rubinstein, I. (1956), 'The effects of moderate sleep deprivation on social influence in the autocratic situation', *American Psychologist*, **11**, 411.

Flanagan, J. C., Levy, S., et al. (1952), *Development of an Objective Form of the Leaders Reaction Test* (Pittsburgh, PA: American Institute for Research).

Fodor, E. M. (1973), 'Group stress, ingratiation, and the use of power', *Journal of Social Psychology*, 91, 345–6.

Fodor, E. M. (1976), 'Group stress, authoritarian style of control, and use of power', *Journal of Applied Psychology*, 61, 313–18.

Gal, R. (1985), 'Combat stress as an opportunity; The case of heroism', Paper, Northeast Regional Conference of the Inter-University Seminar on Armed Forces and Society, Albany, NY.

Gal, R. and Jones, F. D. (1985), 'Psychological aspects of combat stress: A model derived from Israeli and other combat experiences', unpublished manuscript.

Ganster, D. C., Fusilier, M. R., and Mayes, B. T. (1986), 'Role of social support in the experience of stress at work', *Journal of Applied Psychology*, 71, 102–10.

Graham, F. C. (1982), 'Job stress in Mississippi cooperative extension service county personnel as related to age, gender, district, tenure, position and perceived leadership behaviour of immediate supervisors', *Dissertation Abstract International*, 43 (7A), 2180.

Hall, D. J. and Mansfield, R. (1971), 'Organizational and individual response to external stress', *Administrative Science Quarterly*, 16, 533–47.

Hamblin, R. L. (1958a), 'Group integration during a crisis', *Human Relations*, 11, 67–76.

(1958b), 'Leadership and crisis', *Sociometry*, 21, 322–35.

Hammerschlag, C. A. and Astrachan, B. M. (1971), 'The Kennedy airport snow-in: an inquiry into intergroup phenomena', *Psychosomatics*, 34, 301–8.

Harman, D. (1984), 'Lessons learned about emergency preparedness', *Public Management*, 66(3), 5–8.

Hemphill, J. K. (1950), 'Relations between the size of the group and the behaviour of "superior" leaders', *Journal of Social Psychology*, 32, 11–22.

Hermann, C. P. (1963), 'Some consequences of crisis which limit the viability of organizations', *Administrative Science Quarterly*, 8, 61–82.

Hertzler, J. O. (1940), 'Crises and dictatorships', *American Sociological Review*, 5, 157–69.

Herzberg, F. I. (1966), *Working and the Nature of Man* (New York: Crowell).

House, R. J. and Rizzo, J. R. (1972), 'Role conflict and role ambiguity as critical variables in a model of organizational behaviour', *Organizational Behaviour and Human Performance*, 7, 467–505.

Janis, I. L. and Mann, L. (1977), *Decision Making: A Psychological Analysis of Conflict, Choice, and Commitment* (New York: Free Press).

Kalay, E. (1983), 'The commander in stress situations in IDF combat units during the 'Peace for Galilee' campaign', Paper, Third International Conference on Psychological Stress and Adjustment in Time of War and Peace, Tel Aviv, Israel.

Kartez, J. D. (1984), 'Crisis response planning', *Journal of the American Planning Association*, 50(1), 9–21.

Katz, D. (1951), 'Survey research center: An overview of the human relations programme', in H. Guetzkow (ed.), *Groups, Leadership and Men* (Pittsburgh, PA: Carnegie Press).

Katz, R. (1988), 'The influence of group conflict on leadership effectiveness', *Organizational Behavior and Human Performance*, 20, 265–86.

Katz, R., Phillips, E., and Cheston, R. (1976), 'Methods of conflict resolution – a re-examination', unpublished manuscript, Massachusetts Institute of Technology, Boston, MA.

Klein, A. L. (1976), 'Changes in leadership appraisal as a function of the stress of a simulated panic situation', *Journal of Personality and Social Psychology*, 34, 1143–54.

Korten, D. C. (1962), 'Situational determinants of leadership structure', *Journal of Conflict Resolution*, 6, 222–35.

Kugihara, N. and Misumi, J. (1984), 'An experimental study of the effect of leadership types on followers' escaping behavior in a fearful emergency maze-situation', *Japanese Journal of Psychology*, 55, 214–20.

Lanzetta, J. T. (1953), *An Investigation of Group Behavior under Stress* (Task Order V) (Rochester, NY: University of Rochester).

Leighton, A. H. (1945), *The Governing of Men: General Principles and Recommendations Based on Experiences at a Japanese Relocation Camp* (Princeton, NJ: Princeton University Press).

Levinson, H. (1980), 'Power, leadership, and the management of stress', *Professional Psychology*, 11, 497–508.

Lowin, A. (1968), 'Participative decision making: a model literature, critique, and prescription for research', *Organizational Behavior and Human Performance*, 3, 68–106.

McCauley, C. D. (1987), 'Stress and the eye of the beholder', *Issues and Observations*, 7(3), 1–16.

Mileti, D. S., Drabek, R. E., and Haas, J. E. (1975), *Human Systems in Extreme Environments: A Sociological Perspective*, Institute of Behavioral Science, University of Colorado, Boulder.

Misumi, J. (1985), *The Behavioral Science of Leadership. An Interdisciplinary Japanese Research Program* (Ann Arbor, MI: University of Michigan Press).

Misumi, J. and Sako, H. (1982), 'An experimental study of the effect of leadership behaviors on followers' behavior of following after the leader in a simulated emergency situation', *Japanese Journal of Experimental Social Psychology*, 21(1), 49–59 (cited in J. Misumi, 1985).

Mitroff, I. A., Shrivastava, P., and Udwadia, F. E. (1987), 'Effective crisis management', *Academy of Management Executive*, 1, 283–92.

Mulder, M., van Eck, R., and deJong, R. D. (1971), 'An organization in crisis and non-crisis situations', *Human Relations*, 24, 19–41.

Mulder, M., deJong, R. D., Koppelaar, L., and Verhage, J. (1986), 'Power, situation, and leader's effectiveness: an organizational field study', *Journal of Applied Psychology*, 71, 566–70.

Nelson, J. E. (1978), 'Child care crises and the role of the supervisor', *Child Care Quarterly*, 7, 318–26.

Numerof, R. E., Cramer, K. D., and Shachar-Hendin, S. A. (1984), 'Stress in health administrators: sources, symptoms, and coping strategies', *Nursing Economics*, 2, 270–9.

Numerof, R. E. and Gillespie, D. F. (1984), 'Predicting burnout among health service providers', Paper, Academy of Management, Boston.

Nystrom, P. C. and Starbuck, W. H. (1984), 'To avoid organizational crises, unlearn', *Organizational Dynamics*, 12(4), 53–65.

Pines, M. (1980), 'Psychological hardiness', *Psychology Today*, 14(2), 38–9.

Ross, R. B. (1982), 'Emergency planning paid off', *Security Management*, 26(9), 62–5.

Sample, J. A. and Wilson, T. R. (1965), 'Leader behavior, group productivity, and rating of least preferred co-worker', *Journal of Personality and Social Psychology*, 1, 266–70.

Sanders, G. S. and Malkis, F. S. (1982), 'Type A behavior, need for control, and reactions to group participation', *Organizational Behavior and Human Performance*, 30, 71–86.

Sato, S., Kugihara, N., Misumi, J., and Shigeoka, K. (1984), 'Experimental study of escape behavior in a simulated panic situation: III. Effect of the PM leadership conditions', *Japanese Journal of Experimental Social Psychology*, 24, 83–91.

Schweiger, D. M., Ivancevich, J. M., and Power, F. R. (1987), 'Executive actions for managing human resources before and after acquisition', *Academy of Management Executive*, 1(2), 127–38.

Selekman, B. M. (1947), *Labor Relations and Human Relations* (New York: McGraw-Hill).

Seltzer, J. and Bass, B. M. (1990), 'Leadership is more than initiation and consideration', *Journal of Management*, 16, 693–703.

Seltzer, J., Numerof, R. E., and Bass, B. M. (1989), 'Transformational leadership: Is it a source of more or less burnout or stress?', Paper, Academy of Management, New Orleans, LA. Also *Journal of Health and Human Resources Administration*, 12, 174–85.

Simon, H. A. (1987), 'Making management decisions: the role of intuition and emotion', *Academy of Management Executive*, 1, 57–64.

Snyder, L. (1983), 'An anniversary review and critique: the Tylenol crisis', *Public Relations Review*, 9(3), 24–34.

Sorokin, P. A. (1943), *Man and Society in Calamity* (New York: Dutton).

Stouffer, S. A., Suchman, E. A., DeVinney, L. C., Star, S. A., and Williams, R. M., Jr (1949), *The American soldier: Adjustment during army life* (Princeton, NJ: Princeton University Press).

Streib, G. F., Folts, W. E., and LaGreca, A. J. (1985), 'Autonomy, power, and decision-making in thirty-six retirement communities', *Gerontologist*, 25, 403–9.

Tichy, N. and Devanna, M. (1985), *Transformational Leadership* (New York: Wiley).

Tjosvold, D. (1984), 'Effects of crises orientation on managers' approach to controversy in decision making', *Academy of Management Journal*, 27, 130–8.

Torrance, E. P. (1956/1957), 'Group decision-making and disagreement', *Social Forces*, 35, 314–18.

Waldman, D. A., Bass, B. M., and Yammarino, F. J. (1988), 'Adding to leader-follower transactional: The augmenting effect of charismatic leadership' (ONR Tech. Rep. No. 3), Binghamton, State University of New York Center for Leadership Studies.

Watson, B. M., Jr (1984), 'Lawrence, Kansas–before and after "The Day After"', *Public Management*, 66(3), 13–15.

Weinberg, S. B. (1978), 'A predictive model of group panic behavior', *Journal of Applied Communication Research*, 6(1), 1–9.

Willner, A. R. (1968), 'Charismatic political leadership: a theory', Center for International Studies, Princeton University, Princeton, NJ.

Yarmolinsky, A. (1987), 'Leadership in crisis situations', Paper, First Annual Conference on Leadership, Wingfoot, Racine, WI.

9

JOB STRESSORS AND THEIR IMPACT ON
DECISION-MAKING AND LEADERSHIP IN
ORGANIZATIONS

CARY L. COOPER AND MIKE SMITH

ABSTRACT

The relationship between decision-making and stress is clearly a complex one involving many variables and it can be viewed from two perspectives: the implications on stress of decision-making and the implications on decision-making caused by stress. In this chapter we will focus largely on the first perspective by trying to place the activity of making decisions in its context as a cause of stress. But, at the end of this chapter, we will adopt a wider perspective, looking at Kelly's Construct Theory as a model for decision-making and speculating on the impact stress may have on a person's construct system.

Probably the most widely quoted paper on decision-making and leadership as a cause of stress is Karasek's (1979) paper. It is unusual because the data are based on large samples (N's = 911 and 1,896) which were not convenience samples, but carefully constructed representative samples of American and Swedish economically active males. Karasek also developed a model of strain which had two major dimensions: the *demands of the job*, such as the need to work fast, conflict of demands, work overload; and the *decision latitude*, such as freedom to make a lot of decisions, having a say over what happens, and freedom on how to work. In essence, Karasek suggests that stress or strain arises when there is a divergence between the demands and the decision latitude. As figure 9.1 shows, where there are few job demands and few opportunities for decision, or where there are high job demands and high opportunities for decision, there may be higher or lower levels of activity, but there is relatively little strain. On the other hand, where the job makes high demands and there are few possibilities for decision there will be a large reservoir of unresolved strain. Of particular importance to this chapter are the implications for leadership – especially the distinction between formal leaders and informal leaders. Often, an informal leader is subject to high interpersonal demands, yet the direct access to the levers of power is

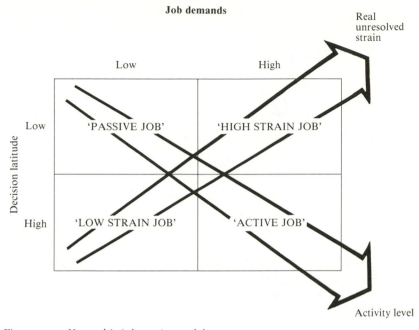

Figure 9.1   Karasek's job strain model

limited and, in that sense, he or she will have less opportunity to make decisions.

Karasek tested this model by extracting data from two large national surveys: one in Sweden and the other in the USA. He derived indices of job demands, decision latitude, and a number of indices of strain, such as job dissatisfaction, life dissatisfaction, consumption of pills, and days off work. The results of his regression analysis are given in figure 9.2. In many ways the results are disappointing. The average of the four beta weights measuring the relationship between decision latitude and strain will be in the order of 0.1–0.2. The average beta weight for job demands is in the order of 0.0–0.05 and the average beta weight for the interaction is in the order of 0.07–0.1. (In strict statistical terms the beta weights should be transformed before performing these calculations but with very low beta weights this transformation makes no practical difference.) Although half of these relationships are statistically significant, this reflects the large sample size rather than the strength of the relationship. Indeed, from the data provided by Karasek, it is doubtful whether 4% of the variance of strain can be accounted for by decision latitude or job demands. Some of the missing variance may be accounted for in an interaction between decision-making and leadership style. Vroom and Yetton (1973) make the

	Strain Indicator			
	USA		SWEDEN	
	Job dissatisfaction	Life dissatisfaction	Pill consumption	Sick days
Decision latitude	− 0.22*	− 0.13*	− 0.01*	− 0.09*
Job demands	0.00	− 0.03	0.07*	− 0.02
Interaction	0.12*	0.11*	0.06	0.02

* statistically significant at 0.01 level or beyond

Figure 9.2   Karasek's results (beta weights)

distinction between *decision quality* – which refers to those aspects of decision which have a direct impact on performance, and *decision acceptance* which is concerned with high commitment from subordinates. Many studies researching the link between decision-making and stress have focussed upon decision quality, and ignored other aspects such as leadership style and decision acceptance.

The question then arises, what accounts for the remaining 96% of the variance? Clearly, the relationship between decision-making and stress is not direct but is probably a melange of several factors.

SOURCES OF MANAGERIAL STRESS

Research has identified at least six major sources of managerial stress that can affect the decision-making process and leadership behaviour (Cooper and Marshall, 1978; Schuler, 1982; Cooper, 1982). These sources of stress are probably applicable to the labour force as a whole. Briefly they include:

Stress from work overload and underload, including factors such as repetitive work, time pressures, and work overload.
Role based stress, such as role ambiguity, role conflict, and responsibility for others.
Relationships with subordinates, colleagues, and superiors.
Career development factors, such as fear of redundancy, obsolescence, and under/over promotion.
Organizational structure and climate, including such factors as office politics, communication, participation, and organizational trust.
Extra organizational sources of stress, which refers to the relationship between work demands and family/social demands, and stressful life events.

These categories of stressors are often blurred. However, they do represent a convenient structure in which to examine sources of decision-making stress. The following section provides a more detailed picture of these issues in terms of past and current research.

STRESS FROM WORK OVERLOAD AND UNDERLOAD

An important source of stress for leaders and decision-making is work overload (Cooper and Melhuish, 1980). French and Caplan (1973) view work overload as being either quantitative (i.e., too much to do) or qualitative (i.e., work that is too difficult). In theoretical terms, overload corresponds to a condition of excess demand. These authors found that managers with more phone calls, office visits, and meetings per unit of work time, smoked significantly more cigarettes. Russel and Zohman (1958) also found a strong association between overload and coronary heart disease. Margolis *et al.* (1974) in a large-scale study, found overload to be associated with low work motivation, lowered self esteem, escapist drinking, and poor decision-making.

More recent studies confirm these relationships (Cooper, Cooper, and Eaker, 1988). Cooper and Roden (1985) examined a representative group of British tax inspectors. They found that qualitative and quantitative overload predicted high levels of anxiety and depression. Indeed, French *et al.* (1982) indicated that qualitative and quantitative overload have been associated with at least nine psychological and physiological responses: job dissatisfaction, job tension, lower self-esteem, threat, embarrassment, high cholesterol levels, increased heart rate, skin resistance, and increased smoking. These responses led to poorer analytical and decision-making processes, which undermined the managerial and leadership role.

The condition of work underload has also been linked to ill-health and poor decision-making (Cox, 1981). Despite limited research, the concept has usually been associated with boring repetitive 'blue-collar' environments. However, research suggests that underload can be a major problem for managerial groups. Davidson and Cooper (1983) identify women managers as a major group 'at risk' from work underload. These authors suggest that due to under-promotion women are more likely to be clustered at the lower levels of most organizations. In an empirical study (Davidson and Cooper, 1983), they found that women were considerably more qualified than their male counterparts of similar management level. Thus, women may represent a large group of underutilized managers.

ROLE BASED STRESS

A great deal of research has concentrated on the managerial role as a source of stress. This has assumed that certain requirements and assumptions of the role can lead to the experience of stress and poorer decision-making. Before examining the empirical evidence, it is worth considering the notion of role from a managerial perspective.

Gowler and Legge (1975) point out that any social position or role, carries specific rights and duties. Also, that these rights and duties may influence the individuals behaviour, values, and feelings. Indeed, the manager is often faced with a range of different role relationships or role sets. These authors suggest that this range of role sets will have their own unique requirements and expectations. Stress will occur when the requirements of one specific role set are inhibited or prevented. This could be due to the complexity of the role itself, or through conflict with the requirements of a different role set. Gowler and Legge (1975) suggest three such possible situations:

Conflict between different role sets.   This may occur when the demands of one role set (e.g. the work environment) prohibit specific required action in another role set (e.g., the home environment). In this situation, the duties of at least one social role will be neglected.

Conflict may occur within a role set.   An individual may be faced with a range of mutually exclusive (or at least conflicting) demands within his role as a manager. For example, he/she may feel a duty to ensure job security for his/her subordinates. At the same time he/she may also have to consider the organization's need for rationalization. This is just one example from an infinite number of situations that can result in role conflict.

Lack of clarity regarding role requirements.   A manager who experiences a lack of clarity about what is expected may be unable to accomplish his/her role requirements. This role ambiguity is not only a source of stress in itself, but also prohibits any clear path to good performance and perceived success.

These situations are likely to become stressful when the individual manager feels unable to cope with the specific role demands. This might lead to either an actual or perceived decline in job satisfaction, and a subsequent decrement in decision-making skills and ultimately in performance. Numerous studies have examined the work and health effects of role ambiguity and conflict. Again, it is worth noting the impact of role ambiguity on leadership. By definition the role of a formal leader is defined and with this definition there will be an at least implied definition of the limits to this authority. In the case of informal leaders, the situation is likely to be less structured and consequently carry greater levels of ambiguity. In the earlier discussion of Karasek's study, it was noted that informal leaders are also likely to be subject to greater role strain because they may also have less opportunity to make important decisions. We now briefly examine the empirical evidence.

Role ambiguity

Kahn *et al.* (1964) found that role ambiguity was associated with lower job satisfaction, job related tension, and less effective decision-making. French and Caplan (1970) conducted a study with engineers, scientists, and administrators. They found that role ambiguity was associated with low job satisfaction and feelings of job related threat to individual well-being. Margolis *et al.* (1974) investigated a representative national US sample of 1,496 employed persons, 16 years of age or older. They found significant relationships between symptoms of physical and mental ill-health and role ambiguity, and ultimately negative decision-making and performance.

Role conflict

Kahn *et al.* (1964) found that men suffering role conflict had lower job satisfaction, higher job related tension, and performed less efficiently. They also found that the greater the status of the individuals 'sending' the conflicting messages, the stronger the relationship between role conflict and job dissatisfaction. Several studies have also related role conflict to physical health outcomes (e.g. French and Caplan, 1970). Shirom *et al.* (1973) collected data on 762 Kibbutz members from a broad range of occupational groups. For the white-collar workers only, they found a relationship between role conflict and coronary heart disease (CHD). Cooper and Marshall (1978) suggest that it is managerial and professional occupations that are more likely to suffer negative effects from such role based stressors.

More recent studies have confirmed these relationships (e.g., Vrenden-burgh and Trinkaus, 1983; Keenan and Newton, 1984; Martin, 1984; Mackay and Cooper, 1987). Kemery *et al.* (1985) applied sophisticated path analysis to data from a sample of accountants. The analysis showed role ambiguity and conflict to have a direct influence on job related tension, job dissatisfaction, poorer decision-making, and propensity to leave an organization.

The approach of person-environment fit

One way researchers have approached role-based stress is through person-environment fit theory. This approach operationalizes stress by calculating the discrepancy between what an individual perceives and desires from various aspects of the work environment. Stress or 'misfit' is defined by either demand exceeding a person's capability or desired level (i.e., the excess demand view of stress) and capability exceeding the demand (i.e., the excess resource view of stress). This latter situation of misfit refers to when the work environment fails to supply the needs of the individual. Qualitative underload would clearly fall into this category.

The Michigan research team (French *et al.*, 1982) used this approach in a large-scale study involving over 2,000 people from twenty-three different occupations. The researchers found relatively strong correlations between several measures of 'work role fit' and various job affect variables (including, job dissatisfaction, workload dissatisfaction, decision-making, and boredom). The results relating to mental and physical health showed low or zero significance.

A further point to consider is that the emphasis on role-based stress and work over/underload may well be inappropriate today. When Kahn *et al.* (1964) originally proposed the concepts of role ambiguity and conflict, industrial society was enjoying economic growth. More recently western societies are emerging from economic recession and it is therefore more likely that a manager's major concerns will stem from the threat of redundancy or obsolescence due to changing technology. Highly competitive markets may also have their impact. Thus fear of mistakes, relationship with the organization and its members, performance of superiors, or even competition within organizations for individual survival, may be 'high pressure' points.

RELATIONSHIPS AT WORK

Relationships with superiors, colleagues, and subordinates have been suggested to be a potential source of managerial stress leading to less effective decision-making, poorer performance, and inadequate leadership (Cooper, 1982). Mintzberg (cited by Cooper and Marshall, 1978) conducted an intensive study with a small sample of chief executives. In a large organization, Mintzberg found that only 22 per cent of time was spent in desk work. The remaining time was spent in scheduled meetings (59 per cent), unscheduled meetings (10 per cent), telephone calls (6 per cent), and other activities (3 per cent). Even in smaller organizations, Mintzberg found that managers spent up to 40 per cent of their time in face to face contacts.

Despite the obvious importance of interpersonal relations, relatively few studies have provided any substantive results (Cooper, 1983). French and Caplan (1970), however, did find that poor relationships at work were positively associated with role ambiguity. These authors suggested that this led to inadequate communications between people, low job satisfaction, job related threat, less effective decision-making, and lowered performance.

Relationships are also important in establishing strong social support (social support is discussed in more detail below). For managers, one would expect support from colleagues and subordinates to be integral for good decision-making and performance (Mackay and Cooper, 1987). Indeed, Payne (1980) makes the point that heterogeneous groups such as 'sales and marketing' are characterized by high rates of social exchange or mutual support. Thus, members of such groups will rely heavily on continuous support in the normal routine of work.

Surprisingly, research into this important aspect of managerial life (i.e., relationships) is relatively scarce. Future studies need to examine the temporal causal networks between work relationships, role ambiguity/conflict, and decision-making/performance.

ORGANIZATIONAL STRUCTURE AND CLIMATE

A major source of managerial stress can arise from the organization itself. These factors include, lack of participation in decision-making, low organizational trust, office politics, poor communications, or even restrictions on behaviour. The main thrust of research in this field has tended to concentrate on lack of participation and stress related outcomes.

In the French and Caplan (1970) study mentioned earlier, it was found that greater participation was related to higher job satisfaction, low job related threat, and higher self-esteem. Buck (1972) found that managers and workers most under pressure tended to have more autocratic leadership. Margolis *et al.* (1974) national US sample found that non-participation was a significant predictor of several negative health indices. These included, poor physical health, escapist drinking, low job satisfaction, low motivation, propensity to leave the organization, and absenteeism. Wall and Clegg (1981) provide evidence from longitudinal data that, when substantive increases in group autonomy and work identity were achieved, they were followed by increased work motivation, performance, job satisfaction, and mental health. The authors discounted a Hawthorne effect because the changes were maintained over a period of at least eighteen months. Also, while performance and motivation increases occurred quickly, the job satisfaction and mental health improvements took several months to appear. This study strongly suggests a causal effect of 'increased participation' on the level of psychological strain.

A study of senior managers by Cooper and Melhuish (1980) factor analysed a broad range of stressors. They found that the 'relationship with the organization', 'job insecurity', and 'poor organizational climate' were all factors predictive of lower mental health and physical health among executives. This study showed that 'poor organizational climate' was no longer the preserve of blue-collar workers. A study from the career development field by Alban-Metcalfe and Nicholson (1984) found similar results. Amongst a sample of British managers, 'challenge', 'creative work', and 'good quality management' were valued as highly important.

A further point to consider is that movement towards greater worker participation (within society as a whole) can in itself become a source of stress. Gowler and Legge (1975) pointed to four main factors which can make participation a source of stress for managers:

1 mis-match of formal and actual power,
2 the manager may resent the erosion of his formal role,
3 increased role conflict due to the need to be both participative and achieve high production,
4 subordinates may refuse to participate.

CAREER DEVELOPMENT

The idea of career progression is often of overriding importance to the individual manager. However, the managerial career has several dimensions and consequent sources of stress. Cooper and Marshall (1978) identified two main clusters of potential career stressors:

1 Lack of job security, fear of redundancy and obsolescence due to changing technology.
2 Status incongruity. This refers to under/over promotion or frustration at having reached one's career ceiling.

Numerous studies have shown these factors to have deleterious health consequences (Cooper, 1983). Studies have also suggested the dysfunctional effects on decision-making and organizational performance (Hall, 1976).

Recent studies also point to the importance of the 'career' in terms of stress outcomes. Martin (1984) found with hospital workers that 'inability to leave' was related to acute and chronic mental health problems. Keenan and Newton (1984) found that 'frustration in organizations' was frequently reported by young graduate engineers in industry. These authors reported frustration as related to a variety of stress outcome variables such as job dissatisfaction and work related anxiety. Despite these studies, the significance of the career as a life-long developmental process has been neglected. Sources of stress will be contingent on this process.

Indeed, career development research has identified at least three distinctive career stages (Hall, 1976) that are relevant to the experience of stress: (1) establishment, (2) advancement, and (3) maintenance. The *establishment* stage refers to the early years of the career. Hall and Nougain (1964) found, in a study of young managers, that in the first year of employment there were strong needs for 'safety', 'gaining recognition', and 'establishing oneself' in the organization. By the end of the fifth year, however, the need for safety had declined significantly.

The next stage they found was one of *advancement*. The individual is less concerned with 'fitting in' than with moving up and mastering the organization. Once established, however, there follows a levelling off period, eventually reaching a managerial plateau. In short, the manager reaches a point of *maintenance*, often adopting a guidance role for new organizational entrants (Hall, 1976).

While perhaps of more relevance to managerial and professional workers, the central point is that different career stages may emphasize different stressors. In the early years, 'relationships', particularly with superiors, may be of paramount concern. This will relate to both feelings of security and also provision of information about the company and the employee's own performance. The individual experiences 'reality shock', moving through a socialization process by learning and acquiring the values and orientations of the organization (Van Maanen and Schein, 1979). Indeed, role ambiguity could also be a major stressor during this phase. Hall and Nougain (1964) found early experiences to affect a manager's future attitudes, expectations, and performance.

During the stage of *advancement*, 'promotion' and 'personal future plans' may begin to dominate. Also, since individuals may have gained higher status, the need for support from colleagues and subordinates may be vital for good performance. Thus, stable positive relationships with these 'support agencies' may be crucial.

Another potential stress source at this stage is from the work:family interface. Preoccupation with the job during advancement years is likely to have disruptive effects on family life during important developmental years (Cooper, 1982).

At the stage of *maintenance*, different factors may become sources of stress. Career frustrations, fears of obsolescence, or even negative organizational attitudes could dominate his/her concerns. A study of police inspectors (a rank equivalent to a first line manager) by Glowinkowski and Nicholson (1984) found the middle-aged group to hold considerable negative attitudes towards the organization (i.e., the constabulary), in terms of their own careers. They also revealed a series of superstitious beliefs and feelings of uncertainty, regarding the workings of the promotion system itself. These authors emphasized the importance of the culture of the organization, which encouraged the idea of promotion as a reward system, and yet provided no feedback or guidance regarding promotion chances.

EXTRA-ORGANIZATIONAL SOURCES OF STRESS

Extra-organizational sources of stress refer to the myriad of interfaces between work and family life that put pressure on the manager. These include family problems, financial difficulties, the disruptive effects of managerial relocation, and so on (Cooper, 1982). However, the major areas of interest have centred around the work:family relationship.

The work:family relationship

The relationship between work and family is usually viewed in terms of the family as 'the social support team'. Gowler and Legge (1975), for example, have stressed the importance of the managerial wife, coining the term 'hidden contract'. Handy (1975) endorses this view, suggesting the necessity of the family bond to career success. However, this relationship is infinitely more complex and has not been effectively integrated within the stress:strain paradigm.

From largely outside the stress literature, three general hypotheses to explain the work:family relationship have been proposed: (1) *spillover*, where the events of one environment affect the other; (2) *compensation*, where the individual attempts to compensate in one environment for what is lacking in the other, and (3) where both environments are said to be *independent.*

Kabanoff (1980) in an empirical review suggested that evidence supports all three hypotheses. However, in a managerial study, Evans and Bartolomé (1980) found the largest proportion of their sample described their own circumstances as one of unidirectional spillover from the work to the home environment. More recently, these authors found several moderating relationships (Evans and Bartolomé, 1984). Spillover into family life occurred mainly from negative work feelings. Also, when work was important to an individual, conflict between the two environments was more likely than when work was less important. The latter tended to result in an 'independent attitude'. They also suggested a mediating role; when work is not important, there will be less spillover of negative work outcomes.

Implications of research for managers

Different job and organizational stressors require different solutions, and only when companies are willing to accept their responsibility and contemplate carrying out specific organizational 'stress audits' will we begin to deal effectively with managerial stress. In the meantime, there are several direct implications of much of this research for organizations. First, the health and well-being of employees depends on managers who are flexible and participative. Training must begin to take place to engender a 'real' rather than 'espoused' participative style of management at work. Second, more effort should be taken to ensure that the 'right manager' is fitted to the 'right job'. Managerial selection should be more comprehensive, with thorough assessment centres, psychometrics, and family circumstance taken into account. And, finally, 'stress' within organizations must cease to be a 'four letter word'. We must help executives in trouble rather than encourage the corporate Rambo or Business Amazon mentality. Stress counselling for executives (and others for that matter) should be a high priority, if the health, decision-making skills, and performance of managers is to be encouraged and developed.

There are also implications for decision-making research in the context of leadership. Most of the existing work has used one type of leadership or allowed the style of leadership to vary uncontrolled. Yet, these differences may act as important moderators of the relationship between stress and decision-making. At the very least we ought to measure, if not control, different types of leadership such as formal, informal, autocratic, participative, and, perhaps, whether the decision concerns an individual or a group.

PERSONAL CONSTRUCT THEORY, DECISION-MAKING, AND STRESS

The debate concerning decision-making and stress is relevant to theoretical developments in cognitive psychology – especially the theory of personal constructs set out by George Kelly (1955). In essence Kelly postulated that all men behave like scientists and as they go about their environment they construct a mental map of their world. When called upon to make decisions individuals refer to these 'maps' and there is considerable empirical evidence that these hypotheses are true. Thus cognitive maps are of direct relevance to the central topic of this paper. Kelly was able to relate these maps both to cognitive decisions and to basic emotions. For example, aggression is an attempt to force reality into a shape which fits the individual's mental map. Anxiety is the emotion produced when an individual realizes that the mental map is inadequate and needs reorganization. The question arises, how does stress alter a person's mental map and thus his or her decision-making? In the absence of empirical evidence, only speculative answers are possible.

The impact of stress is likely to vary with the level of stress. At moderate levels, an individual is likely to attempt to expand his or her construct system, either in terms of expanding the *area* of the domain which is covered, or in terms of *greater detail* or sophistication of the mapping of the present domain. The net result may be to produce a better 'mental map' which is a better reflection of reality and which forms a better basis for decisions about reality. At high levels, the impact of stress could produce a negative impact on decision-making because the individual may feel that their construct system is under threat and needs defending. This defence could take the form of a retrenchment to core constructs and monolithic construing. Core constructs are those very deeply held beliefs which are intimately linked with a person's self-image and their image of their world. Of necessity they are general and not particularly subtle. A retreat to this level of operation would involve a degradation of decision-making where just one or two crude considerations dominate the evaluation of a situation. The details of thought would be directed towards simplicity in which objects were clustered into just one or two monolithic groups and where there is little to differentiate between events, situations, and people. If the situation is truly crude and involves few parameters, decision-making, or at least the speed of decision-making, would be enhanced, but in many circumstances it would lead to suboptimal solutions which lack finesse.

Clearly these ideas need to be worked out and tested but this final section does serve to indicate two things: research into the relationship between stress and decision-making might well take heed of some of the developments in construct theory and, we should not restrict our search to simple linear relationships.

REFERENCES

Alban-Metcalfe, B. and Nicholson, N. (1984), *The Career Development of British Male and Female Managers* (London: British Institute of Management).
Bernard, J. (1968), 'The eudaemonists', in S. Z. Klausner (ed.), *Why Man Takes Chances* (Garden City, New York: Anchor Doubleday).
Buck, V. (1972), *Working Under Pressure* (London: Staples Press).
Caplan, R. D., Cobb, S., French, J. R. P. Jr, Van Harrison, R., and Pinneau, S. R. Jr (1975), *Job Demands and Worker Health*, National Institute of Safety and Health, US Department of Health (Washington DC: US Government Printing Office).

Cooper, C. L. (1982), *Executive Families Under Stress* (New Jersey: Prentice Hall).

(1983), *Stress Research: Issues for the 80s* (New York: Wiley).

Cooper, C. L., Cooper, R. D., and Eaker, L. (1988), *Living with Stress* (London: Penguin Books).

Cooper, C. L. and Marshall, J. (1978), 'Sources of managerial and white collar stress', in C. L. Cooper and R. Payne (eds.), *Stress at Work* (Chichester and New York: Wiley).

Cooper, C. L. and Melhuish, A. (1980), 'Occupational stress and the manager', *Journal of Occupational Medicine*, **22**, 588–92.

Cooper, C. L. and Roden, J. (1985), 'Mental health and satisfaction among tax officers', *Social Science and Medicine*, **21**, 747–51.

Cooper, C. L. and Smith, M. J. (1985), *Job Stress and Blue Collar Work* (New York: Wiley).

Crump, J. H., Cooper, C. L., and Smith, M. (1980), 'Investigating occupational stress: a methodological approach', *Journal of Occupational Behaviour*, **1**, 191–204.

Cox, T. (1981), *Stress* (London: Macmillan).

Davidson, M. J. and Cooper, C. L. (1983), *Stress and the Woman Manager* (Oxford: Martin Robertson).

Evans, P. and Bartolomé, F. (1980), 'The relationship between professional and private life', in C. B. Durr (ed.), *Work, Family and Career* (New York: Praeger), pp. 281–317.

(1984), 'The changing picture of the relationship between career and family', *Journal of Organizational Behavior*, **5**, 9–21.

French, J. R. P. and Caplan, R. D. (1970), 'Psychosocial factors in coronary heart disease', *Industrial Medicine*, **39**, 383–97.

(1973), 'Organisational stress and individual strain', in A. J. Marrow (ed.), *The Failure of Success* (New York: Amacom).

French, J. R. P., Caplan, R. D., and Van Harrison, R. (1982), *The Mechanisms of Job Stress and Strain* (Chichester and New York: Wiley).

Glowinkowski, S. P. and Cooper, C. L. (1985), 'Current issues in organizational stress research', *Bulletin of the British Psychological Society*, **38**, 212–16.

Glowinkowski, S. P. and Nicholson, N. (1984), 'The promotion pathology: a study of British police inspectors', Memo 659, MRC/ESRC SAPU, University of Sheffield.

Gowler, D. and Legge, K. (1975), 'Stress and external relationships: the "hidden" contract', in D. Gowler and K. Legge (eds.), *Managerial Stress* (Aldershot, Hants: Gower Publishing).

Hall, D. T. (1976), *Careers in Organisations* (New York: Goodyear).

Hall, D. T. and Nougain, K. (1964), 'An examination of Maslow's need hierarchy in an organisational setting', *Organisational Behaviour and Human Performance*, **3**, 12–35.

Handy, C. (1975), 'Difficulties in combining family and career', *The Times*, London, 22 September, p. 16.

Kabanoff, B. (1980), 'Work and non-work: a review of models, methods and findings', *Psychological Bulletin*, **88**, 60–77.

Kahn, R. L., Wolfe, D. M., Quinn, R. P., Snoek, J. D., and Rosenthall, R. A. (1964), *Organisational Stress* (New York: Wiley).

Karasek, R. A. (1979), 'Demands, job decision latitude and mental strain: implications for job design', *Administrative Science Quarterly*, **24**, 285–308.

Kasl, S. V. (1978), 'Epidemiological contributions to the study of work stress', in C. L. Cooper and R. Payne (eds.), *Stress at Work* (Chichester and New York: Wiley).

Keenan, A. and Newton, T. J. (1984), 'Frustration in organisations: Relationships to role stress, climate and psychological strain', *Journal of Occupational Psychology*, **57**, 57–65.

Kelley, G. A. (1955), *The Psychology of Personal Constructs* (New York: Norton).

Kemery, E. R., Mossholder, K. W., and Bedeian, A. G. (1987), 'Role stress, physical symptomology and turnover intentions', *Journal of Organizational Behavior*, **8**, 11–23.

Kornhauser, A. (1965), *Mental Health of the Industrial Worker* (New York: Wiley).

Leatt, P. and Schneck, R. (1985), 'Sources and management of organisational stress in nursing sub-units in Canada', *Organisation Studies*, **6**, 55–78.

Mackay, C. and Cooper, C. L. (1987), 'Occupational stress and health: some current issues', in C. L. Cooper and I. T. Robertson (eds.), *International Review of Industrial and Organizational Psychology, 1987* (Chichester and New York: Wiley), pp. 167–99.

Margolis, B. L., Kroe, W. H., and Quinn, R. P. (1974), 'Job stress: an unlisted occupational hazard', *Journal of Occupational Medicine*, **16**, 654–61.

Martin, T. N. (1984), 'Role stress and inability to leave as predictors of mental health', *Human Relations*, **37**, 969–83.

Payne, R. (1980), 'Organisational stress and social support', in C. L. Cooper and R. Payne (eds.), *Current Concerns in Occupational Stress* (Chichester and New York: Wiley), pp. 269–78.

Payne, R., Jick, T. D., and Burke, R. J. (1982), 'Whither stress research? An agenda for the 1980's', *Journal of Occupational Behaviour*, **3**, 131–45.

Pincherle, G. (1972), 'Fitness for work', *Proceedings of the Royal Society of Medicine*, **65**, 321–4.

Russek, H. I. and Zohman, B. L. (1958), 'Relative significance of hereditary diet, and occupational stress in CHD of young adults', *American Journal of Medical Science*, **235**, 266–75.

Schuler, R. S. (1982), 'An integrative transactional process model of stress in organisations', *Journal of Occupational Behaviour*, **3**, 5–19.

Shirom, A. (1982), 'What is organisational stress? A facet analytic conceptualisation', *Journal of Occupational Behaviour*, **3**, 21–38.

Shirom, A., Eden, D., Silberwasser, S., and Kellerman, J. J. (1973), 'Stresses and risk factors in coronary heart disease among occupational categories in Kibbutzim', *Social Science and Medicine*, **7**, 875–92.

Van Maanen, J. and Schein, E. H. (1979), 'Toward a theory of organisational socialisation', in B. M. Staw (ed.), *Research into Organisational Behaviour*, **1**, 209–64.

Vredenburgh, D. J. and Trinkaus, R. J. (1983), 'An analysis of role stress among hospital nurses', *Journal of Vocational Behaviour*, 23, 82–95.

Vroom, V. H. and Yetton, P. (1973), *Leadership and Decision Making* (Pittsburgh, PA: University of Pittsburgh).

Wall, T. D. and Clegg, C. W. (1981), 'A longitudinal field study of group work design', *Journal of Occupational Behaviour*, 2, 31–49.

IO

IMAGE THEORY: DECISION FRAMING AND DECISION DELIBERATION

LEE ROY BEACH, TERENCE R. MITCHELL,
THADDEUS F. PALUCHOWSKI, AND EMILY H. VAN ZEE

ABSTRACT

Image theory, a new, unifying, theory of decision-making for individuals making personal decisions and decisions in the context of organizations is briefly described and two extensions of the theory are explored. The extensions are decision framing, which is the act of placing a decision in an appropriate perspective so that decision deliberation, the second extension of the theory, can take place. The implications of framing and deliberation are described. Finally, a summary of the theory is presented in informal terms in order to demonstrate its commonsensical nature.

In this chapter we will describe an evolving theory of decision-making in organizations, called image theory (Beach, 1990; Beach and Mitchell, 1987, 1990; Mitchell, Rediker, and Beach, 1986), and examine two aspects of the theory that until now have received only secondary attention. The discussion will begin with an informal presentation of the theory's viewpoint in everyday, non-theoretical language in an effort to make clear the commonsensical nature of what the theory is about. Then we will present the theory more formally, extending it to the process by which single decisions are placed in the larger context of the organization's ongoing activities, called decision framing (Minsky, 1968). Finally, we will extend the analysis even further to include the processes involved in deliberations about decision alternatives prior to decision-making.

'INFORMAL' IMAGE THEORY

Theories evolve in a strange way. Observation and experience lead to a rather simple set of notions that, when they are written down, become more abstract and circumlocutious than could ever have been imagined. Further effort to be precise and to tie the theory to existing literature, as well as to make it testable, leads to increasingly defensive formalism.

Soon, what at first seemed to be just good sense becomes so stilted and solemn that even the theorists can hardly detect its humble beginnings. The poor reader, of course, only sees the final product. His or her task is to decode the formalisms in an effort to tie the theory to something he or she has actually experienced. Often this is such a formidable task that things go wrong – and the theorists lament that their simple ideas are being misinterpreted and distorted. Therefore, in an effort to make the reader's task easier and to reduce our future anguish, we have decided to break the rules. We will do the decoding ourselves, and do it prior to presenting the formal theory. What follows is, as close as we can recall, the essence of the simple notions that gave rise to image theory. Of course, there is a reason why we have put work into the formal version of the theory that will follow – we can defend the formal version more precisely and we are willing to submit it to empirical test. This informal version is just that, informal. Perhaps, however, it will help the reader understand the formal version a little more easily.

The general idea is that the decision-making is an individual agent working in the context of a group within an organization, be it a family, a club, or a job. Most decisions are made in concert with colleagues in the group, but the decision-maker has to make up his or her own mind and then the diversity of opinions is resolved in some manner that depends upon the dynamics of the particular organization. Certainly, the colleagues help shape the decision-maker's decision, but that is not the focus of image theory.

The decision-maker has his or her own private principles, goals, and plans, of course, but he or she also knows those of colleagues in the group and the transcendent values of the organization. When engaged in one particular task with one particular group, one set of principles, goals, and plans is relevant, and when working on some other task or with some other group, or when working on a private decision, other sets are relevant. In short, the decision-maker differentiates between what is pertinent in one setting and what is pertinent in a different setting.

The decision-maker possesses values, morals, ethics, and so on that define how things *should* be and how people *ought* to behave. Collectively these are called principles. These are the decision-maker's bedrock beliefs about what the organization stands for and how it does and does not do things. Often these principles cannot be clearly articulated, but they exert a powerful influence on decision-making. Principles run the gamut from the general ('One should tell the truth'), to the specific ('Our products always must meet our quality criteria'), to the compelling ('Our executives must lead by example'), and, as Freud tried to tell us, they are not all especially rational. Whatever they are, they serve as the ultimate criteria for decision-making. Potential goals and actions must not contradict them or they will be rejected, and the utility of decision outcomes derives from them.

In addition to principles, the decision-maker has an agenda of goals to accomplish, as well as timelines for accomplishing them. Each goal has an accompanying plan for its accomplishment, and the various plans are, to a large degree, interleaved in time and coordinated so that they do not interfere with each other. In the best circumstances they facilitate each other.

Potential goals for addition to the agenda come from the need to satisfy principles ('we should adopt quality circles in an attempt to ensure that our products meet our quality criteria'), or from someone who suggests them (a consultant, a customer), or from their being naturally correlated with other goals ('as long as we are reorganizing the office, we should adopt a new computer system'). Potential plans come from past experience (doing this worked before and with a few changes it might work again), from outside sources (a consultant), and, sometimes, from creative flashes of imagination, the mechanisms of which psychologists simply do not yet understand.

Adoption of a potential goal or plan is based, first of all, on whether it is reasonable. That is, does it cause trouble for other goals or plans; is it counter to relevant principles? If the answer is 'yes', how unreasonable is it? If it is not too unreasonable, it might work out all right, but there is some point at which it simply is too unreasonable and must be rejected.

If this initial screening process only involves one potential goal, and if that goal is judged to be not unreasonable, it is adopted and the decision-maker moves on to considering a plan for accomplishing it. If the process involves multiple potential goals and only one passes, the situation is similar to having started with only one and having passed it – it is adopted and a plan is sought. However, if more than one potential goal is involved and if more than one survives the screening, something must be done to break the tie. This something usually involves comparing the relative merits of the survivors and selecting the best of them.

Adoption of plans is similar to adoption of goals except that it also involves imagining what the plan might result in if it were adopted, where the result of particular interest is whether it accomplishes its goal. Thus, plan adoption is in effect a combination of the goal adoption process and the progress monitoring process (both of which basically are screening).

Progress monitoring involves trying to imagine what would happen if a to-be-adopted plan or an already-adopted plan is implemented. Will it create difficulties for other goals and plans? Will it fail to attain its goal? Will it violate relevant principles? If the answer to any of these questions appears to be 'yes', the plan either is not adopted, or if it already is in place the decision-maker considers abandoning it and seeking a replacement. If a satisfactory plan cannot be found to attain a goal, then the goal has to be reexamined to see if it ought to be rejected. That is, if one cannot find an acceptable way to accomplish the goal, it may be necessary to abandon the goal.

Of course, all of this assumes that a decision has to be made at all. If a goal is found to exist in a familiar situation, a plan from the past may already exist to serve as a policy for accomplishing it. Thus, no decision is required – the policy merely needs to be implemented. If the situation is less familiar, but not too different from situations that are familiar, the plans that were used in those familiar situations can be melded and modified to provide a new plan for the new situation. It is knowledge about familiar and fairly familiar situations, together with knowledge about events leading up to the present, that gives meaning to decisions by embedding them in a larger perspective that makes them understandable.

Many decisions, perhaps most of them, are quite straightforward. They require little deliberation and sometimes seem almost to make themselves. This occurs when the screening process reveals that the potential goal or plan (or that progress) fits so well with clearly relevant principles, goals, and plans that there is no question about adoption. Sometimes, however, decisions require more deliberation in order to clarify the relevant criteria and to identify the relevant characteristics of the candidate. This deliberation may consist of sustained, purposeful, and rational thinking, or it may consist of fleeting, scattered, and fanciful thinking. It also may involve strong emotions. Whatever it may consist of, its purpose is to illuminate the decision, to provide perspective, to help the decision-maker know what is important and how he or she feels about the issues. This thinking helps in the identification of the decision's ramifications – the principles, the goals, and the plans that might be affected. It allows the decision-maker to imagine possible futures and to experiment with variations on how to attain desired ends, or on just what those ends might entail. In short, deliberative thinking is, in fact, decision-making, and image theory is an attempt to identify the various aspects of this thinking that occur consistently across different decisions.

'FORMAL' IMAGE THEORY

Many organizational decisions are about whether to change the organization's goals and its goal-directed activities. Image theory is a non-normative, descriptive theory about how such decisions are made. A 'decision occasion' consists of both the social processes in which a decision is embedded and the specific process used by the decision-maker. Clearly the two are intertwined, but it is our opinion that it is profitable to treat them separately for the purposes of theory construction. A number of organizational science discussions focus on the social processes (e.g., Gore, 1964; Weick, 1979); image theory focusses on the individual decision-maker functioning within an organization, usually within a sub-part of the organization. That is, while it is acknowledged that the decision-maker's decision process is influenced by social variables, it is the decision process itself that is of concern.

This focus sometimes makes the theory appear to be describing a decision-maker operating in a social vacuum, but that is not the intent. Indeed, the decision-maker constantly is immersed in a social milieu that strongly influences the way in which he or she frames, deliberates, makes, and implements decisions. The social milieu consists of both the formal organizational structure with its associated culture and the particular sub-part of the organization that is engaged in making the decision, with its informal processes and norms (Barnard, 1938). In an organizational context, individual decision preferences are pooled with those of other sub-part members in any of a number of ways (e.g., voting, consensus, dominance), while all are subject to the authority of the official hierarchy. In what follows, individual decision-makers are understood to be constantly interacting with, and to be profoundly influenced by, their social milieu.

Image theory is based upon the notion that decision-makers utilize schematic structures to organize their thinking about the past, present, and future. These schemata are called *images*, in deference to Miller, Galanter, and Pribram (1960), whose work inspired the theory. There are three images, each of which represents a different kind of decision information. These images are part of the organization's culture (Mitchell, Rediker, and Beach, 1986), and are shared to one degree or another by the members of the organization. In what follows, we are not concerned with the accuracy of the decision-maker's perception of the organization's decision images, we merely require that he or she regards the images as those of the organization and that he or she uses the images when acting as a decision-making agent within the organization.

Images

The *organizational value image* reflects the organization's values, norms, standards, and ethics which collectively are called the organization's *principles*. The decision-maker regards these principles as imperatives for the organization and as rigid criteria for the rightness of any particular decision (e.g., increase market share, quality comes first). Principles serve in the internal generation of new goals and actions, and in guiding the adoption (or rejection) of both internally and externally generated *candidate* goals and actions that fit (or do not fit) the organizational value image.

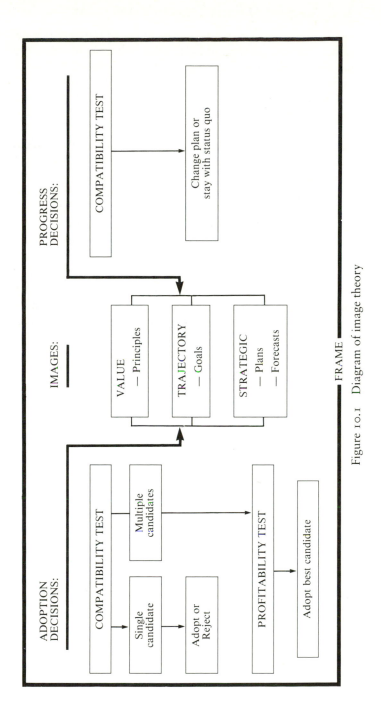

Figure 10.1 Diagram of image theory

The *organizational trajectory image* reflects the organization's agenda for the future, where it should be going and the ends it should be pursuing. This image represents what the organization's members hope it will become and what they want it to achieve: its *goals*. Goals can be concrete, specific events, such as landing a particular contract. They also can be abstract states, such as making the organization a challenging place to work.

The *organizational strategic image* reflects the various *plans* that are in progress for attaining the goals that the organization is pursuing. Each plan is an abstract sequence of potential activities beginning with the goal adoption and ending with goal attainment. The concrete behavioural components of plans are called *tactics*. Tactics are specific, palpable actions that are intended to facilitate implementation of an abstract plan to further progress towards a goal. The second components of plans are called *forecasts*. A plan is an anticipation of the future, and it changes in light of information about the changing environment in which it is (or might be) implemented. As a result, it serves both to guide behaviour and to anticipate what the results of that behaviour will be. By monitoring these forecasts in relation to the goals on the trajectory image, the decision-maker can evaluate his or her progress towards realization of the ideal agenda on the trajectory image. Figure 10.1 contains a diagram of image theory.

Two kinds of decisions and two decision tests

There are two kinds of decisions. *Adoption decisions* are about adoption or rejection of candidates as constituents of the value, trajectory, or strategic images. *Progress decisions* are about whether a particular plan on the strategic image is producing satisfactory progress towards attainment of its goal.

There are two tests by which the two kinds of decisions are made. The *compatibility test* assesses (1) whether a candidate for adoption 'violates' (is incompatible with) the constituents of the various images, and (2) whether the forecasts on the strategic image 'violate' (are incompatible with) the constituents of the trajectory image. The *profitability test*, which is applied to adoption decisions but not to progress decisions, assesses whether the candidate's potential payoffs exceed those of the other candidates that are competing with it for adoption. If a single candidate passes the compatibility test it is adopted without further scrutiny. If more than one candidate passes the compatibility test, they are then subjected to the profitability test, which selects the best. In short, the compatibility test screens out the unacceptable candidates and the profitability test selects the best of the survivors.

Progress decisions require compatibility between the trajectory and strategic images. If they are sufficiently compatible it means that the plans on the strategic image are forecasted to be capable of producing acceptable progress towards their goals and that their continued implementation therefore is warranted. However, incompatibility between the two images means that one or more plan is forecasted to be incapable of achieving its goal and that something must be done to get things back on track.

The compatibility test   The compatibility test makes *adoption* decisions by using the 'fit' between the candidate and the images. In adoption, the candidate's compatibility decreases as a function of the sum of the number of violations, each weighted by the importance of that violation. Each violation is all-or-none and it occurs when an aspect of the candidate negates, contradicts, contravenes, prevents, retards, or in some other way is contrary to or interferes with a constituent of any of the images. The decision rule is that if the weighted sum of the violations exceeds some absolute *rejection threshold*, the candidate is rejected, otherwise it is adopted. The rejection threshold is that weighted sum above which the decision-maker regards the candidate as incompatible with the organization's principles, goals, and ongoing plans (i.e., the constituents of the value, trajectory, and strategic images).

The compatibility test makes *progress* decisions by assaying the 'fit' between the trajectory and strategic images. Here the violations are of the trajectory image's constituents by the strategic image's constituents. The decision rule is that, when the weighted sum of violations exceeds the *rejection threshold*, reevaluation of the plans that generated the forecasts is undertaken and the faulty plan is replaced. Thus, the compatibility test is used for adoption and progress decisions, and it rests upon violations and the rejection threshold (i.e., upon 'fit').

The profitability test   The profitability test is not a single mechanism like the compatibility test. It is a short-hand term for the repertory of strategies (Beach and Mitchell, 1978) that a decision-maker possesses for adopting the best candidate from among a set of two or more candidates, all of which are at least minimally acceptable. The minimal acceptability of the candidates is assured by their having passed the compatibility test before being admitted to the set that is subjected to the profitability test. In this sense, the profitability test serves as a 'tie breaker' when the compatibility test passes more than one mutually exclusive candidate.

EXTENSIONS OF A THEORY

Many treatments of decision-making begin by assuming that the decision-maker has clearly identified his or her decision problem, and then proceed to describe how deliberation and decision-making supposedly take place. From the decision-maker's viewpoint this emphasis is wrong because it usually is easier to make the decision itself than to figure out precisely what the decision is about and what is relevant to it. Indeed, in many cases, once the problem is identified the decision is made, because the decision-maker can implement preformulated policies for dealing with problems of the class to which the presenting decision belongs. The purpose of the following analysis is to use the concepts from image theory to describe how decision problems are identified (i.e., how they are 'framed'), and the role that policies play in resolving many of these problems once identification has taken place.

Framing and policy   To place things in perspective, the concept of framing has roots in two very different lines of inquiry. The sociological and social psychological line begins with the work of Bateson (1972) and Goffman (1974), and is reflected in script theory (Abelson, 1976) and in social schema theories (Hastie, 1981). The cognitive psychological and decision research line begins with the computer simulation work of Minsky (1968), and is reflected in artificial intelligence (Hunt, 1975) and in prospect theory (Kahneman and Tversky, 1979). Unfortunately, neither of these lines is itself sufficient for the present purpose. The social definition of frames is very broad, encompassing the actor's perception of both the social context and its social demands. The cognitive definition is very narrow, concentrating on the ways in which specific characteristics of problems influence how they are interpreted by the problem solver and how these interpretations determine the means by which he or she attempts to solve the problems. The present model acknowledges this entire spectrum of meaning for framing, but its focus is somewhere in the middle – on the framing of decision problems that are more circumscribed than the social definitions admit and less particularistic than the cognitive definitions admit.

Context and events   For convenience we assume that the decision-maker has just arrived on the scene, which consists of a context in which various events are occurring. He or she brings a perspective about the general context that is based upon knowing, for example, that the events are occurring at work (a committee meeting or in a discussion with a co-worker), and a historical knowledge of what has led up to the present situation. The events that occur, together with the contextual perspective

the decision-maker brings, contribute a set of *features* that are conceptually similar to the symptoms that a physician uses to diagnose an illness.
The decision-maker uses these features to frame and categorize (diagnose)
the context and the events in order to determine specifically what is going
on.

Frames Here we borrow from both an old theory of recognition memory
(Beach, 1964) and a new one (Hintzmann, 1986) and from suggestions by
Abelson and Levi (1985) about the role of memory in complex decisions.
The idea is that the features of the context and the events are used by the
decision-maker to probe his or her memory, i.e., his or her past experience. If the probe locates a contextual memory that has features which are
the same as those of the current context and events, the latter are said to be
recognized. If the probe locates contextual memories that resemble, but
are not the same as the current context and events, these memories and all
that is associated with them constitute an *ad hoc* definition of the present
context and events, which then are said to be *identified*. The difference
between recognition and identification is a matter of specificity – both
permit the decision-maker to use existing knowledge from memory to
understand the current situation and to act accordingly.

There are two kinds of frames. The *general frame* places the current
context and events within the perspective of the decision-maker's and the
organization's ongoing activities and classifies it as a particular kind of
situation (work related meeting, idle conversation). Frames of this kind
serve to give general meaning to what is happening and do not themselves
require any action on the part of the decision-maker. The *specific frame*
goes a step further to tie the current context and events, now classified
within a general contextual frame, to the issues that are of specific concern
to the decision-maker, and to define the requirements for action on his or
her part. Specific frames consist of goals and plans, although both may be
quite vague at the moment framing takes place and both may evolve
considerably as a result of deliberation that occurs between the time that
framing occurs and the time that the decision is made and implementation
begins.

Because specific frames are linked to the individual's particular concerns more closely than are general frames, different decision-makers may
derive similar general frames for a given context but derive very different
specific frames for it. For example, consider the famous case of the
intra-board battle at US Steel over corporate investment (Symonds and
Miles, 1985). The communally held general frame consisted of the
industry structure, market conditions, and available resources. Against
this background, the board members all derived a specific frame that had
as its goal component the prudent investment of corporate funds.

However, the different past experiences of the various board members made the plan component of their specific frames very different. Thus, members whose career experience was in production, the 'steelmen', derived plans that stressed production and investment in up-to-date manufacturing facilities. In contrast, members whose career experience was in financial management, the 'money men', derived plans that stressed high profit through investment in promising ventures, even if this meant diversifying away from steel.

Policy   Recognition and identification of contexts and events is possible because they, or situations similar to them, have been encountered in the past. In many cases, interventions also have been required in the past. These interventions are part of the information that is stored in memory and that becomes available when the context is framed. In these cases a goal or a plan that has been used in the past may be usable again. Such a preformulated action is called a habit by students of individual behaviour and a policy by students of organizational behaviour; we use the term policy for both individuals and organizations.

For our purposes, a policy is defined as a goal(s) and its attendant plan(s) that is associated with a particular specific frame. That is, it is a preformulated course of action for a particular problem in a specific frame. This definition assumes that either (a) there previously has been experience with this same frame and that a successful policy has been formulated which can be used again, or (b) that similar frames previously have been experienced and that the knowledge gained from those experiences can be used to anticipate the future and, if necessary, to formulate a policy for dealing with potential problems.

Frequently the goal simply is to make the future compatible with the decision-maker's existing goals, plans, and principles. Plans, on the other hand, are more complex because they consist of both the broad strategy for achieving the goal and the particular tactics that are geared to the unique conditions that arise as the plan is executed. However, plans do not have to be created from scratch every time. On the assumption that a particular specific frame may arise again in the future, plans are stored in memory to be used again when the frame is reencountered.

Policies tend to be evoked automatically when a specific frame is recognized, and this automaticity encourages their inflexible implementation unless they lead to gross and obvious error. In contrast, policies are unlikely to be evoked when the specific frame is merely identified. That is, if a particular situation has not arisen in the past and therefore is merely identified as being similar to frames that have been encountered before (Hintzman, 1986), the decision-maker will resist automatic, blind use of one of the policies associated with one of the similar frames, if only because it may not be clear just which one ought to be used. Instead, in this case it is more prudent to think through the issues and to devise a new plan. In reality, of course, old plans are not blindly followed either, they are tempered by recent knowledge and current conditions. Similarly, new plans seldom are wholly new, they are a synthesis of old plans that have worked for similar past decisions, the advice and example of other people and other organizations, and the decision-maker's creative efforts.

Progress evaluation   When a context is framed and a plan of action is adopted for it, the decision-maker must monitor events to make sure the action is appropriate. To do this, the decision-maker uses the specific frame, and what he or she plans to do in it, in order to make a forecast about what is likely to happen if implementation of the plan is allowed to continue without intervention. If the forecast suggests that the ongoing plan is unlikely to result in anything particularly bad happening, the decision-maker will stick with the plan. Periodic reengagement in this process (forecasting and assessment of potential trouble) serves to monitor events as they develop and to alert the decision-maker if a change in plan becomes necessary.

Assessment of forecasts is performed using the *progress decision mechanism* and the *compatibility test* described by image theory. The progress mechanism involves using the specific frame as a knowledge structure upon which to base a scenario about the future (Beach, Barnes, and Christensen-Szalanski, 1986; Jungermann, 1985; Jungermann and Thüring, 1986; Thüring and Jungermann, 1986; Pennington and Hastie, 1986). This scenario consists of the events that the decision-maker judges will follow from implementation of the plan as the future unfolds. If this future is sufficiently compatible with the decision-maker's existing goals, plans, and principles, no change of plan is required. However, if the events are not compatible, intervention in the plan is in order.

When intervention is in order, the decision-maker must adopt a new plan using the compatibility test described earlier. This involves assessing the compatibility of a new candidate plan with the decision-maker's existing goals, plans, and principles. Because the only goal considered often is that of preventing disruption of the existing goals, plans, and principles, plan adoption may be relatively straightforward. However, plan adoption frequently requires considerably more thought and even may require the decision-maker to choose the best plan from an array of plausible plans, using the *profitability test*. When the plan is adopted, the decision-maker proceeds to implement it and to monitor its progress.

In summary, the features of the present context and events are used to probe memory in order to recognize or identify what is going on. This is called framing. The result is a general frame for the broad context of what is occurring, and a specific frame for those aspects of the context that are related to the decision-maker's particular concerns and which require action on his or her part. If on the basis of a particular past encounter (recognition) the specific frame has a policy associated with it in memory, that policy usually is implemented. If the specific frame has no policy associated with it, or if the frame is diffuse (identification) and there is no single clearly defined policy for it, the decision-maker must procure a candidate plan, perhaps suggested by plans from past encounters with contexts similar to this one. Implementation monitoring involves forecasting what will happen if the current plan is allowed to unfold without change. If the forecast is compatible with the ongoing flow of the decision-maker's other activities and with his or her principles, no change of plan is required. If the forecast is not compatible with these criteria, the decision-maker must identify and adopt a better plan. This consists of reviewing the goal, often simply the goal of not disrupting the flow of ongoing activities or of violating principles, and then adopting a new, more promising plan for achieving that goal. Once adopted, the new policy is implemented and monitored from time to time to make sure it is working.

DECISION DELIBERATION

Decision deliberation is the glue that holds together all the boxes in figures 10.1. It is the cognitive processing in which the decision-maker engages as the decision is framed, as goals and plans are adopted or rejected, and as implementation is monitored and plans and goals are retained or replaced in light of progress. In short, it is what the decision-maker thinks about during decision-making and decision implementation.

Sources of deliberative thinking   Material for deliberation comes most immediately from the decision-maker's own (or knowledge about the organization's) past successes and failures with similar or analogous decisions. Lessons learned from the past are vivid and often have a strong emotional component that makes them particularly compelling.

Another source of material is the arguments and representations of other people who are involved in the decision, either co-decision-makers or resource people. Indeed, when there are differences among decision-makers about what is germane to the decision or about what decision should be made, material is presented both to convey the presenter's position, with whatever social pressure that may contribute, and to persuade the decision-maker through the force of argument and precedent. In contrast to this externally generated and passively received material, other material may be actively generated using mechanisms that foster creative group problem solving (e.g., brain storming).

A third source of material for deliberation is external to the decision, perhaps even external to the organization – such things as inspirational or instructive stories and examples; the sorts of things that are presented in management seminars or published in trade magazines. Too, news stories or conversations with people from outside the organization may foster deliberation that provides perspective on the decision.

A fourth source of material for deliberation is existing rules and regulations, such as precedence, labour contracts, and similar formalized obligations, or legal restraints or requirements.

No doubt there are many other sources, but these give the general idea. Decision-makers tend to think in terms of examples from their own or other people's past experience, from their co-decision-makers' examples of what has happened in the past or what might happen in the future, from suggestions by support persons, or from examples provided by the actions of outsiders. All of this material is used to mull over, to deliberate about, the decision – often being used repeatedly at different phases of the decision, often being reinterpreted or brought to bear on new points, often being rejected as irrelevant only to be resurrected later. In short, decision deliberation involves exploration of the decision in terms of the lessons that can be learned from one's own and from others' past experience and suppositions about the future.

Functions of deliberative thinking   Deliberation serves a number of functions: clarification of issues, generation of new candidates, evaluation of candidates, building confidence about the adopted candidate, and rehearsal and refinement of the manner in which the decision is to be publicly presented and implemented. The major function is to identify and clarify the issues. This involves identifying the relevant subset of principles from all of the constituents of the organizational value image, the relevant subset of goals from the constituents of the organizational trajectory image, and the relevant subset of plans from the organizational strategic image for the decision as it currently is framed. Clearly, not all image constituents are relevant to every decision, and working with subsets reduces the information processing load.

Deliberating also involves identifying the subset of the candidate's characteristics (or the characteristics of the pertinent goal and plan on the trajectory and strategic images in the case of progress decisions) that are pertinent to the aforementioned subsets of relevant principles, goals, and plans. Not all of a candidate's characteristics are pertinent to any particular decision.

In fact, the identification of the candidate's pertinent characteristics and the identification of the relevant principles, goals, and plans are interactive processes. Identifying one places requirements and constraints on what is included in the other. While the frame defines the beginning phase of the process by classifying the decision as being of a particular kind, which means that it touches upon particular principles, goals, and plans, as the process proceeds the candidate's pertinent characteristics influence what is added to or omitted from the initial subsets and vice versa. All of this occurs in the course of deliberation about examples of and analogies with previous decision experiences, and the latter help in the process of identifying relevant subsets.

The second function of decision deliberation is to generate new candidate principles, goals, and plans. These may emerge from such sources as contemplation of past experiences, arguments articulated by colleagues, fanciful ideas and creative thinking, or the perspective provided by constructing scenarios based upon environmental cues, personal life histories, or organizational experiences. Whatever the source, the emergence of new candidates is central to progress towards an appropriate decision.

The third function of decision deliberation is to enable the decision-maker to use the examples and experiences that are thought about to make forecasts about the short- and the long-term implications of adopting a candidate (or of continuing to pursue a particular plan). This involves construction of forecasting scenarios and assessment of the potential violations that might arise from adopting the candidate (or continuing to pursue the current plan).

In addition, forecasting scenarios enable the decision-maker to identify the potential payoffs that may accrue from adopting the candidate (or continuing to pursue a particular plan). This provides information that is useful if it becomes necessary to apply the profitability test to select one from among two or more candidates that have survived the compatibility test. The key to understanding assessment of these payoffs lies in the fact that their worth is tied to the *degree* to which they satisfy, actualize, or facilitate the decision-maker's or organization's principles, existing goals, and ongoing plans. That is, it is this link that gives worth to outcomes, and because of that fact their worth is dependent upon the particular subsets of principles, goals, and plans that have been identified as relevant to the particular decision under consideration.

The fourth function of decision deliberation involves confidence building and appraisal of the risk involved in the decision. Confidence and risk are not identical to the subjective probabilities in subjective expected utility theory, in spite of years of effort to establish such an identity. They are, in fact more fundamental and important than subjective probabilities. Among the decision-maker's and the organization's principles are requirements that candidates inspire some reasonable level of confidence and do not involve undue risk. Refusal to abandon the status quo (Beach, in press; Beach and Mitchell, 1987, 1990) for adoption of what appears to an outsider to be an attractive alternative often stems from the fact that the candidate violates the principles of confidence and risklessness. In the course of decision deliberation, scenarios that forecast success, or that reveal possible (but tractable) difficulties in decision implementation, may increase confidence in the 'appropriateness' of the candidate goal, or the 'potential' of the candidate plan, thereby eliminating violations that earlier threatened its adoption.

The fifth function of deliberation is to consider how the adopted candidate should be presented and implemented. If the decision is a major one involving many changes, the decision-maker will engage in a period of deliberation in which the manner of presentation of the decision to public view is rehearsed and refined. Adoption of a candidate goal triggers a new cycle of deliberative activity as attention shifts to decisions related to implementation.

Evolution of deliberative thinking   The nature and purpose of deliberation changes throughout the decision. Premonitions of the need for a decision may be somewhat casual in character; simple musings about possibilities that are not seriously considered as alternatives to the status quo. As the necessity for a decision becomes clearer, the decision-maker becomes increasingly engrossed in rumination. Often this consists of, as William James (1890/1950) observed, the 'impatience of the deliberative state', which presses for a prompt decision, contending against the 'dread of the irrevocable', which presses for further deliberation – 'One says "now", the other says "not yet"' (p. 530). Eventually, however, vacillation ceases and the decision is made, and in this 'transition from doubt to assurance we seem to ourselves almost passive; the reasons which decide us appearing to flow in from the nature of things, and to owe nothing to our will' (p. 531).

REFERENCES

Abelson, R. P. (1976), 'Script processing in attitude formation and decision-making', in J. S. Carroll and J. W. Payne (eds.), *Cognition and Social Behavior* (Hillsdale, NJ: Erlbaum).

Abelson, R. P. and Levi, A. (1985), 'Decision making and decision theory', in G. Lindzey and E. Aronson (eds.), *Handbook of Social Psychology*, vol. I (New York: Random House).

Barnard, C. (1938), *The Functions of the Executive* (Cambridge, MA: Harvard University Press).

Bateson, G. (1972), *Steps to an Ecology of Mind* (San Francisco: Chandler).

Beach, L. R. (1964), 'Recognition, assimilation, and identification of objects', *Psychological Monographs*, 78, 22–37.

Beach, L. R. (in press), *Image Theory: Decision Making in Personal and Organizational Contexts* (Chichester: Wiley).

Beach, L. R., Barnes, V. E., and Christensen-Szalanski, J. J. J. (1986), 'Beyond heuristics and biases: a contingency model of judgmental forecasting', *Journal of Forecasting*, 5, 143–57.

Beach, L. R. and Mitchell, T. R. (1978), 'A contingency model for the selection of decision strategies', *Academy of Management Review*, 3, 439–49.

(1987), 'Image theory: principles, goals, and plans in decision making', *Acta Psychologica*, 66, 201–20.

(in press), 'Image theory: a behavioral theory of decisions in organizations', in B. M. Staw and L. L. Cummings (eds.), *Research in Organizational Behavior, vol. XII* (Greenwich, CT: JAI Press).

Goffman, E. (1974), *Frame Analysis* (Cambridge, MA: Harvard University Press).

Gore, W. J. (1964), *Administrative Decision Making: A Heuristic Model* (New York: Wiley).

Hastie, R. (1981), 'Schematic principles of human memory', in E. T. Higgins, C. A. Herman, and M. P. Zanna (eds.), *Social Cognition: The Ontario Symposium*, vol. I (Hillsdale, NJ: Earlbaum).

Hintzman, D. L. (1986), '"Schema abstraction" in a multiple-trace memory model', *Psychological Review*, 93, 411–28.

Hunt, E. B. (1975), *Artificial Intelligence* (New York: Academic Press).

James, W. (1890/1950), *The Principles of Psychology*, vol. II (New York: Dover).

Jungermann, H. (1985), 'Inferential processes in the construction of scenarios', *Journal of Forecasting*, 4, 321–7.

Jungermann, H. and Thürling, M. (August, 1986), 'The use of causal knowledge for inferential reasoning', Paper presented at the NATO Advanced Research Workshop on Expert Judgment and Expert Systems, Porto, Portugal.

Kahneman, D. and Tversky, A. (1979), 'Prospect theory: an analysis of decision under risk', *Econometrica*, 47, 263–91.

Miller, G. A., Galanter, E., and Pribram, K. H. (1960), *Plans and the Structure of Behavior* (New York: Holt, Rinehart & Winston).

Minsky, M. (1968), *Semantic Information Processing* (Cambridge, MA: MIT Press).

Mitchell, T. R., Rediker, K. J., and Beach, L. R. (1986), 'Image theory and its implications for organizational decision making', in H. P. Sims and D. A. Gioia (eds.), *The Thinking Organization* (San Francisco: Jossey-Bass).

Pennington, N. and Hastie, R. (1986), 'Evidence evaluation in complex decision making', *Journal of Personality and Social Psychology*, 54, 242–58.

Symonds, W. C. and Miles, G. L. (February, 1985), 'The toughest job in business: How they're remaking U.S. Steel', *Business Week*, 50–6.

Thürling, M. and Jungermann, H. (1986), 'Constructing and running mental models for inferences about the future', in B. Brehmer, H. Jungermann, P. Lourens, and G. Sevon (eds.), *New Directions in Research in Decision Making* (Amsterdam: North-Holland).

Weick, K. E. (1979), *The Social Psychology of Organizing* (Reading, MA: Addison-Wesley).

II

DECISION-MAKING UNDER UNCERTAINTY:
THE EFFECTS OF ROLE AND AMBIGUITY

ROBIN M. HOGARTH AND HOWARD KUNREUTHER

ABSTRACT

In many important decisions, people are uncertain or *ambiguous* concerning the magnitude of the probabilities of events that can affect
outcomes. The classic theory of decision-making argues that people's
decisions should not be affected by whether knowledge of a probability is
precise or ambiguous. This chapter presents a descriptive model of how
people cope with ambiguous probabilities in decision-making. The model
predicts that ambiguity matters. 'Decision weights' associated with
ambiguous probabilities are assumed to be reached via an anchoring-and-
adjustment process in which people anchor on an estimate of the
probability and then adjust this as a result of mentally simulating
alternative values of the probability. The mental simulation process is
affected by both the amount of ambiguity and whether outcomes are large
or small gains and/or losses. One important factor that determines
people's attitudes towards ambiguity is the nature of the role they assume
in making decisions. This interaction between roles and attitudes towards
ambiguity is explored in a series of three experiments which test and
validate explicit predictions of the ambiguity model. The experiments
concern the purchase and sale of insurance, a legal decision-making
situation in which plaintiffs and defendants must decide whether to go or
to settle out of court, and the purchase and sale of industrial equipment
involving warranties and discounts. Finally, recognizing that ambiguity
concerning probabilities is but one source of lack of knowledge in
decision-making, a conceptual framework is suggested to guide future
work on this topic.

The theory of decision-making under uncertainty (von Neumann and
Morgenstern, 1947; Savage, 1954) has proven to be enormously useful
for both helping people make better decisions and understanding how
decisions are made. There are many interesting 'how to' applications
in the literature (see, e.g., Keeney and Raiffa, 1976) and descriptive

implications of the theory have been used extensively in fields such as finance, economics, and public policy. Despite these successes, both the theory's prescriptions and descriptive adequacy have been repeatedly questioned (see, e.g., Einhorn and Hogarth, 1981; Slovic, Fischhoff, and Lichtenstein, 1988). At the origin of these questions are several paradoxical choice situations in which what seem to be reasonable answers turn out to violate the prescriptions of the theory. These paradoxes have been extensively studied and have inspired many prescriptive and descriptive variations of the theory of decision-making under uncertainty (for overviews see Machina, 1987; Weber and Camerer, 1987; Fishburn, 1988).

The starting point of this chapter is one of these paradoxes, first presented by Daniel Ellsberg (1961). To illustrate briefly the essence of Ellsberg's paradox, consider two situations in which you stand to win $1,000 if you correctly guess the outcome of a flip of a coin, i.e., heads or tails. You can only observe the toss of a coin in one of the two situations and it is your task to decide in which of the two situations you would rather guess the outcome. In the first situation you know that the coin is fair, i.e., there are equal chances of observing heads and tails. In the second situation, however, you do not know whether the coin is fair, i.e., the chances of observing, say, heads could be greater, less than, or the same as observing tails. What would you do? Elect to play in the first situation, the second, or would you be indifferent between the two?

When faced with this choice, most people opt for the first situation where they know they have an even chance of winning $1,000. The fact that the odds of winning in the second situation are unknown makes it less attractive. When comparing the two situations, the first has only one source of uncertainty (i.e., whether heads or tails will appear on the toss of a coin), and this can be precisely quantified (the probability of heads is 0.50 as is that of tails). On the other hand, the second situation is characterized by two sources of uncertainty, the first as to whether heads or tails will appear, the second concerning the probability of heads or tails. Ellsberg referred to this uncertainty about the level of one's uncertainty as *ambiguity*.

Many readers may legitimately ask why preferring the situation in which the probability of winning $1,000 is known precisely is paradoxical *vis-à-vis* the theory of decision-making under uncertainty. To see this, ask yourself whether you would pick heads or tails when faced with the opportunity of winning $1,000 if the coin displayed your choice. Most people are indifferent between heads or tails whether or not they know the coin to be fair. Suppose, however, that the game is redefined so that the prize depends on observing heads. In this case, most people would prefer to play with a fair coin where there is no ambiguity. Similarly, if the game were redefined so that the prize depended on tails, most people would still prefer the fair coin. However, since heads and tails are mutually exclusive, how can one rationally defend preferring the coin for which the odds are known?

Whereas Ellsberg's paradox is typically demonstrated using artificial games of chance, the prevalence of ambiguity – and thus the importance of his challenge to the theory of decision-making under uncertainty – should not be underestimated. Indeed, as stated by Ellsberg (1961):

Ambiguity is a subjective variable, but it should be possible to identify 'objectively' some situations likely to present high ambiguity, by noting situations where available information is scanty or obviously unreliable or highly conflicting; or where expressed confidence in estimates tends to be low. Thus, as compared with the effects of familiar production decisions or well-known random processes (like coin-flipping or roulette), the results of Research and Development, or the performance of a new President, or the tactics of an unfamiliar opponent are all likely to appear ambiguous. (pp. 660–61)

In this chapter, we present a descriptive model that shows how people react to ambiguity. Implications of this model are then discussed and illustrated by three different kinds of experiments in which people exhibit different attitudes towards ambiguity. Sometimes they avoid it (as in the example above), sometimes they seek it, and sometimes they appear indifferent to its presence. In some cases, the same person may exhibit all three attitudes when faced with different levels of probability for the same decision-making task. In other situations, a person's role determines his or her attitude towards ambiguity. Finally, recognizing that there are different sources of ambiguity even in simple decision-making tasks, we suggest a framework for an agenda of future research on the effects of ambiguity.

THE AMBIGUITY MODEL

The theory of decision-making under uncertainty assumes that people evaluate the attractiveness of a given alternative by weighting the utility of the outcome by the probability of obtaining it. The basic premise of the ambiguity model is that people do not use probabilities to weight outcomes in ambiguous situations. Instead, probabilities are replaced by subjective weights that do not necessarily have the mathematical properties of probabilities.

The main psychological assumption underlying the model is that the subjective weights given to ambiguous probabilities are the end result of a mental anchoring-and-adjustment process (cf. Tversky and Kahneman, 1974; Einhorn and Hogarth, 1985). People are assumed to anchor on a particular estimate of the probability and then adjust this by imagining, via a mental simulation process, other values that the probability could take. To illustrate, consider a situation in which you are concerned about the chances of an accident occurring in a new industrial facility. A study conducted by technical experts assesses the risk as $p = 0.001$, but they have doubts about the precision of this estimate. In the process assumed here, it is postulated that you would first anchor on a given value of probability (e.g., the 0.001 provided by the experts) and then imagine or 'try out' other values the probability could take, both below and above the anchor. Depending on the circumstances (see below), you would not necessarily accord equal weight in imagination to possible values of the probabilities on both sides of the anchor. For instance, in the present example values above the anchor may well weigh more heavily in imagination than those below (the occurrence of accidents might be salient). The resulting weight given to the ambiguous probability is taken to reflect both the initial anchor and the net effect of the mental simulation process and can be written:

$$S(p_A) = p_A + (k_g - k_s) \qquad (11.1)$$

where p_A is the anchor, k_g represents the values and weight accorded in the mental simulation to values of p greater than the anchor, and k_s corresponds to the weighted values below the anchor.

To make these notions operational, one needs to specify (1) how the anchor, p_A, is established, (2) what effects the amount of mental simulation (i.e., the ranges of alternative probability values considered), and (3) what determines the sign or direction of the adjustment process.

1 In ambiguous circumstances, some initial value of the probability is assumed to be typically available to the decision-maker. This may be a figure based on historical data, provided by experts (as in the example above), or selected from memory.

2 If the decision-maker has sufficient knowledge to assign a unique value to the probability there would be little or no mental simulation (however, see, Hogarth and Einhorn, 1990). When the probability is ambiguous, one would expect considerable simulation, the extent of which is assumed to be positively related to the amount of perceived ambiguity.

3 The sign of the adjustment process is determined by the person's attitude towards ambiguity. This could reflect personal dispositions towards optimism or pessimism, but we argue that it is largely dependent on situational variables such as the sign or size of outcomes or whether the context of the situation induces caution (as when considering insurance) or playfulness (as when gambling).

The manner in which imagination affects the anchor value, p_A, in the ambiguity model can be shown by depicting the judgemental compromise

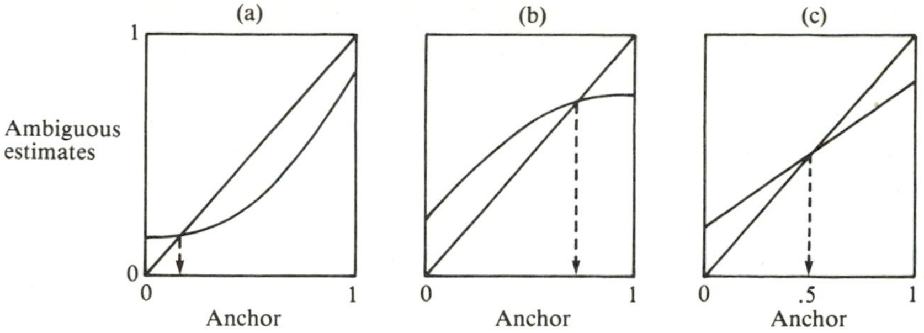

Figure 11.1 Different ambiguity functions. *Note:* In panel (a), values of the probability below the anchor are weighted more heavily in imagination than those above; in panel (b) values above are weighted more heavily than those below; and in panel (c) values above and below are weighted equally. *Source:* H. J. Einhorn and R. M. Hogarth, 1985, 'Ambiguity and uncertainty in probabilistic inference', *Psychological Review*, **92**, 433–61.

that results from the anchoring-and-adjustment process as a function of the anchor probability. This is illustrated in the three panels of figure 11.1.

In interpreting the panels of figure 11.1, recall that two forces cause the final judgement to deviate from the anchor. These are the amount of perceived ambiguity and the person's attitude towards ambiguity in the circumstances. The former determines the amount of mental simulation and thus the extent to which the ambiguity function deviates from the diagonal (45°) line; the more the perceived ambiguity, the greater the deviation. The latter determines the direction of the adjustment and thus the point at which the ambiguity function crosses the diagonal.

Consider first the extreme anchors of $p_A = 0$ and $p_A = 1$. In both cases, the adjustment can only be in one direction, up for $p_A = 0$ and down for $p_A = 1$, thereby illustrating the fact that the location of p_A places constraints on the ranges of values that can be imagined above and below the anchor. Thus $S(p_A) > p_A$ when $p_A = 0$ and $S(p_A) < p_A$ when $p_A = 1$. In general, $S(p_A)$ will overweight small probabilities and underweight large ones; what changes from situation to situation is the point at which the ambiguity function crosses over the diagonal (45°) line, i.e., where overweighting changes to underweighting. In figure 11.1a, values of the probability below the anchor are weighted in imagination more heavily than those above, and the cross-over point lies below $p_A = 0.5$. In figure 11.1b, values above the anchor are weighted more heavily than those below. Here the cross-over point lies above 0.5. In figure 11.1c, values above and below the anchor are weighted equally such that the crossover occurs at 0.5.

To summarize, the ambiguity function shows overweighting of small anchor values but underweighting of larger ones. The point at which the function changes from over- to underweighting depends on the person's attitude towards ambiguity. For example, assuming that people are generally cautious in the face of risk (or engage in something akin to 'defensive pessimism', Norem and Cantor, 1986), the ambiguity function would resemble that shown in figure 11.1a if the decision-maker is concerned with the possibility of obtaining a positive outcome. On the other hand, when faced with the possibility of a loss (e.g., when assessing the risk of a new technology), the function would be better represented by figure 11.1b. This is because caution induces greater concern for possible values of the probability lying below rather than above the anchor in the case of potential gains, whereas the contrary holds for losses. We also argue that the location of the cross-over point will be affected by the degree of caution engendered by the situation. Thus, when facing the ambiguous chance of gaining a very large sum of money, the cross-over point will be closer to $p_A = 0$ than in a case where a small sum is involved. Similarly, when faced with a large potential loss, the cross-over point will be closer to $p_A = 1$ than in a situation involving a small loss.

IMPLICATIONS

An important implication of the ambiguity model is that, relative to anchor probabilities, it does not predict that people will always avoid situations characterized by ambiguous probabilities. Indeed, in some cases people will prefer ambiguity, specifically when faced with either a small probability of a gain (as in figure 11.1a) or a large probability of a loss (as in figure 11.1b). In addition, there will be cases where people are relatively insensitive to the effects of ambiguity, i.e., when the anchor probability is in the region of the cross-over point.

We now describe three experiments in which we exploit the model's implications concerning attitudes towards ambiguity. The experiments are set in three different settings. The first concerns the effects of ambiguity on the purchase and sale of insurance; the second involves a legal decision-making situation; and the third deals with the purchase and sale of industrial equipment. The intention of the experiments is to explore how ambiguity affects competitive situations by having differential impacts on opposing parties. In particular, does asymmetry in the manner in which ambiguity affects the two sides of a decision or transaction confer competitive advantage on one of the parties?

		CONSUMERS	
		Non-ambiguous	Ambiguous
FIRMS	Non-ambiguous	Well-known processes (1)	Typical situation (2)
	Ambiguous	New technologies – inside information for consumers (3)	New technologies – processes poorly understood (4)

Figure 11.2   Classification of insurance situations. *Source*: L. H. J. Hogarth, 1986, 'Decision making under ambiguity', *The Journal of Business*, ...4(2), S225–S250.

Experiment 1

Rationale   In traditional economic analysis of insurance markets (based on the theory of decision-making under uncertainty), two variables are relevant in the pricing of insurance. These are the probability of a potential loss occurring (e.g., the probability of an automobile accident), and the amount of the loss (e.g., the magnitude of the damage). It is further assumed that insurance is bought and sold because buyers (consumers) are more risk averse than sellers (insurance firms) reflecting different levels of wealth (your insurance company is wealthier than you are!). However, we shall argue that the purchase and sale of insurance can also be affected by ambiguity in ways that are not accounted for by the standard theory.

To simplify the analysis, imagine that consumers and firms either are or are not ambiguous about the probability relevant to an insurance contract. These possibilities can be represented in the form of a 2×2 matrix as shown in figure 11.2 together with examples illustrating each cell. Next assume that both firms and consumers have the same anchor probabilities, p_A, but that firms exhibit greater caution in their attitude towards ambiguity than consumers. The rationale for the latter assumption is that there is an important asymmetry in attitude between accepting and transferring a risk. Specifically, compared to the person transferring risk, one would expect the person accepting risk (e.g., an insurer) to give more weight in imagination to possible values of the probability of loss that are greater than the anchor value (see also Thaler, 1980; Hershey, Kunreuther,

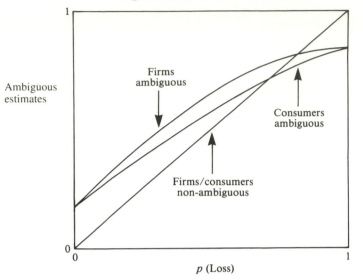

Figure 11.3 Ambiguity functions for insurance decision-making: firms and consumers. *Note*: When firms and consumers are not ambiguous, their ambiguity functions coincide on the diagonal (45° line. *Source*: H. J. Einhorn and R. M. Hogarth, 1985, 'Ambiguity and uncertainty in probabilistic inference', *Psychological Review*, 92, 433–61.

and Schoemaker, 1982). This asymmetry can be translated within the ambiguity model by showing different ambiguity functions for consumers and firms as illustrated in figure 11.3. Note from the figure that the ambiguity function for firms lies uniformly above that for consumers thereby indicating a more cautious attitude in the presence of ambiguity. When neither consumers nor firms are ambiguous, their respective ambiguity functions coincide with the diagonal (45°) line.

Several testable predictions are suggested by figure 11.3. First, consider situations where consumers are ambiguous. For low probabilities more weight is given to values above the anchor than those below; for high values of probability, the opposite is likely to be true. Comparing what consumers would be willing to pay in ambiguous as opposed to non-ambiguous situations, one would thus expect willingness to pay larger premiums under conditions of ambiguity for low probability events (i.e., to avoid ambiguity) but less willingness to buy insurance for high probability of loss events (i.e., exhibiting preference for ambiguity). Second, firms would want to charge higher premiums for ambiguity across most of the probability range. However, aversion to ambiguity would be expected to decrease as probabilities increase. Third, and as a corollary to the preceding, firms are generally expected to be more averse to ambiguity than consumers. We now turn to experimental tests of these predictions.

Subjects   There were two groups of subjects: 101 professional actuaries and 116 MBA students. The professional actuaries were members of the Casualty Actuarial Society and formed a subset of the members residing in North America who responded to different questionnaires as part of a mail survey conducted in 1986. (In total, 489 of 1,165 persons or 42 per cent of the membership provided usable responses in this survey. Mean length of experience as actuaries reported by the respondents was 13.8 years.) The MBA students responded to questionnaires handed out in a class on decision-making at the University of Chicago, Graduate School of Business. All these students had taken prior work in economics and statistics and were 'sophisticated' about the relevant issues, although clearly not as knowledgeable about insurance as the actuaries.

Stimuli and design   The experimental stimulus involved a scenario in which the owner of a small business with net assets of $110,000 seeks to insure against a $100,000 loss that could result from claims concerning a defective product. Subjects assigned the role of consumers were told to imagine that they were the owner of the business. Subjects assigned the role of firms were asked to imagine that they headed a department in a large insurance company and were authorized to set premiums for the level of risk involved. The question was worded to indicate a single risk.

Ambiguity was manipulated by factors involving how well the manufacturing process was understood, whether the reliabilities of the machines used in the process were known, and the state of the manufacturing records. In both ambiguous and non-ambiguous cases a specific probability level was stated (e.g., 0.01). However, a comment was also added as to whether one could 'feel confident' (non-ambiguous case) or 'experience considerable uncertainty' (ambiguous case) concerning the estimate. Uniformity of perceptions of ambiguity was controlled by describing the situations by the same words in both the consumer and firm versions.

Four variables were manipulated in the study. These were role (consumer or firm), ambiguity (ambiguous or non-ambiguous version of the stimulus), probability of loss ($p = 0.01$, 0.35, 0.65, 0.90), and type of respondent (actuaries or MBA students). Subjects were assigned the role of either consumer or firm. Consumers stated the maximum premiums they would be prepared to pay, whereas firms were asked to state the minimum premiums they would be prepared to charge. Each subject responded to both the ambiguous and non-ambiguous versions of the stimuli that related to his or her role but at only one probability level (i.e., responses at the different probability levels were made by different subjects). For the actuaries, the two versions (ambiguous and non-ambiguous) of the stimulus for this experiment were the first and last of several questions they were asked to answer. Each question appeared on a different page of the questionnaire and the order of the ambiguous and non-ambiguous versions was randomized across subjects. For the MBA subjects, the stimuli were included among a series of problems related to decision-making, each on a different page of an experimental booklet in which the ambiguous and non-ambiguous versions were also physically separated by several items. Subjects were instructed to work systematically through the booklet at their own pace without looking back at previous responses.

In summary, the design of the experiment involved four factors: three involved comparisons *between* subjects (i.e., role of consumer or firm, probability level, and type of respondent), and one *within* subjects (i.e., ambiguous versus non-ambiguous scenarios). There were 217 subjects; 10 actuaries and 116 MBA students.

Results   Table 11.1 summarizes the results of the experiment by showing the median prices in all experimental conditions. Medians are shown rather than means because several distributions within cells were quite skewed. Results conformed with predictions of the ambiguity model. Consumers were averse to ambiguity (as measured by willingness to pay higher prices) for low probability events; however, as the probability level increased, the attitude towards ambiguity changed from aversion to preference (compare columns 1 versus 2 for the actuaries, and 3 versus 4 for the MBA students). For firms, there is also aversion to ambiguity for low probability of loss events and the level of the aversion decreases as probabilities increase (compare columns 5 versus 6 for the actuaries, and 7 versus 8 for the students). Firms, however, never prefer ambiguity.

Second, there are differences between prices firms are willing to charge and how much consumers are willing to pay for given probability and loss levels. This is important because it suggests how ambiguity affects the ease with which transactions can be made in insurance markets. Consider the case where, for low probability of loss events, consumers are ambiguous but firms are not (e.g., automobile insurance where firms have statistical data on accidents and thefts which individuals lack. This is the prototypical case in which much insurance is sold – see the upper left cell in figure 11.2). Comparing the entries at the $p = 0.01$ level for columns 1 versus 6 (for the actuaries) and 3 versus 8 (for the MBA students), it is clear that consumers are prepared to pay much more than firms require. However, when firms also become ambiguous (compare columns 5 versus 1 and 7

Table 11.1. *Experiment 1: Median prices ($) of firms and consumers*
Loss = $100,000

		Consumers' willingness to pay					
		Actuaries			MBA students		
Probability of loss	(n)*	(1) Ambiguous $	(2) Non-ambiguous $	(n)	(3) Ambiguous $	(4) Non-ambiguous $	
0.01	(12)	5,000	2,500	(15)	1,500	1,000	
0.35	(14)	46,875	40,000	(15)	35,000	35,000	
0.65	(13)	75,000	65,000	(15)	50,000	65,000	
0.90	(10)	75,000	90,000	(14)	60,000	82,500	

		Firms' supply prices					
		Actuaries			MBA students		
Probability of loss	(n)	(5) Ambiguous $	(6) Non-ambiguous $	(n)	(7) Ambiguous $	(8) Non-ambiguous $	
0.01	(12)	5,000	1,550	(15)	2,500	1,000	
0.35	(10)	50,000	42,674	(14)	52,500	35,500	
0.65	(15)	80,250	70,000	(14)	70,000	65,000	
0.90	(15)	95,000	90,000	(14)	90,000	90,000	

Note: *(n) indicates number of subjects in experimental condition.
Source: R. M. Hogarth and H. Kunreuther, 'Risk, Ambiguity, and Insurance', *Journal of Risk and Uncertainty* 1989, 2, 5–35.

versus 3), it is not clear that it will be easy for consumers to find firms willing to supply insurance at prices they are willing to pay.

A third interesting comparison can be made between the responses of the actuaries and MBA students. On the one hand, the responses of both groups are qualitatively similar in the patterns of their reactions towards ambiguity. On the other hand, the actuaries' prices are generally higher than those of the students when ambiguity is held constant (compare columns 1 versus 3, 2 versus 4, 5 versus 7, and 6 versus 8). The reason for this result is unclear but suggests that actuaries have a greater appreciation of the risks underlying insurance contracts than MBA students and are therefore willing both to pay and charge more. Discussion with actuaries and their comments on the questionnaires revealed that they specifically considered ambiguity in the determination of premiums, taking the price over the level for non-ambiguous probabilities.

These observations are supported by statistical tests involving an appropriate analysis of a variance model with three between-subject factors (probability level, role, and type of subject), the within-subject factor of ambiguity, and the different possible between- and within-factor interactions. This analysis shows significant main effects for probability level ($p < 0.0001$), role (i.e., firm or consumer, $p < 0.0001$), type of subject ($p < 0.01$), and ambiguity ($p < 0.02$). Moreover, there are significant interactions with respect to probability level $\times$ role ($p < 0.0005$), ambiguity $\times$ probability level ($p < 0.0001$), ambiguity $\times$ role ($p < 0.0001$), and ambiguity $\times$ type of respondent ($p < 0.001$).

Experiment 2

Rationale Imagine a case of civil litigation where both plaintiff and defendant must decide whether to accept an out-of-court settlement or risk going to court. For the plaintiff, this decision is naturally framed as either accepting a sure sum (the settlement) or going to court with the possibility of gaining a larger sum or losing all. For the defendant, it is the reverse: either lose money for sure (the settlement) or go to court with the chance of losing either more or nothing. To continue the example, imagine that the two parties agree on both the probability that the plaintiff will win the case and the amount that each is prepared to pay the other to settle out of court. Assume further that this amount is equal to the expected value at stake in the court case. Ignoring consideration of legal costs, what actions do different choice theories predict would be taken by plaintiff and defendant?

The theory of decision-making under uncertainty predicts that, provided the plaintiff and the defendant are risk-averse and agree on the probability of the outcome of the case, they will both prefer to settle out of court (Gould, 1973). This contrasts with the predictions of prospect theory (Kahneman and Tversky, 1979), the leading alternative descriptive theory of decision-making under risk. These are that the plaintiff will take the risk-averse action (i.e., settle out of court) provided the probability of winning the case is not very small; the defendant, however, will take the risky action (i.e., go to court). And indeed, the prospect theory predictions have been upheld in experimental tests of this legal decision-making situation (Hogarth, 1987, chapter 5).

However, what happens if probabilities are ambiguous? First, note that neither the standard theory nor prospect theory make specific predictions concerning the effects of ambiguity. The ambiguity model makes the following predictions: (1) For plaintiffs, when probabilities of winning the case are moderate or large, ambiguity implies underweighting the anchor probabilities (see figure 11.1a) thereby encouraging the parties to settle out of court. In other words, under ambiguity plaintiffs will be more likely to choose the riskless option (i.e., settle out of court) than when probabilities are not ambiguous. (2) For defendants, the predictions are more complex. For high probability of loss events, ambiguous probabilities are underweighted relative to their anchors (see figure 11.1b) such that defendants would be expected to continue to take the risky option (go to court). Indeed, for high probability of loss events the model predicts greater risk seeking under ambiguity when probabilities are ambiguous as opposed to non-ambiguous. However, in the presence of ambiguity, the tendency to take the risky alternative will be reduced, relative to the non-ambiguous case, as the probability of losing the case decreases. This prediction follows from the implication that, for losses, there is over-weighting of anchor probabilities when these are small or moderate (see figure 11.1b). To summarize, defendants are predicted to exhibit risk-seeking behaviour at high probability of loss levels irrespective of ambiguity. At moderate probability levels, however, defendants with ambiguous information about probabilities will exhibit more risk-averse behaviour (i.e., settle out of court) than those with precise probability estimates. The following experiment was designed to test these predictions.

Subjects   Subjects were 80 MBA students at the University of Chicago taking a course in decision-making (these were *not* the same students as those in Experiment 1). As assignments given in the first and second weeks of the course, students were required to complete two questionnaires which contained several decision-making problems that were to be debriefed and discussed later in the course.

Task and method   Subjects were allocated at random to four experimental conditions that were created by crossing two kinds of role (plaintiff or defendant) by two types of probabilistic information (ambiguous or non-ambiguous). In addition, two levels of probability were varied as a within-subject factor by setting the probability of the plaintiff winning the trial at 0.80 in the first questionnaire, and at 0.50 in the second which was completed one week later.

The stimulus consisted of a short scenario which stated: whether the subject was the plaintiff or defendant; the amount at stake in the case (subjects were asked to imagine that this was $20,000 of their own money); an estimate by the party's lawyer of the probability that the case would be won by the plaintiff (see below); and knowledge supplied by each party's lawyer that the opposing party would settle for a given sum (minimum for the plaintiff, maximum for the defendant). This sum was $16,000 in the 0.80 probability condition, and $10,000 in the 0.50

condition. The scenario made no mention of the reasons underlying the litigation and subjects were instructed to ignore legal costs. Subjects were required to decide between accepting the out-of-court settlement (i.e., $16,000 or $10,000) or to risk going to court.

Ambiguity was manipulated in the scenarios by stating, in the ambiguous case, that in response to a query about the chances of winning or losing the case, the lawyer gave a best guess 'after some hesitation' and that 'given the nature of the case, he feels very uneasy about providing you with such a figure'. In contrast, the non-ambiguous version simply stated 'your lawyer believes there is a ... chance that ... '.

Results   Table 11.2 summarizes results of the experiment by reporting the percentages of subjects choosing to settle out of court in each experimental condition. Recall first that, for plaintiffs, the model predicts that ambiguity will act as a force towards risk aversion. For defendants, on the other hand, ambiguity is only expected to induce risk-averse behaviour at low or moderate probability levels, e.g., at 0.50 but not at 0.80. Results show that, at the 0.80 probability level, the vast majority of plaintiffs chose to settle out of court, whereas most defendants took the risky option of going to court. Moreover, there are no differences in responses due to ambiguity, 89 per cent versus 96 per cent for the plaintiffs, and 25 per cent versus 10 per cent for the defendants. However, note that, in the non-ambiguous condition, since almost all plaintiffs chose the riskless option and most defendants the risky option, choices could not be sensitive to effects of ambiguity.

At the 0.50 probability level, the pattern of responses for the plaintiffs is almost identical to that at 0.80 with, again, no effects for ambiguity. However this is not the case for defendants where the difference between the percentages of subjects wishing to settle out of court in the non-ambiguous and ambiguous conditions (6 versus 57) is significant ($\chi^2 = 3.63$, $df = 1$). In addition, whereas there is no statistically significant difference between responses of the same subjects in the non-ambiguous condition at the 0.80 and 0.50 probability levels (25 per cent versus 6 per cent), the difference between responses at these two probability levels in the ambiguous condition (10 per cent versus 57 per cent) is significant (Cochran's test, $Q = 10.00$, $df = 1$, $p = 0.0016$). These results clearly support the predictions of the ambiguous model (for further details, see Hogarth, 1989).

Experiment 3

Rationale   The preceding experiment examined situations involving two parties (defendants and plaintiffs) facing risky situations involving only

Table 11.2. *Experiment 2: Percentages of subjects choosing to settle out of court in different conditions*

Probability level	Percentages of subjects choosing to settle		
	0.80	0.50	(n)*
Plaintiffs			
Non-ambiguous	89	89	(19)
Ambiguous	96	83	(24)
Defendants			
Non-ambiguous	25	6	(16)
Ambiguous	10	57	(21)

Note: *(n) indicates number of subjects in experimental condition.
Source: R. M. Hogarth, 'Ambiguity and Competitive Decision Making: Some Implications and Tests', in P. C. Fishburn and I. H. La Valle (eds.), *Annals of Operations Research*, 1989, 19, 31–50.

losses or gains. It is therefore also instructive to consider what happens when two parties face risky situations involving both possible losses *and* gains. Of particular interest are situations where the structure of a transaction is such that ambiguity has differential effects on the evaluations made by the two parties. Specifically, if ambiguity has little effect on the evaluation made by one party, but does affect the other, competitive advantages can accrue to one of the parties.

To explore this possibility, consider situations where two parties are on opposing sides of transactions that can be thought of as involving risky choices of the following type:

> Party A has: a large probability of a modest gain, and
> a small probability of a large loss.
> Party B has: a large probability of a modest loss, and
> a small probability of a large gain.

To be specific, describe A's situation as involving a 0.9 chance of winning $2,000 accompanied by a 0.1 chance of losing $8,000, and B's situation as a 0.9 chance of losing $2,000 accompanied by a 0.1 chance of winning $8,000.

To evaluate the effects of ambiguity on the situations faced by A and B, recall that figure 11.1a represents a typical ambiguity function for gains, whereas figure 11.1b depicts one associated with losses. This implies that, for party A, an ambiguous 0.9 chance of gaining $2,000 will be evaluated as less attractive than if the 0.9 chance were not ambiguous (see figure 11.1a); in addition, an ambiguous 0.1 chance of losing $8,000 will be evaluated as more aversive than a 0.1 chance that is not ambiguous (see figure 11.1b). In other words, the model predicts that the situation faced by party A is sensitive to the effects of ambiguity. Specifically, since both the loss and gain components of party A's transaction are affected negatively by ambiguity, party A will evaluate the potential transaction as less attractive in the presence of ambiguity.

In contrast to the predictions for party A, the model predicts that party B will be relatively insensitive to the effects of ambiguity. The reason is that the structure of party B's transaction is such that the $S(p_A)$ values associated with the potential loss of \$2,000 and the potential gain of \$8,000 are liable to be in the regions of their respective cross-over points. To see this, consider figure 11.1b for losses and note that, for a large probability (0.9) of a loss, $S(p_A) \approx p_A$. Similarly, for a small probability (0.1) of a gain, note from figure 11.1a that $S(p_A) \approx p_A$. To be more precise, the ambiguity model does not make clear predictions for party B in that it does not specify the exact locations of the cross-over points for losses and gains. However, the net effect of ambiguity on party B's combination of potential loss and gain implies less sensitivity to ambiguity than party A. For example, the structure of party B's transaction could imply contrary forces towards ambiguity, i.e., ambiguity aversion for the gain component and ambiguity seeking for losses. Alternatively, party B might be ambiguity neutral with respect to one component of the gamble, but not the other; and so on.

To summarize, the model predicts that, whereas ambiguity will lead party A to evaluate the transaction less favourably, it will have less impact on the evaluation made by party B. The following experiment was designed to test this prediction.

Subjects and procedure   Subjects were managers in life insurance companies who were attending a residential, professional seminar. They were sophisticated in economic matters and were primarily employed in managing investment portfolios. Their median age was 39. The evening prior to attending a lecture on 'Perceptions of risk', the managers were asked to complete a questionnaire in booklet form (requiring about thirty minutes), the results of which were to be discussed at the lecture. The task was done on an individual basis with managers submitting their completed questionnaires to the course organizers by a specified time. The task described below was included on a separate page in the experimental booklet. Approximately 160 questionnaires were distributed; usable responses were received from 137 managers.

Task and design   The design of the experiment involved four conditions created by crossing two between-subject factors each with two levels. The factors were role (buyers and sellers, see below) and ambiguity. The latter was made operational by two versions of the experimental stimuli where the probabilities of the relevant events were given in either ambiguous or non-ambiguous form. Subjects were allocated at random to the four cells of the 2 × 2 design.

The scenario used in this experiment involved the purchase and sale of industrial equipment valued at about $100,000. Buyers had the opportunity of obtaining the equipment from one of two suppliers (Alpha and Beta) who differed in respect of their terms of sale. Alpha's price included a warranty against a specific type of breakdown. Beta did not offer a warranty but was willing to sell at a discount relative to Alpha. The problem was structured so that the buyer was asked to consider Beta's offer as involving a potential gain of $2,000 (the discount) against a potential loss of $8,000, where the latter was the difference between the $10,000 cost of repairing the breakdown (should it occur) and the $2,000 discount.

In the seller version of the questionnaire, subjects were told that, although their usual policy was to sell machinery with warranties against specific breakdowns, a customer had requested to forgo the warranty for a $2,000 discount. This was described as 'a one-shot deal and would have no repercussions on the rest of your business'. The net effect of the deal was described as 'if you sell the machine with a discount, you are facing a potential loss of $2,000 if no breakdown occurs during the warranty period (i.e., the amount of the discount). However, you also stand to gain $8,000 if a breakdown occurs (i.e., you would save repair costs of $10,000 but allow a discount of $2,000).'

Ambiguity was manipulated in the same manner in both the buyer and seller versions of the scenarios. In the ambiguous case, the machinery being sold was described as being 'based on new design principles' and that, although there was a 'best estimate' of the probability of a breakdown within the warranty period, 'you experience considerable uncertainty about this estimate'. In the non-ambiguous version, subjects were told that 'extensive records' existed concerning the machine's breakdown record and that 'you can confidently estimate the probability of a breakdown occurring within the warranty period'. The anchor probability of the breakdown occurring within the warranty period was given as 0.1 (for both buyers and sellers).

Subjects made two responses to the scenario. Buyers were required to choose between Alpha (i.e., buy with warranty but no discount) or Beta (no warranty but discount). In addition, they were asked to state 'the minimum discount they would be prepared to accept to buy the equipment without the warranty'. Sellers were asked whether they would sell the machinery 'at a discount of $2,000 but with no warranty' or 'without the discount but with the warranty'. Their second question was 'What is

Table 11.3. *Experiment 3: Preferences and discounts of buyers and sellers*

| | Buyers | | Sellers | |
| | Ambiguous | Non-ambiguous | Ambiguous | Non-ambiguous |
Preferences	%	%	%	%
For discount	36	68	53	39
warranty	64	32	47	61
	100	100	100	100
n =	36	28	40	33
Stated discounts	$	$	$	$
Minimum for buyers,				
maximum for sellers				
Medians:	5,000	2,000	1,375	1,000
Means:	4,049	3,011	1,986	1,580

Source: R. M. Hogarth, 'Ambiguity and Competitive Decision Making: Some Implications and Tests', in P. C. Fishburn and I. H. La Valle (eds.), *Annals of Operations Research*, 1989, 19, 31–50.

the maximum discount you would be prepared to grant if you were to sell the machinery without the warranty?'

Results   Following the rationale given above, recall that we predicted that, whereas the buyer's decision should be sensitive to ambiguity, this would not be the case for the seller. Table 11.3 presents the results of the experiment in terms of (a) responses concerning preferences for discounts versus warranties and (b) minimum (for buyers) and maximum (for sellers) amounts that the parties would accept (for buyers) or grant (for sellers) in lieu of a warranty.

Consider first the data in respect of preferences for discounts versus warranties. For buyers, whereas 64 per cent of subjects chose the warranty in the ambiguous condition, the corresponding figure was 32 per cent in the non-ambiguous condition ($\chi^2 = 6.35, df = 1, p < 0.02$). In other words, choices made by buyers were consistent with avoiding ambiguity. For sellers, however, whereas 47 per cent chose the warranty in the ambiguous condition, this figure is 61 per cent in the non-ambiguous condition and the difference is not statistically significant ($\chi^2 = 1.28, df = 1$). To summarize, buyers (party A) were sensitive to ambiguity in this situation as predicted whereas sellers (party B) were not.

Results of the choice data are supported by estimates of minimum (for buyers) and maximum (for sellers) discounts. Median and mean discounts stated by buyers in the ambiguous condition exceed those in the non-ambiguous condition, $5,000 versus $2,000 and $4,049 versus $3,011, respectively. The difference between medians is statistically significant ($p < 0.05$, one-tailed Mann-Whitney test) although the difference between means is not ($t = 1.39, p = 0.086$, one-tailed test). Differences between the mean and median discounts of sellers in the ambiguous and non-ambiguous conditions are both small and statistically insignificant.

DISCUSSION

We first comment on the three experiments reported above and then suggest a framework for an agenda of future research on the effects of ambiguity in decision-making under uncertainty.

The experiments illustrate different aspects of the ways in which ambiguity and role affect decision-making under uncertainty. In Experiment 1, we demonstrated the effects of ambiguity on the purchase and sale of insurance. Although the prices stated by both firms (i.e., sellers) and consumers were sensitive to ambiguity, the two parties differed in their reactions to ambiguity. Firms were generally more averse to ambiguity than consumers. In particular, whereas aversion to ambiguity decreased with increases in the probability of a loss for both firms and consumers, firms never reached the point where they would accept to insure an ambiguous risk for a price less than a non-ambiguous risk with an equivalent anchor probability. Consumers, on the other hand, did show preferences for ambiguity in that they were *not* prepared to pay as much to insure an ambiguous as opposed to non-ambiguous risk when the probability of loss was high.

In addition to illustrating the conditions under which people are averse to or prefer ambiguity, these results help to illuminate some aspects of insurance markets that have puzzled scholars working within the tradition of the classic model of decision-making under uncertainty. One of these puzzles concerns why so many travellers purchase 'flight' insurance at airports even though prices greatly exceed the rates of readily available life insurance (Eisner and Strotz, 1961). There may be a number of reasons why consumers are interested in purchasing such insurance. Whereas the chance of an accident during a particular flight is small, it is ambiguous. Furthermore, when accidents do occur, media coverage is typically extensive such that it is easy to imagine scenarios under which accidents can happen. In short, given an event with an ambiguous probability and the ease with which disastrous scenarios can be imagined, the ambiguity model clearly predicts large upward adjustments of the implicit decision weights associated with the decision to buy flight insurance.

The results of Experiment 1 also shed light on the conditions under which insurance can or cannot be easily acquired by consumers. When both firms and consumers are ambiguous, consumers will have difficulty in finding firms offering insurance at prices they are prepared to pay. On the other hand, for low probability events where consumers are ambiguous, but firms are not, there will be an active market for coverage. Consider, for example, home (theft and fire) and life insurance. For most of us, the probabilities of losses in these domains are experienced as being both low and ambiguous. For insurance companies, on the other hand, the probabilities of these events can be estimated precisely from statistics and there is no ambiguity.

In Experiment 2, we examined how ambiguity affects risk taking in the context of a legal decision-making situation. Our starting point was the asymmetry in risk attitudes predicted by Kahneman and Tversky's (1979) descriptive theory of decision-making under risk. In short, this theory predicts that people tend to be risk averse when faced with risky situations involving gains but risk seeking in the face of potential losses. Translated to the legal scenario examined in the experiment, this means that, whereas plaintiffs (who face potential gains) will have a strong tendency to seek settlements out of court, defendants (who face possible losses) will prefer to take their chances by going to court. However, this analysis ignores the effects of ambiguity and does not square with the empirical observation that the vast majority of civil suits in the USA are in fact settled out of court thereby implying that this option is preferred by both plaintiffs and defendants (cf. Gould, 1973).

In our analysis, we predicted that, for moderate anchor probabilities (about 0.5), the behaviour of defendants would be more cautious in the presence of ambiguity thereby counteracting the tendency to go to court. And indeed, this was what was observed and suggests that, in the presence of ambiguity, parties to civil litigation will typically prefer to settle out of court. Moreover, since most people lack experience with civil litigation and are, perforce, ambiguous about the chances of winning their cases, the ambiguity model provides a rationale for why most cases are in fact settled out of court. We note, parenthetically, that understanding the effects of ambiguity in situations such as these could be important in different types of negotiations. For example, building on Kahneman and Tversky's (1979) work, it has been suggested that in bargaining situations one might be able to exploit asymmetries in risk attitudes towards losses and gains by being able to 'second-guess' the decisions of an opponent (see, e.g., Bazerman, 1983; Hogarth, 1987, chapter 5). Thus in a situation such as our court scenario, a plaintiff could construct his or her bargaining strategy assuming that the defendant would tend to be risk seeking. However, in the presence of ambiguity, this assumption could well be erroneous.

Experiments 1 and 2 illustrated how ambiguity affects certain kinds of decisions and showed that, whereas people tend to avoid ambiguity, there are also situations in which ambiguity is preferred. Experiment 3 demonstrated a further phenomenon. Two parties can be on opposite sides of a transaction that is affected by ambiguity. However, ambiguity only affects the way one but not both parties evaluate the situation. Although the particular task examined in Experiment 3 involved the purchase and sale of industrial equipment, the paradigm of two parties being on opposite sides of a transaction where both could stand to gain or lose (as opposed to only gain or lose) has more general application. One area is the market for protective services where people can hedge risks by different means. Consider, for example, trading in financial instruments, e.g., stocks, bonds, commodities, futures, options, and portfolio insurance. As shown in Experiment 3, if people put themselves into a situation where they have a large probability of gaining a small amount and a small probability of losing a large amount, ambiguity will impact negatively on their position. However, by taking a position that involves a large probability of losing a small amount accompanied by a small probability of gaining a large amount, the subjective evaluation of the position will not be affected by ambiguity. It would be interesting to ascertain empirically what kinds of professional traders tend to structure deals for themselves that are more similar to the first or second type of situation, and whether this leads to strategic advantages in buying and selling. For example, do individuals differ in the types of trades they undertake for different types of institutions?

In summary, we have demonstrated that by incorporating the effects of ambiguity into more traditional models of decision-making under uncertainty we can model and predict many interesting real-world phenomena. In particular, we have shown that attitudes towards ambiguity are largely determined by characteristics of situations people face and/or the roles they are asked to assume and that people do not necessarily exhibit only aversion to ambiguity. However, from a descriptive viewpoint, people face other ambiguities aside from probabilities in decision-making. To illustrate, consider the following scenario:

You receive a telephone call from the department store where you purchased a refrigerator two years ago. The caller informs you that the warranty on your refrigerator has expired and asks whether you wish to renew it an annual rate of $50. The only further information supplied is the minimum cost of labor for someone to visit your home should your refrigerator malfunction ($35). The warranty would cover the costs of both labor and parts. You are quite vague, even ignorant, about the chances of your refrigerator breaking down; you also find it difficult to estimate the costs of possible repairs.

As this scenario illustrates, even in a relatively simple situation involving the purchase of a warranty, decision-makers can experience ambiguity,

Table 11.4. *Situations arising from different levels of knowledge concerning probabilities and outcomes*

		Knowledge about probabilities		
		Known	Ambiguous	Ignorant
Knowledge about outcomes	Known	1	2	3
	Ambiguous	4	5	6
	Ignorant	7	8	9

not only with respect to probabilities, but also with respect to the amounts at stake or outcomes. Moreover, if we define ambiguity as resulting from lack of knowledge of probabilities and outcomes, then it should be clear that there can be a continuum extending from complete knowledge to complete ignorance, for both probabilities and outcomes.

Dividing these continua for probabilities and outcomes into three sections representing 'knowledge', 'ambiguity', and 'ignorance', therefore, we can define a 3 × 3 matrix of situations involving different levels of partial knowledge as illustrated in table 11.4.

Table 11.4 contains nine cells or types of situations for relatively simple kinds of decision tasks. Descriptive work had really only considered two cells, number 1 where both probabilities and outcomes are assumed to be known (as in the classic model of decision-making under uncertainty), and number 2 where, although outcomes are assumed known, knowledge about probabilities is ambiguous (the case considered in this chapter). However, as illustrated in the refrigerator scenario considered above, there must also be many real-life situations that involve the other seven cells of table 11.4.

Building on the work described in this chapter, therefore, table 11.4 suggests a rich agenda for research on understanding the effects of ambiguity and ignorance on decision-making. Contrast, for example, decisions in cell 9 ('Ignorant' – 'Ignorant') with decisions in cells 1 or 2. How does one take risky decisions when lacking even rough estimates of probabilities or outcomes (consider again the refrigerator scenario, above)? What models might best describe behaviour in these kinds of situations? What are the effects of ambiguity concerning outcomes over and above ambiguity with respect to probabilities? Does role (e.g., buyer versus seller) affect ambiguity concerning outcomes in the same manner as ambiguity concerning probabilities? Does ambiguity regarding probabilities of losses help explain the limited interest by insurers in marketing policies such as pollution insurance, earthquake coverage, and political risk protection? These are fascinating and open questions. They are also the kinds of questions we shall be addressing in future research.

NOTE

The research for this chapter was supported by a contract from the Office of Naval Research and grants from the Sloan Foundation and the National Science Foundation. The chapter summarizes work reported in several previous publications notably Einhorn and Hogarth (1985, 1986), Hogarth (1987, 1989), and Hogarth and Kunreuther (1985, 1989).

REFERENCES

Bazerman, M. (1983), 'Negotiator judgment', *American Behavioral Scientist*, **27**, 211–28.

Einhorn, H. J. and Hogarth, R. M. (1981), 'Behavioral decision theory: processes of judgment and choice', *Annual Review of Psychology*, **32**, 53–88.

(1985), 'Ambiguity and uncertainty in probabilistic inference', *Psychological Review*, **93**, 433–61.

(1986), 'Decision making under ambiguity', *Journal of Business*, **59** (4: 2), S225–S250.

Eisner, R. and Strotz, R. H. (1961), 'Flight insurance and the theory of choice', *Journal of Political Economy*, **69**, 355–68.

Ellsberg, D. (1961), 'Risk, ambiguity, and the Savage axioms', *Quarterly Journal of Economics*, **75**, 643–69.

Fishburn, P. C. (1988), *Nonlinear Preference and Utility Theory* (Baltimore, MD: The Johns Hopkins University).

Gould, J. P. (1973), 'The economics of legal conflicts', *Journal of Legal Studies*, **11**, 279–300.

Hershey, J. C., Kunreuther, H. C., and Schoemaker, P. H. H. (1982), 'Sources of bias in assessment procedures for utility functions', *Management Science*, **28**(8), 936–54.

Hogarth, R. M. (1987), *Judgement and Choice: The Psychology of Decision* (2nd edn) (Chichester: Wiley).

(1989), 'Ambiguity and competitive decision making: some implications and tests', in P. C. Fishburn and I. H. La Valle (eds.), *Annals of Operations Research*, **19**, 31–50.

Hogarth, R. M. and Einhorn, H. J. (1990), 'Venture theory: a model of decision weights', *Management Science*, **36**.

Hogarth, R. M. and Kunreuther, H. (1985), 'Ambiguity and insurance decisions', *American Economic Association Papers and Proceedings*, **75**, 386–90.

(1989), 'Risk, ambiguity, and insurance', *Journal of Risk and Uncertainty*, **2**, 5–35.

Kahneman, D. and Tversky, A. (1979), 'Prospect theory: An analysis of decision under risk', *Econometrica*, **47**, 263–91.

Keeney, R. L. and Raiffa, H. (1976), *Decisions with Multiple Objectives: Preferences and Value Tradeoffs* (New York: Wiley).

Machina, M. J. (1987), 'Choice under uncertainty: Problems solved and unsolved', *Economic Perspectives*, 1(1), 121–54.

Norem, J. K. and Cantor, N. (1986), 'Anticipatory and post hoc cushioning strategies: Optimism and defensive pessimism in "risky" situations', *Cognitive Theory and Research*, 10, 347–62.

Savage, L. J. (1954), *The Foundations of Statistics* (New York: Wiley).

Slovic, P., Fischhoff, B., and Lichtenstein, S. (1988), 'Decision making', in R. C. Atkinson, R. J. Herrnstein, and R. D. Luce (eds.), *Handbook of Experimental Psychology: vol. II: Learning and Cognition* (New York: Wiley), pp. 673–738.

Thaler, R. H. (1980), 'Toward a positive theory of consumer choice', *Journal of Economic Behavior and Organization*, 1, 39–60.

Tversky, A. and Kahneman, D. (1974), 'Judgment under uncertainty: heuristics and biases', *Science*, 185, 1124–31.

von Neumann, J. and Morgenstern, O. (1947), *Theory of Games and Economic Behavior* (2nd edn) (Princeton, NJ: Princeton University Press).

Weber, M. and Camerer, C. (1987), 'Recent developments in modelling preferences under risk', *OR Spektrum*, 9, 129–51.

12

JUDGMENT AND DECISION-MAKING

GEORGE WRIGHT, FERGUS BOLGER, AND GENE ROWE

ABSTRACT

This chapter overviews research on the quality of human judgement and decision making. Early research in the psychological laboratory is compared and contrasted with studies of 'expert' judgement. Since judgement is a fundamental input to decision-aiding technologies it follows that a careful evaluation of demonstrations of judgemental bias is important. If judgemental biases and limitations are prevalent it then becomes important to focus evaluation on ways to improve, or debias, judgement. In this review, we assess a variety of approaches to the problem of improving judgement in decision-making and forecasting contexts.

INTRODUCTION

This chapter looks at current research on human judgement. Judgement is a prime input to decision-aiding technologies such as decision analysis and is often used to 'adjust' the output of statistically based forecasting models. Indeed, good judgement and decision-making are seen as major management capabilities.

Interest in the capabilities of human judgement in decision-making became a focus of cognitive psychologists in the 1950s, when Ward Edwards (1955) introduced them to what was, essentially, an economic decision theory. Decision theory basically proposes that two independent types of information are crucial in making good decisions: subjective probabilities attached to the events occurring and subjective values or utilities attached to outcomes of those events at some time in the future. Normative decision theory specifies how subjective probabilities and utilities should be combined to specify optimal decisions (see Wright, 1984, Hogarth, 1987 and Dawes, 1988 for reviews of the behavioural literature and Watson and Buede, 1987, and VonWinterfeldt and Edwards 1986 for more numerical treatments of the intersection of the psychological research and the normative theory). The essential rationale of decision theory is that it improves decision-making by making the best use of the (usually) subjective information the decision-maker possesses, *not* by providing the decision-maker with additional information. This is achieved by dividing a decision problem into its component parts (subjective probabilities and utilities) and recomposing in a normative manner. The simple logic behind this approach is that human decision-makers have limited information processing capacity and so are not able to do all the calculations required by decision theory in their heads. Questions addressed by psychologists working in the general area of decision theory have had to do with evaluation of the quality of the inputs to decision theory and also with comparisons of the prescriptions of decision theory with holistic judgements and decisions (see Wright 1984 for a review of the early research).

In this chapter, we will give an overview of research on human judgement that has concerned us particularly. The issue has to do with the overall quality of human judgement. We shall detail early research in the psychological laboratory and contrast it with studies of expert judgement in real-world contexts. Is human judgement flawed? If it is then both holistic decisions and the required inputs to decision theory need close scrutiny in practice. If judgement is flawed, can biases and limitations be ameliorated in any way? As we shall see, these apparently simple questions are not easily answered.

First we shall trace the history of psychological research on the validity of judgement from the early laboratory studies to more recent research focussing on judgement in real-world work-a-day contexts. In the latter studies, the nature of expert judgement is a major topic of interest. Finally we evaluate procedures and methods for improving the quality of human judgement.

LABORATORY STUDIES

One line of research that has been concerned with the quality of human judgement of probability has stemmed from the work of Tversky and Kahneman (1974). In a major series of papers they outlined some of the *heuristics* that people use for probability assessment. Tversky and Kahneman have demonstrated that we judge the probability of an event by the ease with which relevant information of that event is imagined. Instances of frequent events are typically easier to recall than instances of less frequent events. Thus *availability* is often a valid cue for the assessment of probability. However, since availability is also influenced by factors unrelated to likelihood, such as familiarity, recency, and emotional saliency, reliance on it *may* result in systematic biases. For example, greater media coverage of death by lung cancer leads us to believe that it is a more likely cause of death than stomach cancer. However, in reality, the latter cause is twice as likely as the former. Other heuristics identified by Tversky and Kahneman which may result in biased judgement include *anchoring and adjustment and representativeness*. Anchoring and adjustment refers to a tendency to 'anchor' on a first estimate and then make insufficient 'adjustment' to this initial assessment. For example, one study discovered that people who find gambles basically attractive use the amount to win as a natural starting point in evaluation. They then adjust the amount to win downward to take into account the less-than-perfect chance of winning and the possibility of losing a small amount. Representativeness refers to the dominance of individuating information in intuitive prediction. Here, base-rate information, say on the proportion of football fans who are actually involved in violence at football matches, is downplayed relative to the stereotype of a football fan.

Another paradigm which has been used extensively in laboratory studies of judgement is the measurement of *calibration*. For a person to be perfectly calibrated, his or her subjective assessment of the probability of outcomes should equal the probability calculated on the basis of the actual frequency of those outcomes. A general finding of such experiments is that subjects are *overconfident*. In other words, for a set of events each assessed as having a certain probability of occurrence, say 0.8, less than that probability, say 0.6, actually occur (see Lichtenstein, Fischhoff, and Phillips, 1981, for a review). Other laboratory-based research has argued that it is a misunderstanding of the laws of probability which leads subjects to make unreliable and/or inconsistent estimates of probability and, consequently, results in poor calibration (see Wright, Ayton, and Whalley, 1985; Wright, Saunders, and Ayton, 1988). Subjective probabilities which fail to conform to the axioms of probability theory are said to be *incoherent*. Such findings have led some writers to suggest either training judges in the laws of probability, or providing them with decision support, in order to ensure the coherence of probabilities entered into decision analysis (see Wright and Ayton, 1987).

In general, the conclusion from these laboratory studies is that human judgement is sub-optimal in many respects:

This work has led to the sobering conclusion that, in the face of uncertainty, man may be an intellectual cripple, whose intuitive judgements and decisions violate many of the fundamental principles of optimal behavior. (Slovic, 1982)

However, most of the laboratory-based research has used student subjects who have been required to complete novel paper and pencil tasks within short time periods. Such research has been criticized by Beach, Christensen-Szalanski, and Barnes (1987) as potentially having limited generalizability to work-a-day judgement and decision-making.

More recently the research emphasis has moved away from the psychological laboratory to *ecologically valid* studies of judgement and decision-making by people who care, in situations that matter. The focus has, therefore, been turned to the study of professional experts.

STUDIES OF EXPERT JUDGEMENT

There is some evidence to suggest that the laboratory finding that decision theory does not describe human decision-making, generalizes to non-laboratory situations. For example, Lichtenstein and Slovic (1971) demonstrated that patrons of the 'Four Queens Casino' in Las Vegas were inconsistent in their choice of gambles. Similarly, a number of other studies have demonstrated that professionals do not always select the most appropriate information as the basis for their decisions. For example, a study of Ebbesen and Konecni (1980) of court judges' sentencing decisions found that judges used only a very restricted subset of available dimensions when making their decisions. Further, Gaeth and Shanteau (1984) found that expert soil judges, when categorizing samples, referred to soil materials which were irrelevant to the discriminations they were trying to make.

More positively, other research has shown that some experts are good, relative to novices, at selecting relevant information and utilizing it. For example, Phelps (1977) found that expert livestock judges extract information which novices overlook. Further, Ettensen, Krugstad, and Shanteau (1985) found that expert auditors have an 'enhanced capacity to get to the crux of the problem' in comparison to novices, while Dino (1984) found experts to be better than novices at knowing which problems are soluble and which are not.

More negatively, several judgemental biases have been demonstrated in professionals. For example, in a study of estate agents, Northcraft and Neale (1987) found that deliberately arbitrary valuations tendered by property owners influenced both estate agents' and students' subsequent property valuations thereby demonstrating the *anchoring and adjustment* heuristic. *Availability* of information has also been shown to affect the judgements of experts in the same way as non-experts. For example, research by Christensen-Szalanski, Beck, and Koepsell (1983) found that expert physicians overestimated the risk of certain diseases in a similar manner to a comparison group of students. The source of this particular bias was identified as being the physicians' exposure to patients suffering from the diseases in question.

In support of the positive validity of judgement, good *calibration* has been found amongst experts in a number of domains. For example, Kabus (1976) found bankers to be fairly well calibrated in their predictions of future interest rates. Balthasar, Boschi, and Menke (1978) obtained reasonably well calibrated judgements regarding the success of R and D projects. Also in studies of weather forecasters (Murphy and Brown, 1985), bridge players (Keren, 1987) and horse racing bettors (Hoerl and Falbin, 1974) probability estimates were again well calibrated.

WHY THE CONTRADICTORY FINDINGS OF EXPERTISE RESEARCH?

As we have indicated in the previous section, the 'ecologically valid' studies of judgements by people who care in situations which matter have produced somewhat contradictory findings. Both 'good' and 'bad' judgement has been demonstrated among experts: weather forecasters, bridge players, merchant bankers, and bookies are amongst those exhibiting high performance, while clinicians, personnel selectors, and corn and legal judges demonstrate low judgemental performance. However, the overall impression from the literature is that, in general, expert judgement is sub-optimal and that experts exhibit the same biases as naive subjects. However, there are reasons to question such a conclusion which centres around the issue of whether many of the studies are truly 'ecologically valid'.

In some instances expert performance has been tested outside the particular experts' domain of professional experience. For example, clinicians have been asked to make predictions rather than the diagnoses normally required of them (e.g., Oskamp, 1962; Christensen-Szalanski *et al.*, 1983; Manu, Runge, Lee, and Oppenheim, 1984). Corn judges have been required to predict yield on the basis of an examination of ears of maize, whereas their usual task is to judge the aesthetic qualities of ears presented at shows (Hughes, 1917; Wallace, 1923). Further, restaurant managers have been asked to make judgements about various causes of restaurant failure, many of which they have had no immediate experience (Dube-Rioux and Russo, 1988). It can be argued that in these cases the expert is at no particular advantage over naive subjects and, therefore, liable to the same deficiencies in judgement.

In other studies experts have been required to express judgements in unfamiliar metrics. For example, grain inspectors have been asked to identify percentages of foreign material in samples where they are used to estimating weight of these materials (Trumbo *et al.*, 1962). Also probability estimates have been elicited from R and D managers for the success of pharmaceutical projects over a five to ten year period when they are familiar only with identifying particular successful projects on a year to year basis (Balthasar *et al.*, 1978).

A third reason to question the ecological validity of some expertise research is that the subjects may not have been sufficiently experienced to qualify as 'experts'. The authors of the majority of papers we have reviewed do not specify the professional qualifications of their chosen experts, nor do they specify the length of time spent 'on the job', or describe the nature of the subjects' work duties in any detail. In no instance have we found an attempt to objectively screen potential subjects for expertise. It, therefore, seems likely that, in most cases, expertise is attributed on the basis of role rather than proven performance.

In addition to problems of ecological validity it might also be the case that the nature of some of the task domains in which expertise has been examined is such as to preclude or hinder good judgemental performance. For example, if no feedback about the accuracy of judgement is available, or if there is feedback but it is meaningless or in some other way unusable then, however experienced the judge, s/he can never be any more accurate than a total novice.

From our examination of domains where expert performance has been found to be high, we propose that there are at least three major factors contributing to whether good expert judgement is attainable or not:

> the availability of accurate, relevant, and objective data and/or domain models upon which decisions can be based,
> the possibility of expressing judgements in a coherent and quantifiable manner,
> the existence of rapid and meaningful feedback about the accuracy of judgements.

Of these, we believe that the third, *feedback*, is the most crucial because, as we have already suggested, without usable feedback the decision-maker is unable to improve on his or her own judgemental performance. In order to be usable, feedback must be fairly immediate. A feedback loop of months, or even years, may give the expert little opportunity (or motivation) to revise his or her judgements. This is especially true if the nature of the decision problem changes over time as is the case in many real-world situations (e.g. the development of new drugs requires continual revision of mortality estimates). Keren (1987) also points out that items upon which judgements are made, an outcomes feedback, must be *related* in a way that permits future judgements to be informed by past judgements. In other words, the decision-maker must be able to refine his or her domain model on the basis of feedback received. Thirdly, as Einhorn (1980) makes clear, in many natural settings there is a causal link between judgements and their outcomes so feedback may be unreliable. In order to separate judgement from the effects of actions made on the basis of this judgement it is necessary to perform a controlled experiment. This is often impractical and/or too expensive in real-world situations. Task domains will vary in the degree to which actions based on judgements influence the subjects of the judgements themselves. Thus, for instance, in weather forecasting, a forecast of rain will not affect the probability of rain falling, but the prediction of future values of stocks and shares might in itself influence market trends. In general, a causal link between judgement and outcome will render feedback difficult to interpret and thereby reduce the learnability of the domain.

In summary, we propose that the contradictory findings of expertise research can be explained in terms of characteristics of the *person* making the judgements/decisions (P), the nature of the *situation* in which decisions are being made (S), and the interaction between these two factors ($P \times S$). Specifically, for good judgemental performance to be manifest it is important that:

The expert is experienced (P) at making the type of judgements asked for (S) which can broadly be labelled as the *ecological validity* of the tasks;

It is possible to master decision-making and judgement in the task domain in question by being able (P) to make use of feedback (S) to refine reliable domain models for subsequent judgement; this we term the *learnability* of the decision problem.

In situations where both ecological validity and learnability are high, then we predict that good judgemental performance will be demonstrated by experts. Conversely, in tasks where ecological validity is low and/or the same applies to learnability, then we predict poor judgemental performance in terms of accuracy and reliability. Where both ecological validity and learnability are low, we suggest that the 'expert' is essentially in the same position as naive subjects in laboratory studies. In such a situation, judges will have little or no knowledge relevant to the task in hand and will be forced to fall back upon the heuristics. As we have seen from the work of Tversky and Kahneman (1974), these heuristics can lead to sub-optimal and biased judgements. Our constructs of ecological validity and learnability can be used to analyse tasks so as to allow the identification of situations where judgement is likely to be poor.

IMPROVING PERFORMANCE IN JUDGEMENTAL TASKS

Thus far, from our discussion on the worth of human (and particularly, expert) judgement, we have been led to adopt the conclusion that the adequacy of judgement in decision-making contexts depends upon the interaction of 'person' and 'situation' factors. By analysing the specifics of any given decision-making environment, we may hypothesize as to when factors will allow judgement to be 'good' and when factors may point towards a limiting influence on the proficiency of judgement. This analysis of task environment is particularly important in cases where the presence of biased judgement may not be readily apparent. Such cases include those where the worth of judgement and subsequent decisions, are not easily verifiable, notably when comparative objective data do not exist (or, at least, will not exist for a period of time into the future) against which 'goodness' of decision may be matched.

Having established the presence (or possible presence) of bias, the next step must be to provide the means to correct or ameliorate its influence in order to increase the quality of decisions. However, it would be naive to expect there to be some blanket solution to all biases in all situations. The most appropriate response will vary according to the specifics of the bias and different alternatives may need to be considered before a final technique is selected. Indeed, Keren (1988) views this process of alleviating bias as analogous to medical diagnosis, the first stage being the identification of the characteristics and limitations of bias, followed by the assessment of various corrective procedures and culminating in the monitoring of the ultimately selected technique to ensure its effectiveness (and guarantee the absence of side effects such as other biases). Assuming that bias has already been detected, we turn now to address the possible techniques which may lead to its cure.

Unfortunately, no cookbook of solutions exists to point towards the most appropriate technique for the rectification of all – or even any biases. Considering the vast range of possible situations and influencing variables, it is doubtful whether any such reference manual (at least, a comprehensive one) *could* be produced. In the absence of such a text, the best we can do here is to elucidate some of the more salient findings of the debiasing literature and note some of the most common judgemental aids produced and, further, attempt to clarify where and when such procedures and tools *might* prove useful in the resolution of bias. In doing this, it seems to us that the possible approaches to debiasing readily fall into three major categories, namely: those techniques which seek to debias the judges by improving their cognitive skills, allowing them to retain the role of judge or decision-maker; those techniques which seek to replace the judge or decision-maker (to a greater or lesser extent) by mechanical or statistical procedures; and those preventive procedures which seek to circumvent bias by the selection of appropriate personnel. These categories should not be viewed as being mutually exclusive, since any particular technique or procedure may arguably straddle our selected boundaries, yet we see such a partitioning as a useful organizing procedure for the elucidation of the available judgement-improving approaches.

Debiasing faulty judgement

Within this category we will include those approaches which essentially retain the expert as judge or decision-maker and attempt to overcome bias by some manipulation of the judge or task environment. In this, as in the other two categories, we are assuming that the detected biases are at least partly attributable to some cognitive deficit which exists within the human judge and, hence, that they are not merely artefacts of task situations. This assumption relates to the 'ecological validity' argument which questions the meaningfulness of laboratory findings to the 'real world'. As has already been argued, evidence does exist to suggest laboratory determined biases are 'real'. Further evidence has also been provided by the debiasing literature and has been summarized by Fischhoff (1982), who – in considering research on the overconfidence bias and the hindsight bias (where judges exaggerate the inevitability of what could have been anticipated in foresight) – concluded that manipulations assuming suboptimality of judgement to be attributable to 'faulty tasks' (i.e. inappropriate and misleading tasks), had failed to produce any substantial reduction in bias. By contrast, Fischhoff noted that limited debiasing successes have been achieved in some studies operating under the assumption that at least some blame for poor performance can be levelled at the judges (either assuming that they lack the necessary cognitive skills or that they possess the appropriate skills and yet apply them incorrectly). More specifically, Slovic and Fischhoff (1977), in considering the hindsight bias, found that asking subjects to indicate how they could have explained the occurrences of outcomes which did *not* happen, seemed to reduce the judged inevitability of events. Similarly, in assessing the overconfidence bias, Koriat, Lichtenstein, and Fischhoff (1980) found that a reduction in the subjects' confidence ratings of selected answers could be achieved by having them list reasons why their preferred answers might be *wrong*. These results are interesting in that, by and large, other attempted techniques at bias resolution – such as by simply informing subjects of the nature and presence of a particular bias (e.g. Lichtenstein and Fischhoff, 1980) – have mainly failed. Fischhoff (1982) interpreted these results as indicating task-judge mismatch, reasoning that the contrary evidence (to the subjects' held opinions) must have been available to the judges either in memory or in imagination and yet could not be utilized until the judges had their attention specifically focussed on such information.

Other studies which have been published since Fischhoff's review seem to support the efficacy of procedures aimed at focussing judges' attention on contrary evidence, by such means as providing negative or disconfirmatory feedback. For example, Sharp, Cutler, and Penrod (1988) demonstrated that feedback on confidence levels and accuracy rates improved validity of confidence judgements to a certain extent, while Arkes, Christensen, Lai, and Blumer (1987) found that overconfidence could be reduced by causing subjects to anticipate a subsequent group discussion in which they would have to justify their answers (and suggested that this might motivate the subjects to more carefully consider alternative opinions to avoid being 'humbled' – though it should be noted that this proposed mechanism of what was going on is open to empirical validation).

What each of these studies seems to suggest is that, in the case of certain biases, human judges do possess the ability to fairly rapidly overcome such biases, if only an appropriate environment can be provided to encourage the effective use of our cognitive skills. Arkes *et al.* (1987) suggested that such an environment should be produced using 'indirect' methods, subtly manipulating the variables related to a bias in order to create a more conducive judgemental atmosphere. In contrast, they argued against the use of 'direct' methods (aimed at directly confronting judges with their biases) suggesting that our lack of access to many of our own judgemental processes (i.e. people usually cannot elucidate the exact process by which they derive a judgement or decision) ensures that any provisioning of direct knowledge will be superfluous.

Although this recommendation to debias sounds reasonable, we must be wary of advocating approaches which are too simplistic to do the entire issue justice. Subtle manipulations of a particular task environment may well lead to improved judgement, but, as Keren (1988) has suggested, unless a qualitative improvement in the judges' cognitive skills is achieved, any improvements attained may not be transferable beyond the initial task. In making this point, Keren differentiates between two types of debiasing methods at opposite poles to one another: on the one hand exist procedural or mechanical methods (which aim at producing quantitative judgement changes without requiring the judge to understand the aid – such as by providing a guiding algorithm); and on the other hand there are the structural modifying methods (which seek to make knowledge more explicit, guiding judges to more appropriate representations of the problem space). Keren has suggested that the former procedural approaches are of limited usefulness, whereas the latter type might induce more generalizable cognitive skills which may subsequently be of use in a wide variety of contexts and situations.

This proposal seems eminently sensible: it is far preferable to produce judges with the flexibility to adapt their acquired skills to new and unusual situations, than to rely upon a large number of shallow techniques which basically leave the judge no better off, in terms of cognitive skills, than they were before the debiasing manipulation. Indeed, Keren has suggested that it is precisely because we have concentrated on using procedural methods that so little progress has been made in developing efficient debiasing aids. Part of this problem, according to various authors, lies in our lack of understanding of the underlying cognitive mechanisms responsible for biases (e.g. Wallsten, 1983). In order to develop structural modifying procedures we need to possess more comprehensive cognitive theories. Hence, according to Fischhoff (1982), it is precisely in those places where such underlying theories of cognition have driven research that the most promising successes have been achieved (e.g. Koriat *et al.* 1980).

On the basis of the findings thus far discussed, are there then any simple and pragmatic recommendations that we might make for debiasing judgement? Because certain biases seem to be the product of discounting contradictory evidence and fixating too strongly on evidence supporting our particular views and beliefs, Kleinmuntz (1989) has suggested that encouraging people to document and record their decisions daily might make explicit contrary feedback indicating where our decisions have been poor and thus can be improved. Similarly, Hogarth (1987) has advocated that people should be encouraged to systematically seek disconfirming evidence before making any judgement or decision.

Above, are just a few practical suggestions, which may aid in reducing biases such as overconfidence, the hindsight bias, availability, and so on. However, the research has been somewhat limited and work on a greater scope of biases, in a larger range of situations, is required. If such research can be more properly directed by cognitive theory, then perhaps more wide-ranging structural-modifying methods might be produced and formalized and, subsequently, made available to organizations for appropriate usage.

An alternative approach to improving judgement shifts emphasis away from the debiasing of the individual and on to the amalgamation of individual judgements in group contexts. Of obvious advantage here is the existence and accessibility of a greater range of knowledge and opinion than is available to any one judge. The reason we have retained such group processes under the 'debiasing of faulty judgement' heading is that, from our 'providing contrary feedback' perspective on debiasing, this is exactly what a group may be seen to be doing. That is, through the interaction with other members of a group, each individual is supplied with contrary and unthought-of arguments simultaneously. Perhaps we may view the group organism in terms of a decision-making individual – hopefully one not suffering from certain biases inherent in the individual! However, care is needed in advocating group decision-making as a cure to faulty individual judgement, for the usual committee meeting type environment has been shown to be fraught with problems of its own. Various authors have commented upon the negative aspects of committee decision-making (e.g. Martino, 1983; Lock, 1987; Janis and Mann, 1977), which include aspects such as : the social pressures for individuals to conform to the majority, the unduly large influence of dominant individuals, the repetitions of arguments (quantity of arguments being confused with their worth), premature closure and satisfying of groups (accepting the first decision that no one strongly disagrees with and failing to search further for optimal solutions), the reinforcement of biases, and so on. Thus, although Hill (1982) has argued that '$N+1$ heads are better than one', we must interject a caveat about the word 'better'. 'Better' than 'poor' is certainly an improvement, but doesn't necessarily imply optimality. Practical considerations should also be considered here. The cost (such as in terms of man hours) of assembling a panel of experts may make any improvements in judgement uneconomic for the organization.

However, accepting group decision-making to be a viable option for the organization, other techniques have been developed explicitly for the purpose of retaining those positive aspects of groups, while attempting to do away with the negative side effects. One such approach is the 'Delphi' method (e.g. Dalkey, 1969) which, through the process of polling expert judgement over a number of rounds and providing anonymous feedback to each judge from the other panel members (allowing judgement revision on each new round), seeks to remove many of the social pressures on the individual. At the end of the Delphi process, once a certain stability in judgement is achieved, the group decision may be expressed as a mean or median, with further information arising from the amount of deviation existing in the individual judgements after the final poll (indicating, to a certain extent, the degree of agreement or disagreement). Relatively few empirical examinations of Delphi have taken place, largely due to the fact that the technique was initially introduced as a tool to aid in long-term forecasting of technological and social changes (such as attempting to predict the date of a certain technological breakthrough). Nevertheless, those studies which have been conducted have provided mixed results, some finding Delphi to produce increases in accuracy over rounds (on general knowledge questions and in short-term forecasting) and improved accuracy over techniques like simple conferencing (e.g. Brown and Helmer, 1964; Jolson and Rossow, 1971; Riggs, 1983) and some finding *decreasing* accuracy over rounds and poor performance relative to other techniques (e.g., Gustafson, Shulka, Delbecq, and Webster, 1973; Parente, Anderson, Myers, and O'Brien, 1984). Perhaps these mixed results are unsurprising – after all, Koriat *et al.* (1980) demonstrated that improved accuracy of confidence ratings was brought about by providing subjects with negative information; providing them with positive *and* negative information did not lead to the reduction in the overconfidence bias, probably because the subjects were selectively processing positive over negative information, when the former was present. If this is the case in Delphi also (i.e., judges are selectively interpreting positive information, when this is available), then it is little wonder improvements in judgement are not certain, for the process might be seen as flawed from a 'debiasing of judges' perspective. However, the precise mechanisms of judgement change in Delphi are liable to be complex and further research is definitely needed.

Other techniques for behavioural aggregation exist, such as the 'Nominal Group Technique' (NGT) (Van de Ven and Delbecq, 1971). Here, individuals initially write down ideas related to the given judgemental problem, then present one idea each to the group. A group discussion of all of these points then follows and the process culminates with each judge making an individual assessment of the priorities of ideas by rank ordering or rating, with a final mathematical aggregation yielding the group decision. This technique therefore differs from Delphi in allowing some form of communication to take place between individuals, increasing individual participation. Again, results are variable (e.g. Gustafson *et al.*, 1973; Fischer, 1981) and it is difficult to draw definite conclusions as to why this process should yield improved decisions over, for example, Delphi. Again our suggestion must be that a defining of judgemental mechanisms in this decision-making context is something which should be sought. Until we do produce theories on judgement with considerably more depth, the process of producing debiasing aids will remain a hit-and-miss affair.

In this section, we have been considering techniques which would have us retain human judges and attempt to debias their faulty judgement. Thus, these approaches should be considered in situations where a judgemental aspect is essential, such as in the forecasting domain, where no empirical database exists from which predictions may be made (through mathematical aggregation of past data) or when it may be expected that some change in the future may occur such that past data will not help prediction. Indeed, Coates (1975) has called the Delphi technique a method of the 'last resort' – a technique to be used where no others are available. When you cannot replace the judge, then you just have to try to improve him – either on an individual basis, or by papering over individual biases using a group technique. However, such methods as have been proposed may also be useful to the organization in situations where the human judge may not be so indispensable and where they may be replaceable by some mechanical procedure, for the simple reason of cost. After all, having judges write down contrary points to their professed opinion, before making a decision, may cost little more than a paper and pencil – and would probably be several orders of magnitude cheaper than replacing them with some computer program. Obviously, the economics of the situation of bias must play a role in determining how judgemental improvement is sought, along with aspects such as the availability of appropriate decision-aids and the appropriateness of such aids to the particular judgement situation. Another approach to removing bias is to choose people who are generally good judges or decision-makers. To this topic we turn next.

Pre-empting bias – selecting individuals to suit judgemental situations

As a means of resolving biases in judgement, the most obvious initial step would be to select individuals who were less likely to possess cognitive biases in the first place. However, the key aspect of such biases is that, often, they may be traced to heuristics which normally *do* perform some useful function in our normal lives and hence tend to be virtually universal amongst us, unless specific cognitive strategies have already been learnt which might counter the inherent, or environmentally conditional biases. It would seem then, that what we should realistically be aiming for is, rather than people already bereft of demonstrable bias, people who possess the appropriate capabilities to learn to perform their vocational judgements in a non-biased way. Indeed, Wright and Ayton (1988) have provided some evidence that stable intraorganismic constants (that is, traits or cognitive styles) may be the main determinants of behavioural variation in judgemental forecasting across a variety of task situations (which differed in terms of aspects like length of forecast period, subject-ive desirability of forecast items, etc.) and, consequently, suggested that it may be possible to select people for forecasting ability on the basis of particular traits. However, Wright and Ayton (1987) have noted that, whether there are separable cognitive styles that can describe individual differences in the judgemental forecasting realm, is still an unanswered question. In fact, there has been a paucity of studies of individual differences in judgemental abilities in the behavioural decision research literature. Most investigators have adopted an experimental approach rather than a psychometric one and the result has been an over-emphasis on the situation-contingent nature of decision-making. (See Payne, 1982.)

Nevertheless, it would seem a viable alternative proposition to select personnel on the basis of characteristics possessed by people who have already shown some ability to perform judgemental tasks efficiently, i.e. experts (assuming, of course, that such 'experts' are so classified according to appropriate criteria and are not merely socially determined experts). Such psychological characteristics of experts have been defined by various authors like Shanteau (1987) and Johnson (1988) amongst others (see earlier) and current selection procedures like interviews (for establishing communication skills), intelligence tests, and aptitude tests, would seem to provide potential tools for assessment and selection. Yet, in order to develop more appropriate selection procedures, we must gain more extensive knowledge on the cognitive traits and styles of good judges and decision-makers in order to elucidate the optimal selection criteria (see Wright 1985 for a catalogue of current knowledge on this important but under-investigated area). Much work remains to be done.

CONCLUSION

In this review we have looked at a variety of approaches to the problem of improving judgement in decision-making and forecasting contexts. The complete approach should, ideally, integrate a variety of the techniques mentioned (which represent just a sample of available methods), starting with the selection of more appropriate personnel specifically for their 'judgemental' potential, followed by some form of training where this may be of help (ideally, working to improve the judges' overall cognitive abilities) and utilizing specific judgemental aids where appropriate.

Given the existence of such techniques for improving judgement, we must now address the issue as to their apparent paucity in organizational settings. Perhaps the major reason for this neglect is, simply, the fact that few decision-makers actually know of the existence of decision aiding techniques and are even unaware that any problem in their decision-making may exist in the first place (e.g., Kleinmuntz 1989). Indeed, it is one of the perversities of the situation that those decision-makers who are *most* likely to benefit from judgemental aids, are also those who are *least* likely to realize that such aids may be needed (in the case of forecasting, the lack of feedback on judgements means that judges cannot be expected to learn that they are producing incorrect or biased assessments – and yet this is precisely the sort of situation in which we would expect bias to occur!). Even assuming that organizational knowledge does exist concerning judgemental aids, problems may be seen to exist in terms of cost (financial, as well as in terms of effort and time), while the lack of technical and experimental sophistication in the organization may lead to great confusion as to how to select, develop, test, and monitor any particular aid, such that it becomes adapted to the requisite organizational circumstance (where it is to be employed). Further, as Dawes (1982) has pointed out, our own biases may prevent us from accepting that a need for some form of aid may exist – a form of 'cognitive conceit', with which it is all too easy to dismiss aids as being invalid, or demonstrated empirical findings as being flawed. Indeed, if good judgement and decision-making are valued as the mainstay of good management then few managers would be wise to admit the need for aids to their judgement!

Our aims in this review have been to alert organizations to the fact that judgemental bias may be a pervasive feature of many decision-making contexts, to note that possible techniques for improving judgement exist and to point to some of the areas where further research needs to be done in order to produce more knowledge about biases and how to counter them. Since judgemental inputs are a crucial, and irreducible part of many normative decision technologies, such as decision analysis, we believe that detailed knowledge of the quality of human judgement is fundamental to improving decision-making in real-world contexts.

REFERENCES

Arkes, H. R., Christensen, C., Lai, C., and Blumer, C. (1987), 'Two methods of reducing overconfidence', *Organizational Behavior and Human Decision Processes*, 39, 133–44.

Balthasar, H. U., Boschi, R. A. A., and Menke, M. M. (1978), 'Calling the shots in R and D', *Harvard Business Review*, May–June, 151–60.

Beach, L. R., Christensen-Szalanski, J. J. J., and Barnes, V. (1987), 'Assessing human judgment: has it been done, can it be done, should it be done?', in G. Wright and P. Ayton (eds.), *Judgmental Forecasting* (Chichester: Wiley).

Brown, B. and Helmer, O. (1964), 'Improving the reliability of estimates obtained from the consensus of experts', The RAND Corporation, P-2986.

Christensen-Szalanski, J., Beck, D. E., Christensen-Szalanski, C. M., and Koepsell, T. D. (1983), 'Effects of expertise and experience on risk judgments', *Journal of Applied Psychology*, 68, 278–84.

Coates, J. F. (1975), 'In defense of Delphi: a review of delphi assessment, expert opinion, forecasting and group process by H. Sackman', *Technological Forecasting and Social Change*, 7, 193–4.

Dalkey, N. C. (1969), 'The Delphi method: an experimental study of group opinion', The RAND Corporation, RM-5888-PR.

Dawes, R. (1988), *Rational Choice in an Uncertain World* (San Diego: Harcourt Brace Jovanovich).

Dino, G. A. (1984), 'Decision makers appraising decision making: defining the dimensions of importance', unpublished doctoral dissertation, Kansas.

Dube-Rioux, L. and Russo, J. E. (1988), 'An availability bias in professional judgement', *Journal of Behavioral Decision Making*, 1, 223–37.

Ebbesen, E. B. and Konecni, V. J. (1980), 'On the external validity of decision making research: what do we know about decisions in the real world?', in T. S. Wallsten (ed.), *Cognitive Processes in Choice and Decision Making* (Hillsdale, NJ: Erlbaum).

Edwards, W. (1954), 'The theory of decision making', *Psychological Bulletin*, 51, 380–417.

Einhorn, H. J. (1980), 'Learning from experience and suboptimal rules in decision making', in T. Wallsten (ed.), *Cognitive Processes in Choice and Decision Behavior* (Hillsdale, NJ: Erlbaum), pp. 1–20.

Ettenson, R. T., Krugstad, J. L., and Shanteau, J. (1985), 'Schema and strategy shifting in auditors' evidence gathering: a multi-task analysis', in *Symposium on Audit Judgment and Evidence Evaluation*, USC School of Auditing.

Fischer, G. W. (1981), 'When oracles fail – a comparison of four procedures for aggregating subjective probability forecasts', *Organizational Behavior and Human Performance*, **28**, 96–110.

Fischhoff, B. (1982), 'Debiasing', in D. Kahneman, P. Slovic, and A. Tversky (eds.), *Judgment Under Uncertainty: Heuristics and Biases* (Cambridge University Press).

Gaeth, G. J. and Shanteau, J. (1984), 'Reducing the influence of irrelevant information on experienced decision makers', *Organizational Behavior and Human Performance*, **33**, 263–82.

Gustafson, D. H., Shukla, R. K., Delbecq, A., and Webster, G. W. (1973), 'A comparison study of differences in subjective likelihood estimates made by individuals, interacting groups, Delphi groups and nominal groups', *Organizational Behavior and Human Performance*, **9**, 280–91.

Hill, G. W. (1982), 'Group versus individual performance: are N+1 heads better than one?', *Psychological Bulletin*, **91** (3), 517–39.

Hoerl, A. and Falbin, H. K. (1974), 'Reliability of subjective evaluations in a high incentive situation', *Journal of the Royal Statistical Society*, **137**, 227–30.

Hogarth, R. M. (1987), *Judgment and Choice: The Psychology of Decision* (2nd edn) (Chichester: Wiley).

Hughes, H. D. (1917), 'An interesting seed corn experiment', *Iowa Agriculturalist*, **17**, 424–5.

Janis, I. L. and Mann, L. (1977), *Decision Making* (New York: The Free Press).

Johnson, E. J. (1988), 'Expertise and decision under uncertainty: performance and process', in M. T. H. Chi, R. Glaser, and M. J. Farr, *The Nature of Expertise* (Hillsdale, NJ: Erlbaum), pp. 209–28.

Jolson, M. A. and Rossow, G. (1971), 'The Delphi process in marketing decision making', *Journal of Marketing Research*, **8**, 443–8.

Kabus, I. (1976), 'You can bank on uncertainty', *Harvard Business Review*, May–June, 95–105.

Kahneman, D. and Tversky, A. (1979), 'Prospect theory: an analysis of decisions under risk', *Econometrica*, **47**, 263–91.

Keren, G. (1987), 'Facing uncertainty in the game of bridge: a calibration study', *Organizational Behavior and Human Decision Processes*, **39**, 98–114.

(1988), 'Cognitive aids and debiasing methods: can cognitive pills cure cognitive ills?', in proceedings of 'Cognitive biases: their contribution for understanding human cognitive processes', Aix en Provence.

Kleinmuntz, B. (1989), 'Why we still use our heads instead of formulas: towards an integrative approach', *Psychological Bulletin*, in press.

Koriat, A., Lichtenstein, S., and Fischhoff, B. (1980), 'Reasons for confidence', *Journal of Experimental Psychology: Human Learning and Memory*, **6**, 107–18.

Lichtenstein, S. and Fischhoff, B. (1980), 'Training for calibration', *Organizational Behavior and Human Performance*, **26**, 149–71.

Lichtenstein S., Fischhoff, B., and Phillips, L. D. (1981), 'Calibration of subjective probabilities: The state of the art to 1980', in D. Kahneman, P. Slovic, and

A. Tversky (eds.), *Judgment under Uncertainty: Heuristics & Biases* (New York: Cambridge University Press).

Lichtenstein, S. and Slovic, P. (1971), 'Reversals of preference between bids and choices in gambling decisions', *Journal of Experimental Psychology*, **89**, 46–55.

Lock, A. (1987), 'Integrating group judgments in subjective forecasts', in G. Wright and P. Ayton (eds.), *Judgmental Forecasting* (Chichester: Wiley).

Manu, P., Runge, L. A., Lee, J. Y., and Oppenheim, A. D. (1984), 'Judged frequency of complications after invasive diagnostic procedures: Systematic biases of a physician population', *Medical Care*, **22**, 366–70.

Martino, J. (1983), *Technological Forecasting for Decision-Making* (2nd edn), (New York: American Elsevier).

Murphy, A. H. and Brown, B. G. (1985), 'A comparative evaluation of objective and subjective weather forecasts in the United States', in G. Wright (ed.) *Behavioral Decision Making* (New York: Plenum).

Northcraft, M. A. and Neale, G. B. (1987), 'Experts, amateurs and real-estate: an anchoring and adjust perspective in property pricing decisions', *Organisational Behavior and Human Decision Processes*, **39**, 84–97.

Oskamp, S. (1962), 'The relationship of clinical experience and training methods to several criteria of clinical prediction', *Psychological Monographs*, **76**.

Parente, F. J., Anderson, J. K., Myers, P., and O'Brien, T. (1984), 'An examination of factors contributing to Delphi accuracy', *Journal of Forecasting*, **3** (2), 173–82.

Payne, J. W. (1982), 'Contingent decision behavior', *Psychological Bulletin*, **92**, 382–402.

Phelps, R. M. (1977), 'Expert livestock judgment. A descriptive analysis of the development of expertise', Unpublished doctoral dissertation, Kansas State University.

Riggs, W. E. (1983), 'The Delphi Method: an experimental evaluation', *Technological Forecasting and Social Change*, **23**, 89–94.

Shanteau, J. (1987), 'Psychological characteristics of expert decision makers', in J. Mumpower, L. D. Phillips, O. Renn, and Y. R. R. Uppuluri (eds.), *Expert Judgment and Expert Systems* (Berlin: Springer-Verlag), pp. 289–304.

Sharp, G. L., Cutler, B. L., and Penrod, S. D. (1988), 'Performance feedback improves the resolution of confidence judgments', *Organizational Behavior and Human Decision Processes*, **42**, 271–83.

Slovic, P. (1982), 'Towards understanding and improving decisions', in W. C. Howell and E. A. Fleishmann (eds.), *Human Performance and Productivity* vol XII, Information Processing and Decision Making (Hillsdale, NJ: Erlbaum).

Slovic, P. and Fischhoff, B. (1977), 'On the psychology of experimental surprises', *Journal of Experimental Psychology: Human Perception and Performance*, **3**, 544–51.

Slovic, P. and Tversky, A. (1974), 'Who accepts Savage's axiom?', *Behavioral Science*, **19**, 368–73.

Trunbo, D. A., Adams, C. K., Milner, M., and Schipper, L. (1962), 'Reliability and accuracy: the inspection of hard red winter wheat', *Cereal Science Today*, **7**, 62–71.

Tversky, A. and Kahneman, D. (1974), 'Judgment under uncertainty: heuristics and biases', *Science*, **185**, 1124–31.

Van de Ven, A. H. and Delbecq, A. L. (1971), 'Nominal versus interacting group processes for committee decision making effectiveness', *Academic Management Journal*, **14**, 203–13.

VonWinterfeldt, D. and Edwards, W. (1986), *Decision Analysis and Behavioral Research* (Cambridge University Press).

Wallace, H. A. (1923), 'What is in the corn judge's mind?', *Journal of the American Society of Agronomy*, **15**, 300–4.

Wallsten, T. S. (1983), 'The theoretical status of judgmental heuristics', in R. W. Scholz (ed.), *Decision Making Under Uncertainty* (Amsterdam: Elsevier).

Watson, S. R. and Buede, D. M. (1987), *Decision Synthesis* (Cambridge University Press).

Wright, G. (1984), *Behavioural Decision Theory* (Harmondsworth: Penguin).
  (1985), 'Decisional Variance', in G. Wright (ed.), *Behavioral Decision Making* (New York: Plenum).

Wright, G. and Ayton, P. (1987a), 'Task influences in judgmental forecasting', *Scandanavian Journal of Psychology*, **28**, 113–27.
  (1987b), 'The psychology of forecasting', in G. Wright and P. Ayton (eds.), *Judgmental Forecasting* (Chichester: Wiley).
  (1988), 'Judgmental forecasting: personologism, situationism or interactionism?', in *Personality and Individual Differences*.

Wright, G., Ayton, P., and Whalley, P. (1985), 'A general purpose computer aid to judgmental forecasting: rational and procedures', *Decision Support Systems*, **1**, 333–40.

Wright, G., Saunders, C., and Ayton, P. (1988), 'The consistency, coherence and calibration of holistic, decomposed and recomposed judgmental probability forecasts', *Journal of Forecasting*, **7**, 185–99.

Wright, G. and Whalley, P. (1983), 'The supra-additivity of subjective probability', in B. P. Stigum and F. Wenstop (eds.), *Foundations of Risk and Utility Theory with Applications* (Dordrecht: Reidel).

13

―――――― ❧ ――――――

SOME CONCLUDING REMARKS

FRANK HELLER

To any reader who has gone carefully through the twelve chapters of this book, it will probably seem odd to hear that a well-known scholar who has himself written extensively about decision-making, now questions whether this is a useful concept.

The challenge which is given pride of place in a recent issue of *Organizational Studies* may turn out to be more a whim than a serious challenge, but it gives us an opportunity to have another look at the subject which has been the principal focus of attention of many academics in the present century.

Mintzberg and Waters (1990) claim that, although they and others have spent many years studying the process of strategy formation as a stream of decisions, it 'eventually occurred to us that we were in fact not studying streams of decisions at all, but actions' (p. 2). They argue that the verifiable traces that we actually observe, like the opening of stores in a supermarket chain, or projects started in an architectural firm, are actions and not decisions. Decisions, they say, are much more problematic; they do not seem to leave very clear traces. They may be statements of intent which are recorded in written minutes, but often there is nothing tangible at all. Can one in fact be sure that actions are always preceded by decisions?

This emphasis on the visibility of actions in preference to the allegedly more opaque concept of deciding could with equal or even more force be raised against the concept of leadership. It is therefore appropriate to examine the examples Mintzberg and Waters give to sustain their case. Citing the Canadian criminal code, they argue that the distinction between first and second degree murder accepts that action can occur without a commitment to act. First degree murder requires proof that the act has been planned and deliberated, while second degree murder is killing 'without deciding'. This is a curious argument. The law has an ancient tradition, but is not the best discipline for penetrating the complexities of the human psyche and the elusive concept of motivation. I can bring myself to believe that a killing can occur as a consequence or even during a dream, or while in a semi-conscious state, like sleepwalking, but in other cases a decision will have occurred a short time, maybe only seconds, before the action and this may be interpreted by the law as being different from and less culpable than a carefully premeditated crime.

They give another example, from a film agency that made a decision to put money into a short documentary. It happened that the film became longer than intended and therefore had to be marketed differently. Mintzberg and Walters say that the organization acted without making a decision. My interpretation of such events is to say that they amended their original decision or made a second, more appropriate, decision in the light of new conditions. These are not unusual events and, under favourable circumstances, it is certainly not impossible to find out how one decision replaced another.

An even weaker argument is used to attack the 'conventional management theory (which) falls back on the convenience of implementation' to explain why some firmly taken decisions are subverted by others so that 'there is decision but no action' (p. 4). It is true that the early Mintzberg work (Mintzberg *et al.*, 1976) and most other research on decision-making stopped at the point where the decision is taken and failed to inquire into what happened to the process afterwards. But we have seen in the chapters by Drenth and Koopman and Hickson and Miller, that it is perfectly feasible and indeed necessary to extend the inquiry of organizational decision processes to cover the implementation stage.

Actions are, of course, important bench-marks within decision processes as they are for leadership, but to understand the complex dynamics of actions, as indeed of inaction, it is necessary to establish their critical antecedents and consequences. Even in the case of second degree murder, whether or not it was the result of a split second decision, the parole procedure should take careful notice of the events that followed on the act of killing. Was there rejoicing, regret, or indifference?

Even if we confine ourselves to examining strategic medium- and long-term processes in business or government organizations, the events leading up to a 'no action' outcome can be of great importance. In Britain there have been several major inquiries, supported by elaborate cost benefit analysis, to reach a decision on the siting of London's third airport. In each case, until Stansted was chosen four years ago, successive governments resolved to take no action. The result of these negative decisions have cost the taxpayer vast sums of money and caused enormous inconvenience to thousands of people who lived in the areas designated for the siting of new airports. The scientific study of this 'no action' decision process could be both interesting and useful.

Although, in the particular case of the Mintzberg and Waters argument, the recommended change from a broad decision focus to a much narrower concept of action need not be taken seriously, it is appropriate to look at the various alternative levels of analysis in the literature on leadership and decision-making. Although the necessarily limited scope of a single book does not allow us to cover the whole range of possibilities, the variety of approaches taken by the chapter writers is appropriate and even necessary in the light of our present knowledge. Little is gained by premature foreclosure, but several contributions are usefully complementary.

For instance, Hogarth and Kunreuther's approach is deliberately based on a structural and situational analysis of the effect of roles rather than personality on the perceptions of risk and ambiguity. They reject the possibility that judgements are influenced by differences in optimism or pessimism.

Wright and colleagues, however, highlight the importance of individual differences in the ability to make accurate judgements and consequently argue for more careful selection and training to improve judgemental performance.

Beach *et al.*'s theory also concentrates on the individual's own values, ethical considerations, goals, and plans, rather than on wider concepts, like roles and environmental factors, although they recognize that the image used by individuals is inevitably influenced by social variables.

The individual focus receives further support from the psychologists who investigate the effect of stress on leadership: Cooper and Smith, Fiedler *et al.*, and Bass; while Drenth and Koopman, Hickson and Miller, Yetton and Crawford, Heller, and Janis put more emphasis on group processes, structures, the influence of external factors, and longitudinality.

The reader will have seen that each author makes a distinct contribution to the subject matter of this book. Sometimes the emphasis is more on theory, sometimes more on empirical evidence. There are few contradictions, but ultimately the producers of science, as well as those who use it, will want to see whether and how the different contributions relate to one another.

In medicine, which of course also deals with people, investigations of major diseases at the micro level of organisms, the meso level of individual patient variability, and the macro level of demographic structural factors are seen as complementary and mutually supportive. The knowledge derived from each level is seen as valid in its own right and capable of contributing to a better conceptualization of the appropriate theory and practice relating to a given category of disease.

The social sciences have not yet arrived at this stage of mutual tolerance and support, and maybe the connections across levels of analysis and methodology are more difficult to make. There is as yet little cross-referencing between workers in traditional decision theory and field researchers on organizational processes, though the two chapters by Hogarth and Kunreuther, and Wright *et al.*, provide material for such a dialogue to begin. Similarly, there is not much interaction between the traditional investigations of leadership and those who look at strategic, tactical, or routine decisions. Here, too, the reader may decide that the analysis presented in the introductory chapter could contribute to some cross-fertilization of ideas.

People as well as disciplines become more tolerant as they grow older, and humility often derives from strength. However, we are all trained in relatively narrow disciplines and have invested heavily in bundles of specific skills which tempt us to amortize the investment rather than risk working with other ideas and new tools.

Occasionally, well-known social scientists in the second half of their career, feel the need for adventure and more rapid progress. They are prepared to risk the criticism, sometimes even the wrath, of those colleagues who are preoccupied with amortizing their specific competences. One of these brave men is Kenneth Boulding, who recently published *Three Faces of Power* (1989). It is an attempt to integrate large areas of science under a single umbrella. Boulding, an economist by training, believes that 'the concept of power spans from the physical sciences right through to the social sciences' (p. 9). Although power is very central to all the affairs of people and maybe because it crosses so many boundaries, it 'has tended to slip through the cracks between the different disciplines and never seems to have become a discipline of its own' (p. 9).

I believe that Boulding's attempt to analyse the maximum meaningful breadth one can give to an intellectual concept is eminently worth while, even if one disagrees with the way some of the building stones or the cement are used to build the edifice.

Boulding's choice of integrating concept is particularly relevant to this book, because power can easily be seen as a relevant way of describing and analysing all leadership behaviour and most areas of decision-making. If this is so, then we can begin to build a bridge across these two areas of study which may eventually be of benefit to both.

REFERENCES

Boulding, Kenneth (1989), *Three Faces of Power* (London: Sage Publications).
Mintzberg, H., Raisingham, D., and Theoret, A. (1976), 'The structure of "unstructured" decision process', *Administrative Science Quarterly*, 21, 246–75.
Mintzberg, Henry and Waters, Jim (1990), 'Does decision get in the way? In: Studying deciding: an exchange of views between Mintzberg and Waters, Pettigrew and Butler', *Organization Studies*, 1, 1–16.

INDEX